The Principle of Subsidiarity in Catholic Social Thought

AMERICAN UNIVERSITY STUDIES

SERIES VII
THEOLOGY AND RELIGION

VOL. 308

PETER LANG
New York • Washington, D.C./Baltimore • Bern
Frankfurt • Berlin • Brussels • Vienna • Oxford

Simeon Tsetim Iber

The Principle of Subsidiarity in Catholic Social Thought

Implications for Social Justice and Civil Society in Nigeria

PETER LANG
New York • Washington, D.C./Baltimore • Bern
Frankfurt • Berlin • Brussels • Vienna • Oxford

Library of Congress Cataloging-in-Publication Data

Iber, Simeon Tsetim.
The principle of subsidiarity in Catholic social thought: implications for social justice and civil society in Nigeria / Simeon Tsetim Iber.
p. cm. — (American university studies. VII, Theology and religion; v. 308)
Includes bibliographical references and index.
1. Subsidiarity—Religious aspects—Catholic Church. 2. Social justice—Nigeria. 3. Religion and civil society—Nigeria. 4. Social justice—Religious aspects—Catholic Church. 5. Catholic Church—Doctrines. I. Title.
BX1682.N5I25 262'.02669—dc22 2010014259
ISBN 978-1-4331-1011-5 (hardcover)
ISBN 978-1-4331-1254-6 (paperback)
ISSN 0740-0446

Bibliographic information published by **Die Deutsche Nationalbibliothek**.
Die Deutsche Nationalbibliothek lists this publication in the "Deutsche Nationalbibliografie"; detailed bibliographic data is available on the Internet at http://dnb.d-nb.de/.

This book is dedicated to citizens of Nigeria who are committed to experience and participate in the dialogue of life by building their communities without prejudice to tribe, religion, gender, political, and social affiliations; and to the quest for servant leadership for the nation.

TABLE OF CONTENTS

PREFACE

This book examines the centrality of the principle of subsidiarity in Catholic social teaching, in bringing about social and moral reconstruction of society and in particular the Nigerian social context. The origin of this principle has been traced to the natural human inclination to build a healthy relationship between the individual and society, such that, the society will provide generous help and support to individuals to help one another. Subsidiarity is a way of organizing individuals and social groups in a community to help one another in pursuing their interests with common goals. The ultimate purpose is to assist one another and to uphold the common good.

The vision of the common good sees in the human person the personal dignity proper to one's nature, but is directed essentially to others in society. Hence, the common good and the good of the individual do not oppose one another, but the good of the individual whose nature is personal has a dignity proper to itself, but nonetheless is social in character; that is, it is directed to the well-being of others. Thus, the common good is realized through the participation and contribution of the individual to others in society. In this way, the relationship between the individual and the social group remains a question for everybody in a given social context.

The study carries out a critical analysis of Nigerian society and shows that lack of development at the grassroots, corruption, bribery, ethnic conflicts, failure of leadership, and failure of the rule of law have eaten deep into the fabric of the nation. In order to support individuals and social groups to help each other, the practice of social justice is a necessary component to the common good. Social justice will ensure the building of trust across ethnic lines, protect minority tribes from being taken over by larger tribes, promote grassroots participation of the masses by encouraging self-help tribal, community, kinship, religious, and non-governmental associations as agents of positive social change. Moreover, tribal customs and practices that are unjust may and must be re-evaluated in the light of the Gospel message of Jesus who came to serve and not to be served.

This book is my modest attempt to put on paper many of the issues that have challenged my country of birth since her coming to being by the British colonial power in 1914. My hope is that the views expressed here will add a credible voice to the ongoing quest to make Nigeria the country it ought to be—the giant of Africa. I take full responsibility for any omissions and mistakes, and in the spirit of academic scholarship look forward to your critique.

Simeon Tsetim Iber

ACKNOWLEDGMENTS

In the summer of 2003, I received a scholarship as a civitas scholar from the Center for Public Justice to attend a five-week residential institute on "Christian Faith, Political Thought, and Public Policy," organized for doctoral candidates in Washington D.C. This scholarship was supported by the Pew Charitable Foundation. I am deeply grateful to these organizations for the opportunity given me and the positive contribution it made in the publication of this book.

My sincere thank you goes to Most. Rev. Athanasius A. Usuh, the Catholic Bishop of the Diocese of Makurdi, Nigeria, and his auxiliary Most. Rev. William A. Avenya for their support. Thank you to Jackie Pavlovic, my point person in the production department at Peter Lang Publishing.

Prof. James Hanigan has been an inspiring mentor, an excellent teacher, and a caring friend. I will eternally remember his invaluable advice, critical insights, and encouragement. I owe a special debt of gratitude to Cathy and Ed Moore for their time, selfless sacrifice, and very helpful comments. This same gratitude goes to Gina and Rick Stobaugh for being family away from family. Thank you to the parishioners of St. Anthony parish, Monongahela, PA.

Thank you to my many friends in Port Huron, Michigan, particularly, parishioners of St. Mary and Holy Trinity parishes, and for the personal contributions of Fr. Rene Desmarais (RIP), Sr. Margaret Dowd, IHM, and Sue MacDonald. I spent almost a decade in the Archdiocese of Detroit, and I am eternally grateful for the opportunity given me to have served both as campus minister and pastor of St. Mary parish, Port Huron.

I am most grateful to my many students and colleagues from St. Augustine's Major Seminary Jos where I taught theology from 1994–1997 and to those of St. Thomas Aquinas Major Seminary, Makurdi where I currently teach theology and serve as Academic dean. This book is the result of some of my students' many questions in class, which I always welcome graciously.

Thank you for the moral and personal support received from the following people: my parents Peter I. Iber and Veronica M. Iber and the rest of my siblings with their families. Thanks to Kenneth Agede, Joseph Mali, Louis Yaya, Francis Iber, and Erdoo Ibi. You made the difference in difficult times whether to continue with this project or not. I deeply cherish your friendship and support. Lastly, in June 2009, I received a scholarship and attended a two-week intensive seminar on "Religion and U.S. Foreign Policy," organized by the Institute on Culture, Religion, and World Affairs, Boston University. Thank you to the organizers of the seminar.

Finally, I am very grateful for the moral support I have received from the Rev. Simeon's Community Service Fund, Port Huron, Michigan, and the Center for Development and Social Justice, Makurdi-Benue State.

May God reward you all a hundredfold.

INTRODUCTION

A Theological Inquiry of the Principle of Subsidiary Function in Catholic Social Thought

Background of the Study

The aim of this book is to study the centrality of the principle of subsidiarity in the social and moral reconstruction of the world and in particular the Nigerian context, a principle articulated formally by Pius XI in the social encyclical, *Quadragesimo Anno* (QA), 1931. This task involves examining the principle from various perspectives: theological, philosophical, social, political, and economic, in order to identify the scope and limits of the principle and to establish the proper perspective, in which it was first used by Pius XI. It will also involve an examination of the historical and social context of the drafting of the encyclical, with particular emphasis on why the pope thought it was necessary to embark on a social and moral transformation.

The study pays attention to what it judges to be of enduring value in this encyclical; in particular, the concept of social justice will be examined in relation to civil society and the common good of humanity. The contribution of Nell-Breuning in articulating the position of Pius XI will be examined in detail. The development of the principle in subsequent social encyclicals and its usage also receive some attention. Finally, the study applies the principle of subsidiarity to the Nigerian social context with a view to promoting social justice as an integral part of the common good. Some concrete issues involved in the applicability of subsidiarity both in the Church and society are examined and some proposals recommended.

The question has been raised by some scholars as to why the principle of subsidiarity is still enjoying some relevance in the contemporary world. There are several opinions on the relevance of the principle today, especially in terms of its concrete applications among social groups. In the report prepared for the steering committee on local and regional authorities in Europe, for example, after reflecting on the relative success of the principle today in view of its distant past, the report affirmed that the concept of subsidiarity in Europe is both topical and ambiguous at the same time. This dynamic exists because the principle is "well-suited to a world experiencing not only an economic crisis, but also a crisis of values marked by 'new' ideas and a degree of legal vagueness."[1] Moreover, this concept is the basis on which the report seeks an understanding of the principle that is devoid of its "legal vagueness" by advocating a pragmatic approach and focusing on the political character of the principle as a pivotal point for the sharing of power between the different levels of government. Thus, the well known contemporary nuance of the political character of the principle is that of the 1992 "Maastricht Treaty" in terms of social and economic policy among members of the European Union. In article G of the European Union Charter, the principle is formally introduced by modifying the "Treaty of Rome" and adding article 3b.[2] This study, though, goes beyond this political view of subsidiarity to examine the social and ethical conceptions of the principle beyond the European Union.

Purpose of the Study

This book establishes an understanding and application of the principle of subsidiarity beyond the European Union. While not disputing the social, political, and economic contexts of the depression in Europe and America, and the implications surrounding the initial coinage and usage of the principle,[3] its articulation by Pius XI in the context of the social teaching of the Church has universal significance beyond Europe and America, embracing Africa, Asia, and the Middle East. The question may be asked, what is the basis for taking such a position? The answer lies precisely in the central idea of Catholic social teaching, which is based on the *bonum commune*. The vision of the common good sees in the human person the personal dignity proper to one's nature, but the outlook is directed essentially to

1 Local and Regional Authorities in Europe, No. 55. *Definition and Limits of the Principle of Subsidiarity* (Strasbourg Cedex: Council of Europe Press, 1994), p. 7.

2 Monitoring European Integration, No. 4. *Making Sense of Subsidiarity: How Much Centralization for Europe?* (London: Center for Economic Policy Research, 1993), pp. 19–20.

3 Wilfred Parsons, "The Pope and the Depression," *America* 47 (1932): 37–39 for a concise historical perspective on how Pius XI was critical of "rugged individualism" which was identified by him as the central cause of the economic and social depression of the 1930s in America and Europe.

others in the society. Hence, the common good and the good of the individual do not oppose one another, but the good of the individual whose nature is personal has a dignity proper to itself, but nonetheless it is social in character. In other words, it is directed to the well-being of others.

Thus, the common good is realized through the participation and contribution of the individual to others in society. In this way, the relationship between the individual to the social group remains a question for everybody in a given social context. Here one realizes that the principle of subsidiarity has universal relevance and is not restricted to a unique particular social arrangement of nations in Europe or America, but it is proper to the dignity of the human person wherever he or she resides on earth.

Nell-Breuning has offered a classical understanding of the relationship of the individual to society and vice versa that respects both the principle of subsidiarity and the common good, which is true of all human beings, and is central to Catholic social teaching which will serve as a major guide to this book.

> The relationship of individual and society is more exactly determined by the principle of subsidiarity: society should be helpful to its members especially its ultimate members, the individuals, that is, it should promote their own activity, not suppress or absorb their individual life. This *gravissimum principium* works in two ways: on the one hand it opposes collectivist, especially totalitarian, tendencies, and on this side it must continue to be applied in present-day society; on the other hand—whence its name: *subsidium afferre*—it demands from social groups that they give their members generous help, especially help to self-help.[4]

In the classic text above, one finds a clear affirmation of the universal enduring value contained in Catholic social teaching, which was articulated as the principle of subsidiarity. This book evaluates the principle and applies it to the Nigerian social and historical reality, keeping in mind the fundamental understanding of subsidiarity both as a challenge toward totalitarian tendencies and as help from below geared toward the grassroots. The Nigerian society with its multi-ethnic, multi-cultural, and multi-religious makeup is comprised of many networks of mediating institutions such as the family, churches, mosques, non-governmental organizations, market associations, the press, and labor unions that have kept the people's hope alive for a bright future in the midst of government corruption and misrule.

Thus, this book is unique in the sense that it will engage, in a systematic manner, the integration of a central religious and ethical idea, namely the principle of subsidiarity, as a vision for a just society that contributes to addressing the root cause of the Nigerian question along with local structures of governance and some principles of the classical liberal tradition. This tradition is guided by core prin-

---

4 Oswald von Nell-Breuning, "Social Movements," *Encyclopedia of Theology: The Concise Sacramentum Mundi*, (ed.), Karl Rahner (New York: The Seabury Press, 1974), pp. 1604–1605.

ciples such as the protection of rights through the rule of law, the recognition of human rights and dignity, and the promotion of responsible freedom in political, economic, cultural, religious, and social life.

Any meaningful attempt to promote social justice and civil society in Nigeria needs to begin at the beginning. More specifically, understanding the principle of subsidiarity in the proper context in which it was used by Pius XI in Catholic social teaching as "help to self-help." Indeed, Nigerians and Nigeria need this help to self-help for promoting the *bonum commune* which is at the heart of Catholic social thought.

Acting out of charity, one needs to structure multicultural groups with an interlocking relationship in society so as to engage in social and ethical reconstruction with a view to maximize liberty and still pursue a common good ordered toward the achievement of a just society. This study affirms that the answer to this question demands a holistic study of the principle of subsidiarity, hence the necessity of this book.

Method and Organization

The general approach of this book is to raise fundamental questions within a given context and to proceed with an exposition in order to arrive at some understanding of the questions raised. Since the study is concerned with the relationship existing between the individual and social groups in society and how they can best achieve social justice within a given structural framework toward their common good, the Catholic social encyclicals and biblical texts will serve as primary sources, while other secondary sources, mostly perspectives on the social encyclicals, are reviewed and analyzed.

The book begins with the discussion of the meaning of the principle of subsidiarity. I will explain the concept of subsidiarity as it has been understood in history from different perspectives. The classic sense in which the unity of substantial forms was articulated in Thomistic philosophy and theology and how these have become normative for interpreting subsidiarity in Catholic social thought are examined. Thus, the metaphysics of subsidiarity and its organological vision is discussed. Lastly, I review an African local structure of governance in terms of kinship, family, ethnic group, and the individual and community relationships.

In the second chapter, I will explain the principle of subsidiarity from the perspective of the Catholic social encyclicals. The focus of the chapter is to examine particular areas in these documents that have direct relevance to subsidiarity and other related issues that might enhance its understanding. I begin this review with the social encyclical of Leo XIII, *Rerum Novarum* (RN) 1891, where the background work for the eventual articulation of subsidiarity can be traced leading up to John Paul II, *Centesimus Annus* (CA) 1991, and Benedict XVI's *Caritas In Veritate* (CV) 2009, covering over a hundred years of Catholic social thought.

The third chapter explains the concept of social justice as a theoretical framework for a just society from theological and philosophical perspectives. I examine the biblical meaning of social justice from both the Old Testament and New Testament perspectives without engaging in the details of literary criticism. The philosophies of social justice as an integral part of justice drawing from the useful insights of St. Thomas Aquinas are examined. In addition, I trace the context in which the term "social justice" was formally introduced in Pius XI's *Quadragesimo Anno* (QA) 1931. Finally, the relationship between social justice, society, and the common good is discussed. The aim here is to envision the social context for promoting social justice in a multi-ethnic and multi-cultural pluralistic society and to set forth the essential issues that might form the agenda for building community through healthy participation of persons who imbibe the virtue of social justice as central to the common good.

The fourth chapter engages in a critical and analytical history of the Nigerian social context since the amalgamation of 1914 to the administration of Jonathan Goodluck. In so doing, I look at past mistakes and major efforts toward nationhood within a federal structure by various military regimes and civilian governments since Nigeria's independence in 1960 as well as present challenges and threats to nationhood. I propose an alternative vision for a just society in the Nigerian State. Essentially, the correlation between subsidiarity and the pursuit of a federal governmental structure that respects the complex relationships between local and central administrative units as constitutive parts of the whole is advanced. The goal is to promote grassroots participation and partnership among and between local associations and the government.

The fifth chapter examines the future prospects for subsidiarity in Nigeria. What are some of the concrete issues involved in the applicability of subsidiarity in Nigerian society that can be sustained or not? Will the Church in Nigeria lead the way in the practice of this principle since it is directly connected to the ground upon which it is founded? The aim is to indicate some of the unanswered questions that require further reflection, meditation, and practice to help determine how they will assist persons in the community to help one another and uphold the common good. Finally, the book concludes with a general synthesis of the major findings of this study that will promote the vision for a just society in Nigeria within the framework of the principle of subsidiary function.

1

THE MEANING AND BASES FOR SUBSIDIARITY: AN ORGANOLOGICAL PRINCIPLE

The principle of subsidiarity in Catholic social teaching is formally traced back to Pius XI in his celebrated social encyclical *Quadragesimo Anno* (QA)[1] 1931. What gave explicit rise to this ethical and theological principle? What was the philosophical world view out of which QA pulled and articulated this principle? These questions are raised because of their centrality in locating and rebuilding the structures of thought that gave birth to subsidiarity. In a sense, one is not concerned at this stage with the personal ideologies of those who played a major role in the writing of the encyclical QA.[2] Clearly St. Thomas Aquinas provided the foundational, philosophical, ethical, and theological bases for the doctrine of subsidiarity as it appeared in QA. More specifically, the political, economic, sociological, cultural, historical, and legal dimensions of the principle are ramifications of the philoso-

---

1 Pius XI, *Quadragesimo Anno in Catholic Social Thought: The Documentary Heritage,* (eds.), David J. O'Brien and Thomas A. Shannon (Maryknoll, New York: Orbis Books, 1992), pp. 42–79. Note that all quotations from the social encyclicals will come from this book unless otherwise stated and that this particular papal social encyclical will henceforth be referred to as QA.

2 Oswald von Nell-Breuning, *Reorganization of Social Economy: The Social Encyclical Developed and Explained,* trans. Bernard W. Dempsey (Milwaukee/New York: The Bruce Publishing Company, 1936), p. 203. This is perhaps the best work available in English that explains the encyclical QA. I will make an extensive use of the social encyclicals in the next chapter.

phy, ethics, and theology which actually undergirded the doctrine of subsidiarity. Therefore, it is to this Thomistic metaphysics that one should go to uncover the ideas which so interlock among themselves to generate the principle of subsidiarity. Initially, an analysis of subsidiarity is necessary.

The Term Subsidiarity

The main internal lead pointing to subsidiarity in QA is a solitary note which referred to two texts in St. Thomas Aquinas' two *Summas*.[3] Also, R. E. Mulcahy continued on this vague note when he wrote about the term subsidiarity that: "… this doctrine, though not by name, was taught in the earlier encyclicals of Leo XIII, *Immortale Dei* (ID) and *Rerum Novarum* (RN), and is contained in the writings of St. Thomas Aquinas about the nature of law and the state."[4] Thus, had this clarification been offered by Pius XI, it would have made superfluous our inquiry, but since this was not the case, the relevance of our reconstruction cannot be overemphasized.

Since QA was derived from RN, it may be helpful to trace the actual words in which Leo XIII provided the thought in papal social encyclicals for Pius XI to formally coin the term subsidiarity. Leo XIII, while writing on the idea that civil government should not take over the family except where: "…a family finds itself in great difficulty, utterly friendless, and without prospect for help, it is right that extreme necessity be met by public aid; for each family is a part of the commonwealth… But the rulers of the State must go no further: nature bids them stop here."[5] Leo XIII then states that "Paternal authority can neither be abolished by the State nor absorbed; for it has the same source as human life itself;"[6] Leo XIII quotes from St. Thomas Aquinas' statement, "…The child belongs to the father

3 QA Par. 47, p. 78. These references are found in St. Thomas Aquinas, *Summa Contra Gentiles,* 3, 71, trans. Vernon J. Bourke (New York: Image Books, 1956), pp. 238–239; and St. Thomas Aquinas, *The Summa Theologica,* trans. Fathers of the English Dominican Province (New York: Benziger Brothers, 1947), I, q. 65, a.2, c. Note that all quotations from St. Thomas Aquinas will come from these texts unless otherwise stated. In both notes, Pius XI took for granted that those who read the encyclical should be able to notice the obvious connection between subsidiarity as a term and the sources out of which emerged the doctrine of the principle of subsidiarity. The research will show that such a link was not as obvious as it seemed and that further clarification was needed to articulate the proper foundational basis for the term.

4 R. E. Mulcahy, "Subsidiarity," *New Catholic Encyclopedia,* vol. 13, (ed.), William J. McDonald et al. (New York: McGraw Hill Book Company, 1967), p. 762.

5 RN Par. 11, pp. 18–19.

6 Ibid.

(parents)..."[1] The purpose of Leo XIII is to protect the right of the human person (whether such a person is a child or an adult) from being taken over by the State. Thus, Leo XIII upheld the natural right of the parents to look after their child, a duty which a higher collectivity like the State need not embark on when responsible parents are there to take up such a task. One can notice here, in Leo XIII, how the obvious connection between the quote from Aquinas and subsidiarity is somewhat vague. How can one make this link much more nuanced? Perhaps, some understanding of the foundational ground for subsidiarity might provide a step in the right direction.

The clearest understanding of the root meaning of the term subsidiarity, which was discovered in the process of this study, is that provided in *Andrew's Latin Dictionary*, cited by Benjamin Llamzon. The root meaning of *subsidium:* the troops stationed in reserve in the third line of battle (behind the Principes); subsidium dicebatur quando milites subsidebant in extrema acie labentique aciei succurebant. Hence the essential idea of an auxiliary force and the synonym suppetiae.[2] According to the above Latin meaning of the term, the function of the principle of subsidiarity is similar to that of reserve troops in time of war or rescue mission; in other words, it has to come to the rescue, to help out where regular troops are inadequate.

The *Oxford English Dictionary*, paraphrasing Pope Pius XI in QA 80 describes subsidiarity as: "...the quality of being subsidiary; the principle that a central authority should have a subsidiary function, performing only tasks which cannot be performed effectively at a more immediate or local level."[3]

Similarly, Manno's working definition of subsidiarity further articulates the meaning of the term in this way:

> Subsidiarity refers to a way of organizing and ordering groups to pursue common purposes and objectives. The etymology of the word includes notions of support, aid and help in standing up. The term, then, points to a particular manner of organizing communities to assist each other in the task of standing up and pursuing common goals. To accept this principle is to imply something inherently good about groups organizing around interests and helping each other seek common ends, the ultimate end being to put things right and help everyone stand on their feet.[4]

---

1 Ibid. cf., St. Thomas Aquinas, *The Summa Theologica*, II-II, q. 10, a. 12. The word in bracket is mine.

2 Benjamin S. Llamson, "Subsidiarity: The Term, Its Metaphysics and Use," *Aquinas* 21(1978): 48; *Andrew's Latin Dictionary* (New York, 1907), n.p.

3 *The Oxford English Dictionary*, 2 ed. vol. XVIII, (eds.), J. A. Simpson and E. S. C. Weiner (Oxford: Clarendon Press, 1989), p. 59.

4 Bruno V. Manno, "Subsidiarity and Pluralism: A Social Philosophical Perspective," *Toward Vatican III: The Work That Needs to Be Done*, (eds.), David Tracy, Hans Kung & Johann B. Metz (New York: Seabury Press, 1978), p. 320.

Manno's understanding of subsidiarity specifically reveals it as a principle of justice by which individuals and groups formulate and pursue true social order: "... Even though groups have varying interests, subsidiarity implies that common ends are not antithetical to the pursuit of particular interests. In fact, the common good is defined through the interaction of these varying interests conducting themselves with an eye to social charity."[5]

Mulcahy further upholds an understanding of the term subsidiarity, which seeks to link the different spheres of society by insisting that one must look to the nature of the state and society:

> Man is a social person, who achieves his perfection only in society. The state exists to help the persons who live within the society. This is the meaning of the Latin word, *subsidium*, aid, and help. Normally, this aid is indirect by the care of the complex of conditions that enable the subordinate societies and the individuals to care for their own needs.[6]

This was the sense in which Pius XI formulated the *subsidiarii officii principum*, the principle according to which the State must fulfill a subsidiary function with respect to the family and organically developed socio-ethical life. Thus, the complex of conditions in a given society is geared toward the common good of all members of the society. The present research will show the many conditions necessary to enable the individual to achieve his or her social and economic welfare. At present, the term subsidiarity is understood as dealing broadly with the "...limits of the right and duty of the public authority to intervene in social and economic affairs."[7]

Daniel Wincott[8] has also offered an understanding of the term subsidiarity in the context of Catholic social thought that takes into consideration the limited role of government; the place of private institutions; and society as an organism comprising a hierarchy of organs. In so doing, Wincott highlights the major themes which surround a holistic understanding of subsidiarity as a term in this way:

> The purpose of subsidiarity in Catholic Social Theory was on the one hand to limit the role of government as a whole in order to vindicate and protect the place of private institutions including the Church itself, while, on the other hand, justifying some role for government. This notion of subsidiarity was enmeshed in an understanding of society as an organism characterized by a hierarchy of organs. Subsequently, subsidiarity has been used as a quasi constitutional concept in some federal or federal-type political systems to provide a rationale for the allocation of powers between various levels of government. Wherever possible powers are given to the least aggregated level of gov-

5 Ibid.

6 See Mulcahy, "Subsidiarity," p. 762.

7 Ibid.

8 Daniel Wincott, "Subsidiarity," *Oxford Concise Dictionary of Politics*, (ed.), Iain McLean (Oxford: Oxford University Press, 1996), p. 482.

ernment; only when a particular task cannot be undertaken adequately by a 'low' level of government will it be handed 'up' to a higher level.[9]

Both Leo XIII and Pius XI quoted St. Thomas Aquinas as the basis for the term subsidiarity. This research indicates that the term subsidiarity has always been linked to an organic structure within the human community, and that subsidiarity values both individual liberty and community. It supports the growth and development of human identity and community through the effort of groups that are free of domination, compulsion, invasion, and intrusion by large outside forces. What was missing in the position of both Leo XIII and Pius XI was the fact that they presumed an obvious link in their readers between the metaphysical framework in Aquinas which gave birth to this term and its subsequent articulation as a papal term in the social encyclicals. The next section will unearth the metaphysics in Aquinas from which the term subsidiarity was derived.

The Metaphysics of Subsidiarity[10]

In taking a metaphysical position as basis for subsidiarity in Aquinas, one is aware of attacks from linguistic positivists, especially on the issue of God and similar questions. This approach should not be perceived as a return to and glorification of Pre-Kantian dogmatism. This investigation is based on two related principles: an understanding of Aquinas which rejects essentialistic parts coined out of any type of purely conceptual arguments; a reflective Thomism with its roots firmly established in the existential judgment which is directly related to the act of being itself—*esse* as absolutely a priori to essence and everything else in existence. These philosophical claims transcend both the perceived rigidity of Kant on metaphysics to empty concepts, and the demand of the Positivists that meaning and understanding be limited simply to empirical phenomena. The examination of some key Thomistic positions[11] will clarify further why it is appropriate to use Aquinas's metaphysics as a basis for subsidiarity.

First, one begins with the position that God is First Cause. God is the wise and provident governor of all creation which He governs with Divine goodness. Second, the Divine governor provides order and harmony to the plurality of beings in the universe. Third, the Divine governor has created the human person with the aim that human beings pursue their ultimate end in a self-directed way. Fourth,

9 Ibid.

10 See Llamson, 44–62. This study was an important attempt to articulate the metaphysics of subsidiarity from a philosophical perspective. One will draw some insights from the arguments made here and sharpen them toward establishing the foundational basis for subsidiarity as an ethical and theological principle in human history.

11 St. Thomas Aquinas, *The Summa Theologica*, I, a. qq. 103–119; Paul J. Glenn, *A Tour of the Summa* (Rockford, Illinois: Tan Books and Publishers, 1978), pp. 84–96.

with the Divine primary causality, the human person freely actualizes himself as secondary causality (concurrence). In this conjoined causality, the secondary causality itself remains intact and is never lost. Fifth, God as divine goodness, orderer, and governor sometimes intervenes to produce effects which are at once called for but are for the moment beyond the capacity of the lesser causalities. Thus, preservation or conservation is fundamental to the divine governor. These positions are so interlocked in Aquinas that they are to be understood in concert rather than separately. In what way do these positions simultaneously provide the basis for subsidiarity?

The act of being—*esse*—is that by which any lesser creature, by itself only potential to existence, exists. It is not possible for any secondary creature to be the origin of this *esse*, because that would possess the quality of a purely potential being actualizing itself. God is the only Being, *Ipsum Esse,* that causes the existence of other beings and that sustains their activities. It follows then that in the Divine simplicity, causality is identical to wisdom, providence, and government. This means that "God preserves all creatures…by positive sustaining power; that is, God conserves all creatures directly. But He does not conserve all things immediately, that is, without using any creatural means or medium."[12] This means further that God guides all created beings toward divine goodness according to their mode of being. God is then in created beings just as the "…archer is present in the arrow…" that flies from the bow toward an appointed target.[13] So, while God is present in the human person as energizing his act of selecting his target, God is in no way responsible for the sinful acts of the human being. One notes particularly how Aquinas was able to resolve this paradox in the analogy of the limping man. The power of locomotion is meant to cause the man to walk, not to limp. The limp is due rather to the "crooked limb."[14] In the same way, human beings exist and carry out their free choice which is sustained by divine causality. But the acts proper are imputable to the human agents. The pertinent point is that the Divine governor, in directing created beings to their ultimate end unequivocally respects their own natures. In particular, God wills the human being to be "master of his own destiny." This is precisely the focal point where subsidiarity emerges in Aquinas,

> The best thing in any government is to provide for the things governed according to their own mode, for the justice of a regime consists in this. Therefore, as it would be contrary to the rational character of a human regime for men to be prevented by the governor from acting in accord with their own duties except, perhaps, on occasion, due to the need of the moment so, too, would it be contrary to the rational character of the

12 St. Thomas Aquinas, *The Summa Theologica,* I, q. 103, art. 6; cf. Paul J. Glenn, *A Tour of the Summa,* p. 86.

13 cf., St. Thomas Aquinas, *The Summa Theologica,* I, q. 103, art. 1.

14 Ibid. I, q. 49, a. 2, art. 2.

divine regime to refuse permission for created things to act according to the mode of their nature.[15]

What is the point of making the analogy that human government reflects Divine government? It seems reasonable to say that Aquinas made room for diversity of opinions in human society as it is reflected in the universe; one can then begin to see why the idea of subsidiarity was considered to be intrinsic to wise and just governance. Special consideration was given to the role of the administrators, who act as facilitators by maintaining a healthy balance between the ruled and the ruler:

> Besides, in things ruled by human providence, it is to be observed that someone is placed at the head who has charge of the general matters of great importance, and by himself devises what arrangements to make with regard to them; while he himself does not devise the order of minor affairs but leaves this to others lower than himself. Now this is owing to a defect on his part, in as much as he is ignorant of the conditions of particular matters of less importance, or is himself incompetent to decide the order of everything because of the labor and delay required for the purpose.[16]

Aquinas opines that creaturely causality remains intact and active, not outside the Divine government but in view of it, and within it. Also, the independence of the individuals within human society is promoted within the ultimately sustaining perspective of society and the guidance of its ruler who necessarily work hand in hand in the exercise of individual causality. The central role of the ruler, then, is to assemble individuals with different talents and to seek their cooperation with the main aim of building the common good of the society. Aquinas makes this point very clear:

> Furthermore, he will have to gather together the men who must be appointed to suitable places according to their respective occupations. Finally, he must provide for each one what is necessary for his particular condition and state in life; otherwise, the kingdom or state could never endure. These are, then, briefly, the duties that pertain to the office of king in founding a city or kingdom, as divined from a comparison with the creation of the world.[17]

An important analogy that Aquinas used in emphasizing how unity in diversity can be maintained in a given State or kingdom further exemplifies the significance of subsidiarity. It is the analogy of the parts and whole of a living body:

> The fact that all parts of the universe are directed to the perfection of the whole is not in contradiction with the foregoing conclusion, since all the parts are directed to the perfection of the whole, insofar as one part serves another. Thus in the human body, it is clear that the lungs belong to the body's perfection in that they serve the heart;

---

15 *Summa Contra Gentiles,* 3, 71.

16 Ibid. 3, 76.

17 St. Thomas Aquinas, *De Regime Principum,* rev. ed. & trans. Gerald B. Phelan (London/New York: Sheed & Ward, 1938), I, 12.

> and thence there is no contradiction in the lungs being for the sake of the heart and for the sake of the whole animal. In like manner, that other natures are omitted for the sake of intellectual ones is not contrary to their being for the perfection of the universe; for without the things required for the perfection of the intellectual substance, the universe would not be complete.[18]

There seems to be a major connection here between Book XIX of St. Augustine's *City of God* and Thomas Aquinas's *De Regime Principum*[19] in the understanding associated with order and peace. According to Augustine, order is intrinsic to the good of the society in the sense that it provides the opportunity for the allocation of roles according to the proper position of each thing. Peace, which is the "tranquillity of order," is the peaceful order which exists among the things themselves-their cooperation, harmony, support, mutual enrichment, accessibility, shared responsibility, shared benefits and burdens.

> The peace of the body...is a tempering of the component parts in duly ordered proportion, the peace of the irrational soul is a duly ordered repose of the appetites; the peace of the rational soul is the duly ordered agreement of cognition and action. The peace of body and soul is the duly ordered life and health of a living creature; peace between mortal man and God is an ordered obedience, in faith, in subjection to an everlasting law; peace between men is an ordered agreement of mind with mind; the peace of a home is the ordered agreement among those who live together about giving and obeying orders; the peace of the Heavenly City is a perfectly ordered and perfectly harmonious fellowship in the enjoyment of God, and a mutual fellowship in God; the peace of the whole universe is the tranquillity of order...[20]

What is emerging from this study is the multiplicity and plurality of existential levels among creatures. At the same time, these creatures are somehow bonded in such a manner toward the achievement of a common finality. The universe then is the composite of a natural pluriverse, arranged and organized according to the Divine governor's disposition and willingness to allow for the proper enhancement of the various beings, each according to their nature. One can deduce from this analysis the metaphysical basis for the doctrine of subsidiarity on four grounds:

1. Since God does not do away with secondary causality from creatures in their pluriform actions and activities in the world, states or governors, as they carry out their civic responsibilities, should not overrun individual enterprise, overtly or covertly through the use of deputies, or by the imposition of a hidden ideology or agenda.

2. Moreover, it is pertinent that the different roles, hobbies, and trades of the citizens in a S tate be the products of individual initiative from below, not of assignation from the top, no matter how cleverly hidden to appear

---

18 *Summa Contra Gentiles*, 3, 113.

19 *De Regime Principum*, I, 3; 9; 4.

20 St. Augustine, *City of God* (Penguin Classics, 1984), XIX, 13, p. 870.

otherwise. This is the true sense in which individual causality is retained and promoted. Thus, it is only in emergency situations and for a limited time and with a concrete aim and goal that the individual causality could be overruled. Even here, such an intervention must be for the sole purpose of protecting the common good.

3. Accordingly, God's intent is that thinking beings should be able to direct themselves to their end, struggling in their diversity toward a common ground. The creator gives human beings the will to decide whether to move ultimately in the direction of the governor.

4. Since, at the core of their being, humans enjoy the capacity and freedom to choose how to go about attaining their ultimate end, humans are able to claim inalienable rights in society. No society can interfere on this deeper level of their existence. This means that though humans are in the State, it is impossible for the state to assimilate them totally as in Dostoevsky's *Grand Inquisitor* or Hobbes's *Leviathan.*[21] Ontologically, human beings are prior to the State with a freedom that is before and beyond the power of the State; the individual has no less than a divine mandate, at this level of one's existence, to fulfill himself through his initiative. Thus, his or her participation in society should be through the exercise of his inalienable capacity to choose. At this point, one encounters the deepest and profound realization that human beings are in partnership with the State as its building blocks. They should not just be seen as parts of the whole, but their transcendent capacity to choose remains intact before the Divine governor, and *a fortiori* before any human governor.

Challenges to the Metaphysics of Subsidiarity

Some challenges emerge in this inquiry about the metaphysics of subsidiarity in two ways. The first issue has to do with relationality in a substantial form. Whereas traditional Thomistic thought emphasizes unity of form and substance, it tends to minimize the interrelation of substances. In what respect can a holistic notion of substantial forms go beyond making wholes more than the sum of their parts and endow them with new characteristics, properties, and behaviors which cannot be found in the isolated parts? The second issue is closely related to the first one: it

21 Thomas Hobbes, *Leviathan,* (ed.), C. B. Macpherson (New York: Penguin Classics, 1985), 150–168; Fyodor Dostoevsky, *The Grand Inquisitor,* Intro. Anne Fremantle (New York: Continuum, 1998), pp. 1–22 address three key issues: human freedom, human conscience and human unity, which groups in society are constantly dealing with both as individuals and communities that are central to a proper understanding of subsidiarity that will stand out in the later part of this work.

has to do with the nature of the parts of a given system or substance and in their relation to the whole. Thomas affirmed that the substantial form informed prime matter directly and that in an organism no more than one substantial form emerged

> ...For there are not different substantial forms in one and the same thing...Since, if the first form were to make the being a substance, the following forms would be accruing to that which already is actually a definite something *hoc aliquid*, and subsisting in nature; thus, the later forms would not make a definite something, but would be in the subject which is a definite something as accidental forms.[22]

Perhaps, some understanding of substantial forms as organisms, which inform the matter of an organism as parts of the substance, rather than accidents in the process, might offer some perspective toward a holistic presentation of the degrees of subsidiarity. One may then discover that some subsidiary forms might be more independent, others more interdependent of the larger whole than others, some less independent than others. Could the understanding of substantial form as organism in terms of relationality and levels of subsidiary functions offer some insights to the principle of subsidiarity? The next section will address this question and similar issues as one considers the organological vision of subsidiarity.

The Organological Vision of Subsidiarity

The term "organological vision" is not found in any of the major reference works today. But one does find the term "organology": "...the study of the organs of animals and plants,"[23] and so the term "organological:" means "of or relating to organology" and is used as the adjective of organology. Thus, the term "organological vision" is derived from the understanding of "...organism: as an organic structure, something felt to resemble a living plant or animal"[24] in the following ways:

> -an entity having existence independent of or more fundamental than its elements and having distinct members or parts whose relations and powers or properties are determined by their function in the whole (the nation is not merely the sum of individual citizens at any given time, but it is a living organism, a mystical body...of which the individual is an ephemeral part-Joseph Rossi);
>
> -a being in which every part is at once a means and an end to every other, something arising and developing in an organic manner (whether the whole of reality is an organism or a machine-Weston LaBarre);

22 Thomas Aquinas, *Summa Contra Gentiles* (Notre Dame, IN: Notre Dame Press, 1975), 4, 81, 303.

23 *Webster's Third New International Dictionary of the English Language*, ed. Philip Babcock Gove (Springfield, Massachusetts: Merriam/Webster Publishers, 1993), p. 1590. See details of the meaning of the term "organology" that one has adopted in this work.

24 Ibid.

-an individual constituted to carry on the activities of life by means of parts or organs more or less separate in function but mutually dependent: a living being/system.[25]

Thus, Ad Leys, who used the term "organological vision" in relation to subsidiarity and from whom I have borrowed the term, understood it in terms of the "concept" of the society: "The organological vision of society understands society (and other forms of associations) as one whole, as a unity. This vision rejects the idea that such an association would be a solitary reality and that associations are based purely on agreements."[26] In this study I use the term "organological vision" both in the sense understood by Leys as a vision of society and association embracing an innate relationship between the parts and the whole, as a unity, and in the sense articulated in *Webster's International Dictionary* as a living being or system where the parts and the whole have different functions but are mutually dependent on each other.

Leys tells the fable of Menenius Agrippa, the Roman senator, who tried to quiet the uprising of the people in order to place them once more under the guidance of the Senate. Tradition has it that this fable helped to restore peace in Rome and provided a reasonable forum for the Senate to operate while at the same time providing checks and balances for the protection of the people against the abuse of power. The fable is that:

> Long ago the human body was not yet one whole reality, but each part had its own life, its own will, and its own thoughts. One day the members asked themselves why they were so busy the whole day long. They concluded that the reason was to be found in the stomach, which is situated at the center, and which was being served by all other members, while it did nothing. The other members thought this was crazy and they decided to stop. The feet no longer walked, the hands no longer held anything, and the mouth refused to chew. But when this had gone on for a whole day, the members did not feel happy. It became clear that the stomach was not just being fed, but that the food was transformed into strong blood which coursed through the arteries to the members and which was necessary for them. In the new situation the members were in dan-

25 Ibid.

26 Ad Leys, *Ecclesiological Impacts of the Principle of Subsidiarity*, trans., A. Van Santroord (Kampen, Netherlands: Kok Pharos, 1995), p. 2. cf. VII n. 49, p. 127. The work of Ad Leys is a major study on subsidiarity from an ecclesial perspective, which serves as a response to the request made by the Synod of Bishops of 1985 for an in-depth study on the theoretical and practical applications of subsidiarity for the Church. This work has provided one with very useful insights for this research. Perhaps one major difference between Leys' work and this study lies in the perspectives. Leys examined the Church from a European view point while my understanding of Church is colored by my African experience. What is central to both works is that the principle of subsidiarity has universal relevance and is common to all human communities.

> ger of becoming victims of an action which was intended only to affect the stomach. The members realized this, began to function again, and were no longer unhappy.[27]

What can one learn from this fable that is related to the organological vision? How does this fable help one describe the organological vision? In what way is the organological vision both similar to and different from subsidiarity? Can the organological vision provide some fundamental basis for understanding the principle of subsidiarity? The next section will address these pertinent questions.

The fable of Menenius Agrippa stressed the reality that peace and harmony were necessary ingredients for healthy associations in a given community. It also underscored the importance of having a united association, while rejecting an association where members of the group live disjointedly without relating in some way with the other members of the group. There is a connection between this fable and the organological vision since they convey the meaning of maintaining interdependence of the parts to the whole and vice versa. Ad Leys tells us that Ambros[28] provided the context and foundation on which the organological vision and more concrete organological concepts are based. They include:

1. The notion that wholeness and unity are in opposition to a simple collection of unrelated organisms;
2. The notion that individual realities are parts and not self-sufficient;
3. The notion that the parts belong to the whole structure in which their particular role and relation to the whole is constantly being determined, and at the same time determines the whole.

It would seem then that the organological vision on associations should include, among other things, some fundamental characteristics: the idea of some kind of unity in diversity; the idea of interdependence of the parts rather than self-sufficiency, and the idea that the structure of the whole be kept intact at all times.

What is meant by calling an association an organism? In general, organisms convey the meaning of a concrete, individual, independent, living reality: a single cell, a plant or an animal or a human body. These are largely biological and physiological realities, where the concrete existence of the parts and of the whole is constantly dependent and interdependent on one another. Does this situation apply in the case of associations involving human persons? One can argue, for instance, that human beings are capable of some form of withdrawal from their society, without necessarily losing their biological or physiological existence. In a

---

27 The fable of Menenius Agrippa, probably from the fifth century B.C., is a prototype and classical expression of the organological vision on associations, such as the family, church, society as a whole, organizations within society, and the state. Cited in Dohm 1978, 526; See Ad Leys, p. 1.

28 See Ambros 1963, 15–16; cited in Ad Leys, *Ecclesiological Impacts of the Principle of Subsidiarity*, p. 2.

situation where groups of people form a social organism, there is not such a substantial unity as in a biological union; the same directness and necessity of mutual relationships is lacking. That is why political, social, cultural, religious, and economic interests are often opposed: "...Individuals and groups do not always work together harmoniously, they often oppose each other; yet that does not necessarily lead to disintegration of the state or of society."[29] The position expressed by Leys with regard to social harmony is pertinent because it raises two critical implications: first, one must admit that some measure of conflict is vital for the healthy functioning of society; second, the existence of absolute harmony in a social setup is unattainable anywhere except as a utopian project.

Dohrn and Kluber, cited by Ad Leys,[30] have shown that the State and society have often been called an "organism" for as long as people have practiced political reflection, and have pointed out the similarities between the biological and the social organism in this way:

1. There is a certain unity, connection, and interaction between the whole and the parts. Political, economic, and social processes show that;
2. Society as such survives change and/or even interchange of its parts: there is continuity and history;
3. Society as such has its own goals which can be achieved by the (organized) parts.

Having discussed the similarities between biological and social organisms, one sees the context in which one could apply the term "organism" to a concept beyond the normal biological connotation. Scholars such as Gundlach and von Nell-Breuning are pioneers whose works are still being supported by those of Ad Leys and Manno in making an analogous use of "organism" in connection with associations,[31] a position which I find both useful and relevant for some understanding of the principle of subsidiarity. What is most appealing in the analogous use of "organism" is its communal character which allows one to expand the meaning of organism beyond biological organisms. In view of this development, Ad Leys says, the organological vision takes on a broader meaning: "In this vision one makes a choice for the way one sees the human being, not the isolated individual, the monad, who only secondarily affirms his coexistence with subjects, but as a person who knows that being human and becoming subject is essentially a communal

29 See Ad Leys, *Ecclesiological Impacts of the Principle of Subsidiarity*, p. 3.

30 Dohrn 1978, 519–623; Kluber 1968, 848–849 cited in Ad Leys, *Ecclesiological Impacts of the Principle of Subsidiarity*, p. 4.

31 Gundlach 1931/2, 1614; Nell-Breuning 1947, 9–11; cited in Ad Leys, *Ecclesiological Impacts of the Principle of Subsidiarity*, p. 5; Bruno V. Manno, "Subidiarity and Pluralism," pp. 321–322.

project."[32] By designating an association as an organism, one is only at the primary level of comprehension, for the full content of how an association will play out as an organism has not been clearly articulated. One is pointing here to issues like the relationship between persons, between partial groups, between persons and partial groups, between partial groups and the whole group. Thus, any talk about an "organism" or an organological vision should be understood as something more formal and more concrete.

Leys points out, for instance, how Schlanger in her study of "organism" as *analogon* in the 18th and in the 19th centuries concluded that the concept is a variable: "...especially in the texts on political questions it is not possible to indicate precisely what the meaning of (organism) is."[33] Schlanger did offer a pertinent function of analogy: the *fonction de facilitation*. This analogy offers a perspective which includes expressions, arguments, and models that perform a heuristic role. Thus, the central role of an organism is clarified when Schlanger says that an "Organism has a political or rhetorical meaning: by describing society or the state in this way one wants to indicate that harmony, integration, and solidarity are more important, more fundamental than opposition of interests or classes, and are in fact prior to these."[34] Thus, in an organological vision, emphasis will be placed on social harmony and unity, which does allow for the existence of opposition which might give allowance for conflict. No doubt, opposition could lead to some form of conflict and to safeguard that conflict does not reign, the judicious use of the rule of law and public authority are employed in areas of conflict and disharmony.

Challenges to the Organological Vision

Nell-Breuning has examined the limitations of the organic analogy in the context of the role of the organism in the moral order by taking a cautious approach in applying this analogy to the social organism, especially with respect to the human person. Accordingly, one cannot expect that the human person like the cell in an organism should remain indefinitely in the place it happens to occupy by nature of its function: "...This would actually bring us dangerously near guilds of birth. In reality the moral-legal organism of society, demanded by nature, but for whose development we are given a large degree of freedom, is freer and less rigid than the physiological organism."[35] Thus, one advocates an understanding of organism in the social arena that is much more fluid and accommodating, to guard against "...

32 See Ad Leys, *Ecclesiological Impacts of the Principle of Subsidiarity*, p. 5.

33 See Schlanger 1971, 27 and 31: "les continus de la representation, eux, varient selon les epoques;" cited in Ad Leys, *Ecclesiological Impacts of the Principle of Subsidiarity*, p. 6.

34 Cf. Schlanger 1971, 33, 91–99 and 256, cited in Ad Leys, p. 6.

35 See Nell-Breuning, *Reorganization of Social Economy*, p. 220.

The performance principle of liberal competition, under which I must struggle for my social position and must expect to lose it as a result of temporary inefficiency."[36]

Similarly, Ad Leys maintains that the major difficulty with the organological vision is that it allows some room for a centralist concept of the State:

> Such centralistic concepts could be: in a totalitarian system the power of the state (and/or the party) is seen as unassailable; principles of tolerance, of free development of the person, and of autonomy of the various spheres of life and culture are denied...an authoritarian system (is) seen as a mild form of the totalitarian system. Collectivism not just gives preference to the collective over the individual, but denies also the inalienable proper value of the individual and human rights.[37]

Thus, the tendency to centralize is enhanced by appealing to the individual, the particular, to subject to the whole just as in the fable of Menenius Agrippa- the theory shifts its hierarchy of importance from the stomach to the head, and all the other parts of the body are made subject to the head:

> By giving so much emphasis to the head or to the whole, the organological vision can easily become a centralistic vision of state and society, in which the individual person is subject to the whole and cannot claim any rights from that whole. The "head" (authority) determines everything and, in order to let the whole function well, the "members" (individuals or groups) must subject themselves: the interest of the whole prevails sometimes even at the cost of the "members."[38]

Thus, centralism appears to be inherent to the organological vision. Ad Leys has explained that, in the history of the West, this centralism was expressed in terms of a *corpus theory*,[39] and has shifted from one age to another. In the beginning, unity in diversity was emphasized; then the Roman Empire and Emperors became synonymous with the emperor as the head or the soul; the Middle Ages also insisted on the leading role of the head, over and against the other members, in a body like State and Church; while in the beginning of the 19th century some totalitarian tendencies become manifest in this vision. Is there any way by which the centralism discovered in the organological vision could be countered, so that the positive elements of this vision are maintained as bridges to understanding the

---

36 Ibid. p. 220. Nell-Breuning argued further that corporate and vocational activity in a state should involve both a "performance society" and an "area society." "Wherever people live close together they establish numerous contacts that lead to social life. It is necessary for the welfare of the state that these economic and cultural centers maintain their independent significance and, as separate groups, form the building stones of the state structure," pp. 221–222.

37 See Ad Leys, *Ecclesiological Impacts of the Principle of Subsidiarity*, n. 23, p. 7.

38 See Kluber 1968, 849; Bockenforde 1982, 16–17; cited in Ad Leys, *Ecclesiological Impacts of the Principle of Subsidiarity*, p. 7.

39 Ibid.

principle of subsidiarity? One can turn to Immanuel Kant's understanding of "organism" to find some basis for responding to this question.

Immanuel Kant and the Organological Vision

Kant's organism[40] theory has been articulated and applied to society by some scholars[41] as providing some general understanding of the organological vision. Kant's three *Kritiken* provide us with major understanding on the preconditions of human knowledge and the key issues involved with cognitive power. The questions of Kant's epistemological difficulties are far beyond this work. Thus, one can specifically examine the usage made by Kant's views on "organism" without going into the larger perspective of his *Kritik der Urteilskraft*.[42] Kant uses the analogy of the tree[43] to explain an organism. According to him, a tree is capable of developing within itself the capacities of cause and effect, as it grows from its genus. The true reality is that the permanence of the different parts of the tree depends on their mutual interaction; just as the whole is dependent on the parts, so too are the parts dependent on the whole, and the leaves as products of the tree as well help the trunk to grow and the tree to survive. In case of an accidental damage to the tree, the tree relies on its innate ability to recover and continue its growth. Following these arguments, Kant posited that a natural goal could be simultaneously cause and effect of itself.[44]

There are two interlocking necessary conditions for a thing to be goal in and of itself: the form and existence of the parts are possible only in relation to the whole, but this is not a sufficient determinant because such a thing could also be influenced externally; the parts then must mutually form cause and effect of their own. In this way, the whole is able to determine and inform the coherence of all the other parts.

40 "*Organisierte Korper*" is the equivalent of organisms, because they are "*Gewachse und Tiere*," Immanuel Kant, *Kritik der Urteilskraft*, Hrgb. W. Weischedel 57(Frankfurt a. M.: Suhrkamp, 1974), par. 292 cited in Ad Leys, *Ecclesiological Impacts of the Principle of Subsidiarity*, p. 8, n. 31–32.

41 See Ad Leys, p. 8, n. 29–30 for the tribute paid to the works of Bockenforde 1982, 16; Schlanger 1971, 200; Ambros 1963, 17, and Greiffenhagen 1971, 201 on the importance of Kant's thoughts on organism.

42 The edition used is the English translation, Immanuel Kant, *Critique of Judgment*, trans. Werner S. Pluhar (Indianapolis/Cambridge: Hackett Publishing Company, 1987). The general areas that deal with organism which are appropriated in this work include: The Translator's Introduction pp. lxxvii-lxxxii; Part II, Par. 64–66. The other more specific areas are indicated in subsequent footnotes.

43 Ibid. Par. 64, pp. 249–250.

44 Ibid. Par. 65, p. 251.

Essentially, the position of Kant adopted here is that an "organism" which has an inner cause and effect is that whereby each part exists through the other parts and for the other parts and for the whole. Here, each part plays an equally productive part as the other parts. Hence, one can affirm a goal in and of itself without any external influence. Thus, Kant defined the organism as: "...an organized product of nature is one where everything is a purpose and reciprocally also a means. Nothing is gratuitous, purposeless, or to be attributed to a blind natural mechanism."[45]

What is the significance of Kant's vision against centralist tendencies in organological thought? There appears to be some positive contribution, arising from Kant's use of the "original contract"[46] theory, which one can link with that of the organological vision of the State. Kant maintains that a people constitute themselves into a State by means of an "original contract" which legitimates the existence of the State. The "original contract" is understood as the inner cause for the people coming together to found the State. Thus, the link between the "original contract" and the organological vision of the State lies in the inner causality for the existence of the State. Notice here some correlation between the inner dynamism of an organism which is central to the proper understanding of the organological vision, and the existence of the State without any external cause articulated by Kant in the "original contract."

Ad Leys supports the understanding that Kant's organism theory agrees with a non-centralist organological vision and thus provides a healthy perspective for articulating the organological vision of the State that is devoid of centralist tendencies like the "corpus theory" alluded to earlier:

> The parts (the members) are mutually each other's cause and effect and maintain, therefore, a relative independence. No part is pure means, not even in relation to the whole, which exists only thanks to the parts: as such the whole is no more than the sum of the parts and their mutual interplay...In Kant's organism theory the relations between the parts and with the whole are mutual and continuous and so the parts retain their own position.[47]

Thus, the interaction between the parts and the whole allows room for a common goal, a holistic goal that embraces unity in diversity. The chapter discusses the fact that the inner dynamism of an organism to exist is far more essential than any form of external causation. Thus, an organological vision of the State with centralist tendencies needs to be reformulated to reflect a mutually interdependent conception of the State or society, where the parts and the whole work together in an organic and harmonic unity, respecting the worth of each other in being part

45 Ibid. Par. 66, p. 255.

46 Immanuel Kant, *The Metaphysics of Morals.* trans. & ed., Mary Gregor (Cambridge: Cambridge University Press, 1996), Par. 47, pp. 42–43.

47 See Ad Leys, *Ecclesiological Impacts of the Principle of Subsidiarity,* p. 10.

of the whole. The next section will examine the bases for the organological vision of society from the African perspective.

The Organological Vision in African Societies

The study of the organizational arrangements of traditional African societies has been carried out in depth by various scholars from different perspectives.[48] It is beyond the scope of this book to examine African traditional practices of self-government on the whole of the African continent. The research is restricted to the Nigerian context, and particularly to the Tiv people of the middle belt of Nigeria. The study will, however, cite examples of practices of tribal, family and kinship activities around the African continent that are related and relevant to the topic. The goal is to highlight some of the key issues around which African societies were able to organize themselves prior to the colonial encounter and to examine the impact of modernity on these institutions; to ascertain the role of the individual and the community in the African society; to see how some of the positive values support the organological vision of the State; and to examine the stabilizing role that the principle of subsidiarity plays in the ethical, social, political, religious, cultural, and economic reconstruction of the Nigerian State.

John S. Mbiti is of the opinion that, in African societies, the sense of a people, society, and nation is centered on a person's understanding of 'tribe':

> A person has to be born a member of it, and he cannot change tribal membership. On rare occasions he can be adopted ritually into another tribal group, but this is seldom

48 Chinua Achebe, *Things Fall Apart* (London: Heinemann, 1958). This is one of the earliest books that captures so vividly and dramatically the organization of Igbo ethnic society and how the British colonial conquest put asunder the organizational arrangements of the society. John S. Mbiti, *African Religions and Philosophy* (London: Heinemann, 1969), pp. 15-27, 100-110; Cheryl Johnson, "Grass Roots Organizing: Women In Anticolonial Activity in South-Western Nigeria," *African Studies Review* XXV/2&3(June/September, 1982): 136–157; P. O. Bodunrin, (ed.), *Philosophy in Africa: Trends and Perspectives* (Ile-Ife: University of Ile-Ife Press, 1985), pp. 128–228.; A. Adu Boahen, *African Perspectives on Colonialism* (Baltimore: The Johns Hopkins University Press, 1987), pp. 1-26.; Tesemchi Makar, *The History of Political Change Among the Tiv in the 19th and 20th Centuries* (Enugu, Nigeria: Fourth Dimension Publishers, 1994), pp. 8–30; Elochukwu E. Uzukwu, *A Listening Church: Autonomy and Communion in African Churches* (Maryknoll, New York: Orbis Books, 1996), pp. 12–20, 35–46; Ali A. Mazrui and Alamin M. Mazrui, *The Power of Babel: Language and Governance in the African Experience* (Chicago: University of Chicago Press, 1998), pp. 1–28.; John L. Comaroff and Jean Comaroff, (eds.), *Civil Society and the Political Imagination in Africa: Critical Perspectives* (Chicago & London: The University of Chicago Press, 1999), 72–103, 124-159.; Coulibaly Cheibane, "On Subsidiarity in Western Africa: A Contribution to Institutional Problem-Solving in Africa," Paper for *The Workshop on the Workshop* 2. Bloomington (Indiana: Indiana University, 1999), pp. 1–32; Kwasi Wiredu, "An Akan Perspective on Human Rights," *The Philosophy of Human Rights: Paragon Issues in Philosophy*, (ed.), Patrick Hayden (St. Paul, Minnesota: Paragon House, 2001), pp. 298–314.

> done...Tribal identity is still a powerful force even in modern African statehood, although that feeling of tribal identity varies like temperature, from time to time, depending on prevailing circumstances.[49]

The meaning of the term 'tribe' is to be understood in the context of a kin-bonded community:

> ...Composed of several villages recognizing a traditional relationship to each other based upon a shared name, a common language and culture, marital boundaries that are isomorphic with the boundaries of the village ensemble, and possibly recognizing supra-village religious authorities...
>
> Such a society is classless, functions through designated kin or quasi-kin associations.[50]

An examination of the different facets of the tribe helps to further determine the different organizational arrangements that have stood the test of time in the historical experience and existence of these communities.

The Kinship System

According to Mbiti the major reason why tribal ties are still very strong in African modern Statehood can be traced to the influence of kinship:

> The deep sense of kinship, with all it implies, has been one of the strongest forces in traditional African life. Kinship is reckoned through blood and betrothal (engagement and marriage). It is kinship which controls social relationships between people in a given community: it governs marital customs and regulations; it determines the behavior of one individual towards another. Indeed, this sense of kinship binds together the entire life of the 'tribe,' and is even extended to cover animals, plants and non-living objects through the 'totemic' system. Almost all the concepts connected with human relationship can be understood and interpreted through the kinship system. This it is

49 See Mbiti, *African Religions and Philosophy,* p. 104.

50 Stanley Diamond, "Tribal Society," *A Dictionary of Marxist Thought,* 2nd ed., (ed.), Tom Bottomore (Oxford: Blackwell Publishers, 1991), p. 545. While one agrees with this description by Diamond, concerning the 'tribe,' his subsequent comments in the same text are somewhat vague: that such a tribal society "...has no civil structure and no civil authority," but is somehow able to "...maintain an internal egalitarianism so they relate to other villages in a non-[exploitative] framework. Cooperative work groups, military and/or hunting units may also cross-cut villages in a 'tribal' context." There are two issues that deserve some attention in the course of this study that may help clarify the vagueness: to show that some tribal administrative arrangements particularly in the Middle belt region of Nigeria were both civilly structured and authoritative given their context and historical experience; to show that it is much more relevant and enduring to build on some of the tribal arrangements that are in existence in order to make the case today for a stronger model of civil society, rather than a blanket claim that there was nothing in existence, as if to say, that some of the tribal cooperative groups alluded to earlier did not emerge out of a concrete historical experience.

> which largely governs the behavior, thinking and whole life of the individual in the society of which he is a member.[51]

The activities enumerated above deal with the kinship system and explain the complex web of relationships and interrelationships that exists within the social system that can be likened to that of the relationship existing between the parts to the whole and vice versa. Some concrete general observations can be made that will give understanding of the issues at stake in terms of an organological vision of the State. According to Mbiti, the kinship system is to be understood as embracing a network stretching both horizontally and vertically. Horizontally, kinship ties are extended to many 'brothers,' 'sisters,' 'uncles,' 'nephews,' 'mothers,' 'fathers,' etc. There appears to be some fluidity in the arrangement and extension of kinship rights within the tribe. Vertically, the kinship system is extended to include the departed and those yet to be born. Hence, the position of ancestors is of paramount importance in the African social systems as will be shown in the next section.

The Ancestorship System

According to Alyward Shorter, an ancestor can be described as:

> A deceased blood relative who in life was responsible as head of lineage for the continuation of the descent group and who in death continues to exercise this responsibility in a new way, in solidarity with other deceased blood relatives.[52]

Ancestors are departed members of the family, clan, and community who continue to have some influence on family and social affairs. That is why Mbiti was able to describe the personal and communal roles of ancestors in this manner:

> They return to their human families from time to time and share meals with them, however symbolically. They know and have interest in what is going on in their family... They are guardians of family affairs, traditions, ethics and activities.[53]

Thus, genealogical ties to ancestors serve social purposes by establishing both inter-family and inter-communal relationships. In some ethnic societies, ancestral genealogical ties are traced as far back as the mythological symbol of the ancestral founder or 'first' in the order of existence or national hero. This is significant because "...it is also on genealogical basis that organizational divisions have evolved among different peoples, demarcating the larger society into 'clans,' 'gates,' families, households and finally individuals."[54] Perhaps, an example of the Tiv People

---

51 See Mbiti, *African Religions and Philosophy*, p. 104.

52 Aylward Shorter, "Ancestor Veneration Revisited," *African Ecclesial Review* 25/4 (August, 1983): 198.

53 See Mbiti, *African Religions and Philosophy*, p. 151.

54 Ibid. p. 105.

of the Middle Belt of Nigeria and their social and political organizational set up, which is based on their ancestral genealogies, might help illustrate better the issues at stake.

The Tiv Tribe and Social Organization

The Tiv people are an ethnic group in Benue State of Nigeria. The term Tiv connotes a triple heritage: an ethnic group, the ancestral father figure of the people and the language spoken by the people. The population of the tribe is over three million, which makes them the largest ethnic group in the Middle Belt of Nigeria and the sixth largest ethnic group in Nigeria. While a majority of the Tiv people resides in Benue State, some of them are scattered in neighboring States such as Taraba, Adamawa and Nasarawa. The concern of this study is not to offer here a comprehensive perspective of Tiv cultural, social, religious, and political heritage, but to articulate some of those organizational practices and customs that are relevant to the scope and limits of this research. Details about the Tiv people and some of the issues raised in this study can be read in the works cited.[55]

Makar[56] has shown how the Tiv People organized their social system in the 18th and 19th centuries before the British arrived on Tiv territory. What follows will be an attempt to capture the major components of Tiv social organizational arrangements during the 18th and 19th centuries. It is pertinent to State from the outset that some of these social arrangements have been in place as long as the Tiv people have existed and continue to serve as the cornerstone upon which the community is built. The Tiv people believe that they are descendants of one ancestral Father Tiv. Dominic Yuhe quotes M. Mead as saying:

> All the Tiv were one in the person of the ancestor Tiv. The individual was continuous with his community and his community was continuous with the ancestors, who diminished in actual count until the whole society was limited to the two sons of Tiv, and finally, to Tiv himself.[57]

---

55 L. Bohannan and P. Bohannan, *The Tiv of Central Nigeria* (London: International African Institute, 1969), pp. 1–50; E. Rubingh, *Sons of Tiv: A Study of the Rise of the Church Among the Tiv of Central Nigeria* (Grand Rapids: Baker Press, 1969), pp. 70–75; Mvendaga Jibo, *Tiv Politics Since 1959* (Katsina, Ala: Mandate International, 1993), pp. 10–20; Tesemchi Makar, *The History of Political Change Among the Tiv in the 19th and 20th Centuries*, pp. 3–40.

56 See Makar, *The History of Political Change Among the Tiv in the 19th. and 20th. Centuries*, pp. 12–53, for the historical details of the various social arrangements that were in place before the coming of the British and the consequences of the British colonial impact among the Tiv people.

57 Dominic Yuhe, *The Encounter of Tiv Religions and Moral Values with Catholicism in the Time of Secularization* (Makurdi: Government Printer, 1978), p. 14.

Tiv had a brother named *Uke* and their father was *Takuruku*.[58] Tiv had two sons from who emerged the social and political organization of Tiv land. The two sons were *Ichongo* and *Ipusu*. Among the Tiv, territorial and social organization is construed in terms of *Tar*. Tar is the Tiv word for the cosmos or world and country. This includes the individual entities, visible and tangible and also the unseen forces that advance and retard the affairs of humanity. *Tar* embraces the past and present, the people and their customs, habits and built-in traditions of the ancestors. The *Tar* was divided according to territorial strata and social grouping into units named after a common ancestor and was further subdivided into many segmentary units called *ityar*. Figure 1 below presents the major ancestral genealogical groupings among the Tiv:

Figure 1

A. The Ipusu Ityar genealogies are:

1. Shittire
2 Ukum
3. Mbaikor
4. Jemgbagh
5. Jechira

B. The Ichongo Ityar genealogies are:

1. Ugondo
2. Tongov
3. Ikurav
4. Nongov
5. Iharev
6. Masev
7. Turan

One of the amazing stories of social cohesion among the Tiv people is that in spite of the many impacts of colonialism, the various Tiv social segmentary units have survived to this day in the 21st century and still serve as the basis for choosing their paramount leader the Tor Tiv, the distribution of political power and the maintenance of law and order. The diagram below provides a structural and patriarchal representation of the different ancestral segmentary units which make up the social organizational network among the Tiv people. The Tiv segmentary units also help define the degree of marital relationships in terms of the levels of consanguinity.

58 To read more about *Takuruku* and his relationship with *Aondo,* God in Tiv, read Simeon T. Iber, "The Concept of Life After Death Among the Tiv in the Light of Christian Eschatology," (unpublished master's thesis, University of Calabar, 1994), pp. 26–30.

Figure 2

Shon
Takuruku
Awange
Tiv
Mbaipusu
Mbaichongo
Shitire
Ukum
Kparev
Ugondo
Tongov
Ikurav
Nongov
Iharev
Masev
Turan
Kpav
Gambe-tiev
Gambe-ya
Torov
Ingenev
Ucha
Mbaterem
Ikor
Kprev
Usar
Maav
Kendev
Utange
Nyiev
Ukan
Ikov
Mbaikyaa
Mbagba
Mbagwa
Jemgbagh
Mbatierev
Mbatiav
Kusuv
Mbayion
Ishorov
Mbagen
Ipav
Yandev
Mbakor
Tombo
Mbatie
Mbalagh
Jecira
Kunav
Kyan
Tiev
Ute
Ningev
Mbaduku
Mbakaange
Mbara
Mbayongo
Tsambe
Mbagbera
Gaav
Mbavaa
Iwarev
Shangev
Shangev-ya
Shangev-tiev
Ikurav-ya
Ikurav-tiev
Kaambe
Saghev
Ndzoyov
Raav
Mbakpa
Sherev
Nyev
Mbagwen
Mbawa
Utondo
Mbasaan
Mbasai
Injiriv
Yonov
Ingahar

Tiv Traditional Administrative Council Systems

The *tar* was the largest social unit among the Tiv and was divided into many *ityar*. However, for the purposes of administration, these segmentary *ityar* units were further subdivided into subordinate or subsidiary units to act as administrative councils and charged with social, economic, political, and cultural functions. Thus, there were four major councils with traditional administrative functions: *Ya, Ingyor, Ityo, and Tar* councils.[59] A brief examination of how these councils were organized and administered follows.

The *Ya* or family or compound council was headed by *Orya*, literally the caretaker, who was normally the oldest male in the family or compound. He also had an assistant *ordondon* (singular) or in some cases many assistants *mbadondon* (plural), to whom he could delegate the power of governance. The council was responsible for the maintenance of proper marital laws within its jurisdiction, the admission, entertainment and expulsion of strangers, women who had left their marital homes and went back to their ancestral homes, and the recovery of various forms of debts. These political, social and economic roles of the *Orya* were, however, restricted and limited to only his council and not beyond. But one did perform some useful service of governance at his level. Makar has described the important role played by the *Orya* in the *Ya* council in this manner:

> So vital is the role of *Orya* that he was expected to be fair, kind, impartial, and sympathetic in dealing with his subjects. The failure of *Orya* as a ruler might lead to the disintegration of his *Ya*, the compound, leaving him and his wife and children alone… a *Ya* which continued to exist and flourish several years even after the death of *Orya* was a sign that the successive *mbayaav* (plural of *Orya*) had been very successful rulers. It was a sign of a successful government and administration of the lowest level of the society.[60]

The *Ingyor* council was responsible for taking up any political, social or religious issues that could not be handled by the *Ya* council discussed earlier. Thus, the *Ingyor* council acted as a support group to the *Ya* council. The *Ingyor* council was made up mostly of leaders from the different family or compound units that made up the different *Uya* (plural of *Ya*). Here, too, the senior elder acted as the leader of the group. But the role of the leaders was limited and they could not discuss issues that were related to traditional religious rites and those connected to death. These issues were considered beyond their power of jurisdiction and had to be passed on to the council next in rank, the *Ityo*.

The *Ityo* was a much larger group than the other councils under discussion so far. This council was responsible for evaluating the problems of the larger society.

---

59 See Makar, *The History of Political Change Among the Tiv in the 19th and 20th Centuries*, pp. 23–27 for details on the organizational arrangements of these councils.

60 Ibid. p. 24.

It was made up of prominent leaders and elders from the various *angor* (plural of *ingyor*) groups. The head of the *Ityo* council wielded both political and religious powers. Sometimes, two elders were chosen as co-leaders, one with political authority and the other with religious authority. This arrangement created an interesting cooperative venture between political leaders and religious leaders that is best described in these words:

> This religious expert and co-equal of the president of the *Ityo* council had a unique and very important role. This is because any social wrong or crime was regarded as an evil and a violation of the traditional religious order. A political settlement was therefore followed by a religious settlement. The society was politico-religious hence a man with priestly powers was needed in every segment of government.[61]

The *Ityo* council had judicial functions and tried cases of major crimes including murder. It also intervened in both internal and external disputes like those involving peer groups and those involving the status and rights of foreigners, *atoatiev*. According to Makar, the organization of the *Ityo* group among the Tiv "...facilitated the holding together of the Tiv society for purposes of social control, basic societal behavior, religious rites and cultural unity."[62]

The *Tar* was the highest council of elders. It was in charge of both the internal and external security and defense of the Tiv people in general. It also settled disputes between members of the other council groups discussed earlier. The *Tar* council was, therefore, the stabilizing council and the last resort. It also settled land disputes and was responsible for nominating and screening members of the community who were selected for the award of titles and initiation into religious leadership positions. The council units are represented in a schematic arrangement in Figure 3.

These council units operated from the bottom to the top and not from the top to the bottom, which has important implications for subsidiarity which encourages that decisions are best made by those at the level closest to them, the local level. That is why the Tiv people believe that power lies with the people and not the authority figures. The above perception of authority might help explain why in the beginning the Tiv people functioned without a central chief of the whole tribe but through local decentralized leaders with voting rights in the general council of local chiefs. Thus, the Tor Tiv (Chief of Tiv) was a later creation which took place in 1948 to meet the changing social circumstances that were taking place among the Tiv and Nigeria in general. People in authority are chosen from among the community, to perform particular roles on behalf of the group. The famous Tiv saying: *tahav ka ityo*, power lies or belongs to the community, conveys the people's understanding regarding power. Once the community support is withdrawn, one loses his or her power base and by implication, whatever power one wielded.

61 Ibid. p. 25.

62 Ibid. p. 13.

Figure 3

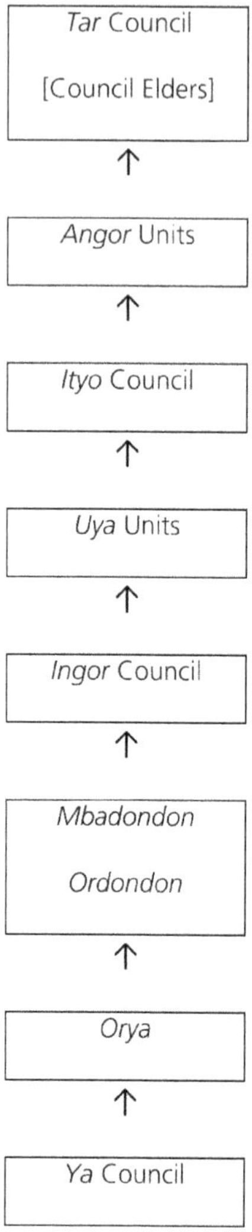

The Clan System

Another significant subdivision of the 'tribe' is the clan. Clan systems vary from one tribe to another and they can be either patriarchal or matriarchal depending on the section of Africa under consideration. Clan systems further help define the extent to which marital engagements are permitted. Clan systems also help provide human cooperation, market conditions, social, and security issues. In some ethnic societies, these clans are further subdivided into sub-clans: "…these localize clan matters, and deal with affairs which need not concern the whole clan. It is probably this subdivision which, in the course of time, grows into a full clan of its own. The 'gate' is made up of members from a common ancestor up to six or eight generations back."[63]

Elochukwu E. Uzukwu[64] has pointed out how, among the Igbo tribe of Eastern Nigeria, the general pattern of social organization is that of village-groups. These village-groups consist of a federation of clans composed of kindred and the kindred made up of extended families. An important point for this study, in supporting a basis for subsidiarity, is the fact that decision making involves a process of consultation at the different levels of the village-group: family, kindred, and clan levels.

Through kinship, ancestorship, councils, the clan and gate are born to deal with specific issues that do not have relevance to the larger society, but are limited to particular families or households. In this type of kinship arrangements, one sees some organological institutions that practiced the spirit of the principle of subsidiarity: where the clan, council, and gate would deal with the issues within their social setting without outside interference from the larger kinship group. The larger kinship group was only invited to participate in decision making when the clan could not handle matters at their own level or when it became necessary that lack of intervention on the part of the larger kinship group could place the existence of the clan in jeopardy. Notice that in the spirit of subsidiarity the larger kinship group could intervene in the smaller groups to protect the common good of the clan. Uzukwu supports this position in his examination of the organization of African societies with authority in many hands when he opined that "...in these societies there is an experience of what some have called republicanism or direct democracy... The power of these groups lies in persuasion rather than in coercion."[65] An examination of how such kinship arrangements played out in the relationship between the individual and the community follows.

The Community and the Individual in African Experience

In African tradition community life consists of the family, household and the individual.[66] The family setup includes both the immediate family and the extended family structures. The extended family generally means that two or more brothers

63 See Mbiti, *African Religions and Philosophy*, p. 106.

64 Elochukwu E. Uzukwu, *A Listening Church: Autonomy and Communion in African Churches*, pp. 14–15 for details of the various organizational practices in some ethnic groups of Nigeria.

65 Ibid. p. 16.

66 See Mbiti, *African Religions and Philosophy*, p. 106.

(in patrilocal societies) or two or more sisters (in matrilocal societies) set up families in one compound. The household is the smallest family unit: "...if a man has two or more wives, he has as many households since each wife would usually have her own house erected within the same compound where other wives and their household live."[67] Having discussed the major components that make up the community, one might seek to know, what is the place of the individual within the community?

According to Mbiti, the role and place of the individual within the community is shaped by a fundamental African philosophical concept: "I am, because we are; and since we are, therefore I am."[68] The individual does not exist alone except corporately. The individual is part of the whole community and is shaped by the community. On the one hand, the individual depends on the support of the corporate group; on the other hand, the individual is conscious of his or her own being, duties, responsibilities and privileges, but insofar as they are connected toward other human beings. Mbiti sums up the various webs of interrelationships in this manner:

> When he suffers, he does not suffer alone but with the corporate group; when he rejoices, he rejoices not alone but with his kinsmen, his neighbors and his relatives whether dead or living. When he gets married, he is not alone; neither does the wife 'belong' to him alone (figuratively). So also the children belong to the corporate body of kinsmen, even if they bear only their father's name. Whatever happens to the individual happens to the whole group, and whatever happens to the whole group happens to the individual.[69]

This pivotal point in the understanding of the African view of the human person provides a central basis for the recognition of how the social and political setups in Africa were organized. The philosophy of I am, because we are; and since we are, therefore I am, defines to some degree the interconnectedness between the social, political, religious, and economic setups of African societies. The interplay between the whole and the parts and the parts with the whole is echoed in the relationship which the individual has with the community, and that of the community with the individual. One can examine the issue of corporate personality in a given African social context.

67 Ibid. p. 107. The practice of monogamy and polygamy has existed almost side by side in most African communities. Today, while there is a major shift toward monogamy largely due to the influence of Christianity, polygamy is still practiced in some households. It is beyond the scope of this project to discuss the issue of marriage practices in Africa.

68 Ibid. p. 108.

69 Ibid.

The Concept of Corporate Personality in Tiv Experience

The issue of corporate personality in the traditional Tiv society was taken up recently in a critical research work.[70] The meanings associated with Tiv convey some major understanding about the elements of social cohesion, communal heritage and identity and corporate personality in society. Thus, the individual does not consider himself as an individual person as such, but as a member of the group. It does appear that the individual is somehow submerged both in the immediate and extended families and the larger ethnic community. Rubingh puts it more forcefully: ". . . It is through the community that the individuality of each person becomes recognized and finds expression. To be unique, therefore, is to set the entire community into jeopardy."[71] The extent to which such an understanding of the person in community could affect a proper vision of the integral relationship between the parts and the whole in the context of the organological vision of society will be explained. There are other views associated with the concept of corporate personality worth noting.

Both Rubingh and Tseayo have agreed that the reality of a common genealogical heritage among the Tiv provides further basis for communality or corporate personality. Hence, most social activities are mandatory realizing that "...the efficacy of the individual is reflected in the lives and fortunes of all members of the community," just as the destiny of one is shared by all. Thus, the Tiv "minimize individuality in the interest of the larger community."[72] The famous Tiv saying: *aya tutu ka unyo, ka se,* conveys the meaning of unity is strength; united we stand; that which a people stands for in spite of their differences and difficulties; the recognition and support for both the least and most privileged of the community; it is the distinguishing mark of the clan, community or society; joining hands together for a common purpose, a clear affirmation of solidarity. Thus, the social and political organization of traditional Tiv society was very much influenced by the view of corporate personality.[73]

This chapter has shown how Tiv social system was divided into *ityar* (segmentary lineage, *tar* named after a common ancestor) units. Further, *Tar* is the largest

---

70 Terwase H. Akaabiam, *The Proclamation of the Good News: A Study of LK 24 in Tiv Context,* XXIII/673(Frankfurt am Main: Peter Lang/European University Studies, 1999), pp. 155-157; On the relationship between the individual and the community from another African perspective, cf. Benezet Bujo, *African Christian Morality: At the Age of Inculturation* (Nairobi: Paulines Publications Africa, 1998), pp. 95–102.

71 See Rubingh, *Sons of Tiv,* pp., 67, 85–86.

72 Rubingh, *Sons of Tiv,* p. 85; cf., Terwase H. Akaabiam, *The Proclamation of the Good News,* p. 156.

73 See Maker, *The History of Political Change Among the Tiv,* pp. 12–30; cf., Akkaabiam, *The Proclamation of the Good News,* pp. 157–159.

genealogical unit remaining among the Tiv people that have retained group consciousness and organization. One major reason for this group consciousness is due to the experience of survival tactics by members of the group. The group must have migrated together and experienced common difficulties, which have made them territorially and traditionally bonded. Significantly, among the Tiv people, these genealogical groups still influence social and political life today.[74] E. Rubingh captured this attitude when he said, among the Tiv, "…to be unique is evil; the-I should forever be swallowed in the non-I."[75] This study challenges such a social and cultural philosophy as promoting centralist practices that could inhibit individual self-realization. That is why the position taking by Moti and Wegh is most refreshing and offers a perspective for articulating the African understanding of the individual and the community in Tiv context that could be properly enhanced to promote the existing social and political arrangements and, to embrace a holistic organological vision devoid of centralist tendencies.

> Community, however, does not mean an absence of individual self-consciousness or the annihilation of the individual in the face of kinship ties, traditional customs and religious beliefs. Tiv thought is that true development of the individual self is achieved in activating oneself in one's relationship with others.[76]

Challenges to the Organological Vision in African Tradition

Benezet Bujo[77] had raised a very pertinent question: "Is the African, whose acting and thinking is always in solidarity and almost identical with his or her tribal community, able to make as an individual, an ethical, responsible decision at all?"[78] Another closely related question could be, "Is the individual absorbed by the com-

74 See Maker, pp. 225–239 on how the conflict between individual and communal interests ravaged Tiv society from 1960 to 1964 which was responsible for the worst political anarchy in Tiv society. Notice that the continuity of the individual with the group implies that the effects of individualism are visited on all members, hence there is the constant attempt to control individualistic tendencies. cf. also, Jibo, *Tiv Politics Since 1959*, pp. 16–20.

75 Rubingh, *Sons of Tiv*, pp. 69–70.

76 James Shagba Moti and Shagbaor F. Wegh, *An Encounter Between Tiv Religion and Christianity* (Enugu: Snaap Press, 2001), p. 102.

77 Benezet Bujo, *African Christian Morality: At the Age of Inculturation* (Nairobi, Kenya: Paulines Publication Africa, 1990), pp. 95–102 presents some key arguments for understanding the relationship between the individual and the community in the context of African morality. One will paraphrase some of these arguments as they relate to our topic, outlining in the process some of the inherent challenges to the inter-play between the individual and community in African communities.

78 Ibid. p. 95.

munity to the extent that such an individual is unable to express his or her personal freedom?" These questions are integral to some of the issues one has discussed in terms of 'corporate personality' and the interrelated nature of the individual and community in African societies.

The major challenge which the individual faces in a pluralist State is that the major African philosophical concept of solidarity, 'I am because we are, and since we are, therefore I am,' is constantly undermined and in some respects even destroyed. Thus, new sets of ethical norms are required in a pluralist world beyond the tribal setting. The ties of kinship do not seem to have the same force in social settings where people are tied together by different languages, ethnic groups, professions, associations, trade unions, sports, political parties, and Church denominations. How might the individual balance his or her loyalties between the kinship community and the larger community?

Bujo has argued that individual name-giving in African communities defines and categorizes persons as unique individuals. Thus, the circumstance of one's birth, the family situation at the time of a person's birth and the condition of the clan, all play important roles in the name that is given to a person at birth. A person's name contains, then, both the pre-history and the history of the individual, family and clan. If, for example, a person was born at the time when the family was in a crisis situation, the moment was captured in the name of the child. A personal illustration might be helpful here. The author's ethnic name is *Tsetim* (*Tse* means 'lineage,' while *Tim* means 'destroy.' He was born at a time when his Father had just lost all his parents, hence the name *Tsetim* literally 'lineage is destroyed' was given in memory of what had happened). Thus, the ontological reality of the individual in African societies is made up of a network of relationships. According to Bujo, this means, "On the one hand, the individual cannot be thought of outside of his or her community, though, on the other hand, he or she is obviously a unique and irreplaceable being who has his or her own rights and non exchangeable tasks within the community."[79]

However, the mere fact that the individual is not thought of outside of his or her ethnic community raises some fundamental moral and social challenges about the extent to which a person might be accepted outside of his or her ethnic community. How might a people structure a given African State that evolves a national solidarity which builds on the individual tribal solidarity without excluding other tribal groups? This might be an instance where subsidiarity could help serve as a stabilizing principle between the different ethnic groups in Nigeria. In this way, subsidiarity might help check centralist and totalitarian tendencies aimed at domination of the individual, minority ethnic groups or associations and putting into jeopardy the capacity of human persons in community to model their lives accord-

79 Ibid., p. 97; cf. also Eugene Hillman, *Toward an African Christianity: Inculturation Applied* (New York & Mahwah, New Jersey: Paulist Press, 1993), pp. 11–16 on the tension which existed between Missionaries and the Kikuyu names in Kenya.

ing to the rule of law, freedom, justice and liberty. Uzukwu has also raised the issue of the tendency toward dictatorship and autocracy among some ethnic groups in Nigeria with centralized authority such as the Hausa kingdoms who were greatly influenced by the Islamic culture after the Dan Fodio jihad.[80]

Even within a person's ethnic community, the question may be raised as to how the individual might act in solidarity with others in the community and at the same time be able to maintain personal individual responsibility? The question of how the individual is supported and promoted within the community in the African context is a very contestable issue that deserves some serious consideration, because there continues to be major instances of abuses both in the family, clan, community and society at large that require some major overhauling. How does the concept of 'corporate personality' practiced by the Tiv for instance constitute a serious danger to individual self-realization in a pluralist society? Can one draw some positive lessons from the Tiv views of *aya tutu ka unyo, ka se,* beyond Tiv tribal community to embrace other ethnic groups? My personal position is that this type of social philosophy enunciated by the Tiv will have to recognize and embrace other tribal groups in a pluralist society. This is one sure way of breaking down deep seated inter tribal animosity. Discussion will ensue in the course of the research, how some of these issues have played out concretely in the Nigerian context in areas like tribal and inter-tribal conflicts, communal and boundary disputes, corruption and nepotism, majority and minority rights, women's rights, social and class warfare, religious fundamentalism and political uncertainty.[81] These are significant areas where the principle of subsidiarity could play some major stabilizing role in shaping the proper relationship that should exist between the individual and the community in a given African civil social context in the light of Christian ethical and social principles. The bases for the practice and understanding of the principle of subsidiarity as an organological principle of the family, household, clan, community and State have been established on the following grounds:

1. The central point of convergence for subsidiarity would necessarily begin with the relationship between persons in community. Thus, this principle has universal relevance and application wherever human beings are gathered on earth. In this regard, the contribution of St. Thomas Aquinas was a novel one when he maintained that human beings are willed by their creator to enjoy the capacity and freedom to choose and have a say in their ultimate end.

80 See Uzukwu, *A Listening Church,* pp. 16–17.

81 Eghosa E. Osaghae, *Crippled Giant: Nigeria Since Independence* (Bloomington and Indianapolis: Indiana University Press, 1998), pp. 1–30. Osaghae has provided a concise historical and analytical overview of the Nigerian State that captures some of the major struggles toward nationhood, which have stood as stumbling blocks, thereby making Nigeria a crippled giant. Some of these issues will be addressed more critically in a later chapter on civil society and the Nigerian state.

2. Subsidiarity seeks to help, support, and aid persons to organize and order their communities to assist each other in the task of pursuing common goals. While recognizing that communities are made up of people with different interest groups, this principle promotes the healthy interaction of these varying interest groups with a view toward the common good of all.
3. The principle maintains that a central authority such as the State should have a subsidiary function, performing only tasks which cannot be performed effectively at a more immediate or local level.
4. On the one hand, the organological vision of associations like the family, church, and society provides the ground for a holistic understanding of subsidiarity since it understands society and all other forms of associations as a unity and not just a collection of loose and unrelated groups. On the other hand, this vision could be employed to wrongly support centralist and totalitarian tendencies. Hence, subsidiarity, as a principle of competencies, could be developed to maintain tolerance, freedom of persons, and the autonomy of the different groups which make up a given community.
5. In view of the existing different social arrangements in the African community, subsidiarity could be developed to help the social structures that will promote healthy interaction between the different ethnic groups in a given multiethnic/religious and socio-political plural context like Nigeria.

Questions for Further Reflection

1. How would you describe the relationship existing between the individual and the community in your own experience? Is it more positive or more negative?
2. Given your local context, which of the many challenges that have been posed to your community do you find to be most serious?
3. What type of support do you seek from your community? What happens when that support is not forthcoming?
4. How might you contribute positively to your community?
5. In your experience, discuss the understanding associated with the fact that the common good and the good of the individual are not opposed to each other.

2

THE PRINCIPLE OF SUBSIDIARITY IN PAPAL SOCIAL ENCYCLICALS: ORIGIN AND DEVELOPMENT

The term encyclical letter is:

> ...A word derived from the Greek which means a letter that goes the rounds, an encyclical letter. In the early beginnings of the Church many bishops referred to their peace and communion letters as such; these letters were given by bishops to members of the laity traveling abroad, with the indication that they were 'in communion:' i.e. received communion in their local Church and were recommended to other local Churches. Thus, since the sixteenth century, the title has been used to refer to papal letters concerned with doctrinal or moral matters, exhortations, warnings or recommendations.[1]

It is beyond the scope of this study to examine all the different issues with which the encyclicals were concerned or the conditions under which the papal social encyclicals under review were articulated. The focus of the study is to examine particular areas in these documents which have direct relevance to the principle of subsidiarity, and other related issues that might enhance its understanding.

---

1 Rodger Charles, *Christian Social Witness and Teaching*, vol. 2. (Gracewing: Fowler Wright Books, 1998), p. 12. See Leo F. Stelten, *Dictionary of Ecclesiastical Latin* (Peabody, Massachusetts: Hendrickson Publishers, 1995), p. 305 "*encyclica epistola*: encyclical letter; a formal pastoral letter written by the Pope for the entire Church and not used for dogmatic definitions, but rather to give counsel or to shed greater light on points of doctrine that must be made more precise or that must be taught in view of specific circumstances in various countries."

This study affirms, among other things, that the human quest for self-actualization and the interplay between social groups in society were at the center of the social and moral reconstruction, which gave rise to the formulation of subsidiarity in the social encyclicals. Oswald von Nell-Breuning,[2] the great German moral theologian and social philosopher, undertook the noble task of writing QA and offering critical interpretations on the document. In examining the social encyclicals, attention is focused on the contributions of each document to the development of the principle of subsidiarity, in the larger framework of integrity and responsibility that are the hallmarks of Catholic social teaching in three ways:

1. The contemporary documents need to be examined in the light of the continuing historical effort to relate Christian faith to the problems of modern society, that is, to Catholic theology, broadly understood.

2. The documents need to be examined as well in the context of the overall life of the contemporary church; these teachings are one, but only one, important expression of Catholic faith and life. They can be understood and evaluated only in relation to other expressions of Catholicism, from the spiritual lives of individuals through the worship and fellowship of congregations to the ongoing development of Catholic theology.

3. The documents are best read and evaluated from the viewpoint of the laity. More than other formal documents of the church, these are located at the intersection of the church and the world, the sacred and the secular. Of their very nature they deal with the problems of living the Christian life in the midst of ordinary human relationships.[3]

---

2 Oswald von Nell-Breuning, S.J. at age 40 (1890-1991), was the one chosen by the Jesuit General, Wlodimir Ledochowski, to prepare an encyclical for Pius XI on the 40th anniversary of *Rerum Novarum*. Nell-Breuning was a moral theologian, canon lawyer and political economist. He wrote his theology dissertation on "The Morality of the Stock-Market," (1928) under Joseph Mausbach. He was the emeritus professor of social and economic ethics at the Hochschule Sankt Georgen in Frankfurt am Main. He developed the encyclical QA in complete secrecy but was greatly influenced by the works of Heinrich Pesch and the resources of the *Königswinterer Kreis*. Nell-Breuning was an icon of Catholic social thought, who died on August 21, 1991 at age 101 in the Jesuit College of St. George in Frankfurt, leaving a corpus of eighteen hundred books, monographs, and articles. To read more about Nell-Breuning see: Oswald von Nell-Brening, S.J., "The Drafting of Quadragesimo Anno," *Readings in Moral Theology No. 5: Official Catholic Social Teaching,* (eds.), Charles E. Curran and Richard A. McCormick (New York/Mahwah: Paulist Press, 1986), pp. 60-68; Philip J. Chmielewski, S.J., "Nell-Breuning, Oswald von," *The New Dictionary of Catholic Social Thought,* (ed.), Judith A. Dwyer (Collegeville, Minnesota: The Liturgical Press, 1994), pp. 676-678; Francis X. Murphy, "Oswald von Nell-Breuning: Papal Surrogate," *America* (October 26, 1991): 293-295.

3 David J. O'Brien and Thomas A. Shannon, eds., *Catholic Social Thought: The Documentary Heritage* (Maryknoll, New York: Orbis Books, 1992), p. 6. Note that all the papal social encyclicals discussed in this chapter will be quoted from this text unless otherwise stated.

Thus, the social encyclicals are read and understood in three complementary ways: 1) the moral guidance they give on human rights stems from the dignity of women and men made in the image and likeness of God, and it is the central basis for assessment in every school of thought and every policy and practice of its teaching; 2) they are promulgated primarily for members of the Church who have faith in her teaching, but also for all women and men of good will; 3) they provide moral judgments at the ordinary teaching level of the Church, which means that they are binding in conscience.[4] What follows then is an analysis of the central indicators for subsidiarity in the major social encyclical of Leo XIII.

The Encyclical of Leo XIII, Rerum Novarum (RN) 1891: Foundation for Subsidiarity

The social encyclical of Leo XIII RN clearly was the first papal social document to appropriate the teaching of St. Thomas Aquinas as the foundational basis for its theoretical framework, which points toward an understanding of the principle of subsidiarity in Catholic social teaching. One can trace the structures of thought in this social encyclical that ground the doctrine of subsidiarity from the following points of view.

Leo XIII provided the first basis for understanding subsidiarity in the context of human dignity. The human capacity to exercise choice distinguishes human beings from any other animal. Human beings are capable of being masters of their acts, making decisions in freedom out of their own personal human experience and from their God-given talents. Hence, the power of reason makes human beings the custodians of the earth and places them at the level of existence which is prior to the State. "Man is older than the State, and he holds the right of providing for the life of his body prior to the formation of any State."[5] This is the basis from which the rights of the family are advocated in the social encyclical.

Thus, the human family is "...a society limited indeed in numbers, but a true 'society,' anterior to every kind of State or nation, with rights and duties of its own, totally independent of the commonwealth."[6] The human family has a natural right, then, to own property. The inner dynamism by and through which a family is governed must be respected. "A family, no less than a State, is, as we have said, a true society, governed by a power within itself that is to say by the father (Mother)."[7] The document maintains that the family has equal rights as the State insofar as

4 Cf., Roger Charles, *Christian Social Witness and Teaching*, vol. 2, pp. 12–13 on how the social encyclicals are generally explained and understood.

5 RN Par. 6, p. 16.

6 Ibid. Par. 9, p. 18.

7 Ibid. Par. 10, p. 18; words in brackets are mine.

the pursuit and preservation of liberty are concerned. Consequently, both the State and any other type of association which human beings participate in must necessarily seek to help promote their well-being rather than place their capacity for self-actualization in jeopardy.

> ...Since the domestic household is anterior both in idea and in fact to the gathering of men into a commonwealth, the former must necessarily have rights and duties which are prior to those of the latter, and which rest more immediately on nature. If the citizens of a State - that is to say, the families - on entering into association and fellowship, experienced at the hands of the State hindrance instead of help, and found their rights attacked instead of being protected, such associations were rather to be repudiated than sought after.[8]

Furthermore, the document challenges any civil government that seeks to take over the functions of the family and the household. It called such reasoning and policy a grave mistake. What the document recognizes is limited intervention by government in affairs of the family in a situation of dire need and for a specific period, and a targeted goal: "...but the rulers of the State must go no further: nature bids them stop here. Paternal authority can neither be abolished by the State nor absorbed; for it has the same source as human life itself; the child belongs to the father (Mother)."[9] Also, the document encourages the formation of multiple organizations that will help promote the claims of the working class. This is to be carried out as a cooperative venture between the different ranks of the working class themselves and the State: "...social and public life can only go on by the help of various kinds of capacity and the playing of many parts, and each man, as a rule, chooses the part which peculiarly suits his case."[10] This should also be the underlying principle for the relationship between the employer and the employee. Here one notices how Leo XIII made use of the analogy of the human body earlier discussed in chapter one both in Aquinas and the fable of Menenius Agrippa. Thus, Leo XIII affirmed that:

> Just as the symmetry of the human body is the result of the disposition of the members of the body, so in a State it is ordained by nature that these two classes should exist in harmony and agreement, and should, as it were, fit into one another, so as to maintain the equilibrium of the body politic. Each requires the other; capital cannot do without labor or labor without capital. Mutual agreement results in pleasantness and good order; perpetual conflict necessarily produces confusion and outrage.[11]

Moreover, the document holds on the one hand that there are some functions that are better carried out by organizations such as the Church, whose 'heroism of charity' through various institutions for help and mercy is a novelty in human experi-

---

8 Ibid.

9 Ibid. Par. 11, p. 19; words in brackets are mine.

10 Ibid. Par. 14, p. 20.

11 Ibid. Par. 15, p. 20.

ence. Thus, to resort to "...a system of State-organized relief,"[12] is an attempt to substitute for the many avenues of charity that have stood the test of time in human history. On the other hand, the proper role of the State is to promote the well-being and common good of its citizens. This is ensured by providing justice toward all members and recognizing that each person has an important role to play. In this connection, the relationship between the parts and whole which St. Thomas Aquinas articulated is employed to provide a credible argument for distributive justice:

> ...The State must not absorb the individual or the family; both should be allowed free and untrammeled action as far as is consistent with the common good and the interests of others. Nevertheless, rulers should anxiously safeguard the community and all its parts; the community, because the conservation of the community is so emphatically the business of the supreme power, that the safety of the commonwealth is not only the first law, but is a government's whole reason of existence; and the parts, because both philosophy and the Gospel agree in laying down that the object of the administration of the State should be not the advantage of the ruler, but the benefit of those over whom he rules.[13]

Even here, the role of government should be limited to the correction of a particular anomaly in society. Paragraph 29 then points out the different exceptional cases under which government intervention would be appropriate. Nevertheless, the document insists that: "The limits must be determined by the nature of the occasion which calls for the law's interference - the principle being this, that the law must not undertake more, nor go further, than is required for the remedy of the evil or the removal of the danger."[14]

Another instance for subsidiarity is envisaged in the area of "just wages" for workers. The document maintained that where there was a clear case of injustice by way of refusal to pay just wages to workers, the State should intervene to remedy the situation. It considered such an action on the part of the State to be pertinent because the worker's wages were both personal and necessary to him. However, the process for further negotiations should be discussed directly between the contractor and workers' unions: "...in order to supersede undue interference on the part of the State, especially as circumstances, times and localities differ so widely, it is advisable that recourse be had to societies or boards such as we shall mention presently, or to some other method of safeguarding the interests of wage earners; the State to be asked for approval and protection."[15]

> The call for the formation of the "workmen's associations," is one major area where the basis for subsidiarity is laid. The document thought of these associations as, soci-

---

12 Ibid. Par. 24, p. 25.

13 Ibid. Par. 28, p. 27.

14 Ibid. Par. 29, p. 28.

15 Ibid. Par. 34, p. 31.

> eties for mutual help; various foundations established by private persons for providing for the workman, and for his widow or his orphans, in sudden calamity, in sickness, and in the event of death; and what are called 'patronage,' or institutions for the care of boys and girls, for young people, and also for those of more mature age.[16]

The associations for mutual help are the basis for building a civil society. Here, the document, drawing on the work of St. Thomas Aquinas, makes an important distinction between "public society" and "private society." The former is related to civil society and exists for the common good, and is concerned with the interests of all in general. The latter is related to the State, its primary purpose is the private advantage of the associates.[17] Thus, the document upheld the natural right of persons to enter into associations of their own choosing:

> Particular societies, then, although they exist within the State, and are each a part of the State, nevertheless cannot be prohibited by the State absolutely and as such. For to enter into a "society" of this kind is the natural right of man; and the State must protect natural rights, not destroy them; and if it forbids its citizens to form associations, it contradicts the very principle of its own existence; for both they and it exist in virtue of the same principle, viz., the natural propensity of man to live in society.[18]

The document does allow, however, that there are instances when it would be appropriate for the State to ban associations that are harmful to persons and the common good of the society from existing. Even here, there are some words of caution.

> There are times, no doubt, when it is right that the law should interfere to prevent associations; as when men join together for purposes which are evidently bad, unjust, or dangerous to the State. In such cases the public authority may justly forbid the formation of association, and may dissolve them when they already exist. But every precaution should be taken not to violate the rights of individuals, and not to make unreasonable regulations under the pretense of public benefit.[19]

The document sets forth important principles of organization for the State to help bring about harmony between the different classes of workers' associations with different interests. By so doing, the State will help provide individuals and families with better conditions for their mutual support. Another word of caution is emphasized: " Let the State watch over these societies of citizens united together in the exercise of their right; but let it not thrust itself into their peculiar concerns and their organization, for things move and live by the soul within them, and they may be killed by the grasp of a hand from without."[20]

16 Ibid. Par. 36, pp. 32–33.

17 See Par. 37, p. 33.

18 Ibid. Par. 38, p. 33.

19 Ibid.

20 Ibid. Par. 41, p. 35.

Lastly, the document maintained that each organization is to fashion its own mode of governance depending "on national character, on practice and experience, on the nature and scope of the work to be done, on the magnitude of the various trades and employments, and on the circumstances of fact and of time…[21] The aim of these associations is still to promote the well-being of individuals, families, and the community. These are some of the major ideas in Leo XIII's social encyclical, *Rerum Novarum,* which were taken up by Pius XI in *Quadragesimo Anno* to formally formulate the principle of subsidiarity as a papal term.

Having examined some of the thoughts which served as background to the eventual formulation of subsidiarity as a papal term, the following observations are necessary to help highlight some of the issues that were fine tuned in subsequent social encyclicals.

First, Leo XIII embraced the organic model of the social order without many reservations, which has grave implications for subsidiarity. It would seem, for example, that he supported the paternalism of the time which was very oppressive especially toward women and sought to perpetuate their subjugation in society based on their God-given condition, which Leo considered restricted their role in society. "Women, again, are not suited to certain trades; for a woman is by nature fitted for home work, and it is that which is best adapted at once to preserve her modesty, and to promote the good bringing up of children and the well-being of the family."[22] This type of reasoning could be interpreted, today particularly, as a negation of the understanding that all human persons are created equal with a God-given dignity to exercise their own choices without unnecessary human limitations. This is the central basis upon which the principle of subsidiarity is itself based, since it allows persons in community to contribute to the common good without undue interventions from other quarters. In view of the restrictive role of the woman that the document could be said to have promoted, "…work which is suitable for a strong man cannot reasonably be required from a woman or a child,"[23] one might argue that its ground for understanding subsidiarity was laid on a somewhat shaky foundation. In general Stephen J. Pope supports this position when he opines "…in Leo's paternalistic view, the 'rulers' hold responsibility for the common good of the entire society, and their fatherly guidance is needed by those whom Leo regarded as the ignorant and undisciplined masses."[24]

Second, while on the one hand Leo XIII called for changes in the socio-economic order that will improve the working conditions of the workers against exploitation, on the other hand, the process which he advanced for this transformation raised some difficulties for subsidiarity. Leo held that the State had a duty to pro-

---

21 Ibid. Par. 42, p. 35.

22 Ibid. Par. 33, p. 30.

23 Ibid.

24 Stephen J. Pope, "Rerum Novarum," *The New Dictionary of Catholic Social Thought,* p. 838.

tect the rights of workers by ensuring that ownership of property is much more widely distributed. But how was this to be effected? Dorr supports the view that "Leo wanted these changes to be initiated 'from the top down,' that is, by the very people or classes who were benefiting from the existing liberal-capitalist order. If they failed to introduce a more equitable society, Leo was not prepared to encourage the poor or workers to engage in confrontation."[25] The challenge lies in the fact that if Leo had defended the rights of workers to form unions, why did he not wish the unions to play a political role in changing society which would have revised its *modus operandi* "from the top down" to " from the bottom up," which is favored by the principle of subsidiarity? The issue of the role of unions and their relationship with the State in the context of the subsidiarity principle is so pertinent that it will be taken up by QA in fashioning the proper place of unions in the relationship between the State and civil society.

Third, in general, one would agree that while Leo XIII was concerned with "superseding undue interference from the State, he unequivocally rejects the laissez faire doctrine of noninterference."[26] In so doing, Leo clearly anticipated the doctrine of subsidiarity by insisting that while self-help of the individual was necessary, organized self-help was much more important and this issue was taken up by Pius XI in QA.

The Encyclical of Pius XI, Quadragesimo Anno (QA), 1931: Formal Definition of Subsidiarity

The principle of subsidiarity was formally introduced into Catholic social teaching in the social encyclical QA by Pius XI. At that point in time, the 40th anniversary of Leo XIII's landmark social encyclical RN was being commemorated and great tribute was given by Pius XI to the work of Leo XIII. The need for a social order animated by justice and characterized by the decentralization of wealth and power in the socio-economic world, which Leo XIII advocated, was reaffirmed by Pius XI. The section of QA that one needs to focus on is that entitled "Reconstruction of the Social Order, 76–80." Even here, one's attention is limited particularly to Par. 79–80:

> It is indeed true, as history clearly shows that owing to the change in social conditions, much that was formerly done by small bodies can nowadays be accomplished only by large organizations. Nevertheless, it is a fundamental principle of social philosophy, fixed and unchangeable, that one should not withdraw from individuals and commit to the community what they can accomplish by their own enterprise and industry. So, too, it is an injustice and at the same time a grave evil and a disturbance of right order

25 Donal Door, *Option for the Poor: A Hundred Years of Catholic Social Teaching,* rev. ed. (Maryknoll, New York: Orbis Books, 1992), p. 33.

26 Stephen J. Pope, "Rerum Novarum," p. 835.

> to transfer to the larger and higher collectivity functions which can be performed and provided for by lesser and subordinate bodies. Inasmuch as every social activity should, by its very nature, prove a help to members of the body social, it should never destroy or absorb them. (Par. 79)
>
> The State authorities should leave to other bodies the care and expediting of business and activities of lesser moment, which otherwise become for it a source of great distraction. It then will perform with greater freedom, vigor and effectiveness, the tasks belonging properly to it, and which it alone can accomplish, directing, supervising, encouraging, restraining, as circumstances suggest or necessity demands. Let those in power, therefore, be convinced that the more faithfully this principle of "subsidiarity" is followed and a hierarchical order prevails among the various organizations, the more excellent will be the authority and efficiency of society, and the happier and more prosperous the condition of the commonwealth. (Par. 80)[27]

In this social document one finds more than a mere validation of a fundamental principle of social philosophy. Rather, as a Christian document, one finds a view of the dignity and destiny of the human person, a view enlightened by Revelation, and, therefore, much broader in perspective than one would find in a philosophical, sociological, or political text. The document articulates a view of the human being as one who knows, strives and is deserving of justice and opportunities for integral human development including, of course, one's relationship with God. This view is fundamental to the Church's understanding of how one is to live as both Christian and citizen in a civil society, promoting social justice for the common good.

Oswald von Nell-Breuning comments that the principle of subsidiarity is central to the Christian social doctrine because of its distinctive character that is "… different from every collectivistic and one-sidedly exaggerated universalistic social philosophy."[28] Accordingly, this fundamental principle of Christian social doctrine leads one to understand the working relationships between member associations and the larger society. Nell-Breuning maintains that the interrelationship existing between these groups involves three key principles: autonomy, intervention, and hierarchy.[29] These principles help explain the rights of the larger society to the member associations and vice versa. Indeed, some understanding of the inner workings of the principles of autonomy, intervention, and hierarchy is necessary to help provide a balanced perspective of the subsidiarity principle.

---

27 QA Par. 79–80, p. 60.

28 Oswald von Nell-Breuning, *Reorganization of Social Economy: The Social Encyclical Developed and Explained,* trans. Bernard W. Dempsey (New York: The Bruce Publishing Company, 1936), p. 206.

29 Ibid. note 3. pp. 206–207.

The Principle of Autonomy

The principle of autonomy maintains that:

> Since member societies are societies in the true sense of the word, having their own purpose, there follows first of all that all the legal conditions peculiar to each social organization will in their case exist and be effective, valid by themselves, and independent of a superior social authority investing them with their original, and therefore social, rights of individuals. A member society must above all take care that it does attain its particular, special purpose and must regulate the affairs determined by this special purpose. This is the natural right of self-government which is an attribute of the member societies for the sake of realizing their special purpose and the fulfillment of their own vital tasks.[30]

The autonomy principle stresses the fact that some degree of independence is necessary for both member associations and individuals to be able to operate in a given society. Such independence should be from within the social organism itself and not from without. This is the sense in which such autonomy would be conceived as both authentic and valid for upholding the rights of the members of the organization. Thus, the right to self-government emerges from this inner dynamism and flows from its participation and fulfillment of this role in society. In terms of subsidiarity, the autonomy principle helps explain to some degree the individuality of the person and associations to make free choices without any form of external coercion.

The Principle of Intervention

The principle of intervention defines the extent to which the autonomy principle could operate:

> This autonomy, however, cannot be absolute, but is subordinate to the moral end, therefore, to the whole social order. According to the law of unity of authority within society, it follows that the supreme authority, which must care for the common good of the entire society, must also possess the right to supervise the activity of the member societies, to regulate the indispensable contributions of the member societies toward the society as a whole and to intervene against violations of the public welfare committed by member societies.[31]

One major distinction that has emerged is the non-absolute nature of autonomy both for the individual and the association. This independence must be accountable to the common good of the entire society. This calls for some form of mutual supervision both on the part of the small associations and the larger society. It is

30 Ibid.

31 Ibid.

in this context that some form of intervention could be permitted when there are clear cases of violations against the common good.

The Principle of Hierarchy

The principle of hierarchy helps explain the levels of authority in society especially as they participate in different ways in their associations and societies. Thus, hierarchy is understood as:

> The order of social authorities itself is in conjunction with the order of special objectives within the general social objective; the good to be realized by member societies within the framework of public welfare will be the greater, the more they participate in the social authority. As a result, we have a subordination and superordination of the multifarious authorities in society which we designate as the principle of hierarchy.[32]

The principle of hierarchy underscores the various levels of participation among the social groups that promote the individual values of their associations, while at the same time upholding the social objectives of the larger society. This process necessarily involves limited power sharing among the member societies in view of the common good of all, and leaves some room for putting in check any arbitrary use of such powers. In this way, the principle of hierarchy is related to subsidiarity in the sense that it allows for some degree of authority according to the level of participation. There are, no doubt, instances of hierarchical abuse that might demand prompt intervention. In such a situation, it is in the nature of subsidiarity to act as a stabilizing principle.

Furthermore, Nell-Breuning explains that all the three principles discussed, namely, autonomy, intervention and hierarchy, are geared towards the fulfillment of a common goal.

> The social order does secure for individuals as well as member groups that free play which they need in order to fulfill their natural tasks, and that the entire society as a whole, superior and overlapping as it is, can devote itself to those tasks only which the individuals or the subordinate member groups cannot administer by their own power. Consequently, the law prevails that each and every social activity is by its nature and concept subsidiary.[33]

This is precisely the context in which the principle of subsidiarity finds its clearest articulation as it is formulated in QA 79-80. There are some component parts of subsidiarity that needs proper explanation.

32 Ibid.

33 Ibid.

The Essential Parts of Subsidiarity

Nell-Breuning has offered five essential parts that are central to the principle of subsidiarity.[34] These essential parts of subsidiarity are discussed below with two additional components: the principles of social education and tolerance.[35]

1. The essentially social individual
2. Subsidiarity protects essential rights
3. Subsidiarity rehabilitates State authority
4. Subsidiarity and solidarism
5. Subsidiarity and social justice or social charity
6. Subsidiarity as the principle of social education
7. Subsidiarity as the principle of toleration

The Essentially Social Individual

The essentially social nature of the individual emphasizes that the individual is at the heart of the social system; hence, both the economy and social life are at the service of the individual. The individual is not understood here as an independent entity living entirely for his or herself, but rather one who is social by nature and living in community. Thus, to view the individual in relation to the community is at the heart of the principle of subsidiarity and conveys an intrinsic quality of the individual. Hence, "...the double relationship of the individual to society and of society to the individual has been intended by the Creator, and we must not only recognize it but make it the basis of scientific investigation."[36]

James P. Hanigan[37] has also offered a standard understanding of the relationship between the individual and the community or social groups which employs subsidiarity:

34 Ibid. pp. 207–209.

35 The principles of social education and tolerance are discussed in relation to the principle of subsidiarity drawing on the useful insights provided by John H. Walgrave, *Person and Society: A Christian View* (Pittsburgh, PA: Duquesne University Press, 1965), pp. 158–178.

36 Ibid.

37 James P. Hanigan, *As I Have Loved You: The Challenge of Christian Ethics* (New York and Mahwah: Paulist Press, 1986), pp. 81–83 deals specifically with the relationship of the individual to social groups, and explains the relevance of subsidiarity; however, two chapters in this work: chapter three "The Person As Moral Agent," and chapter four "The Moral Agent in Community," provide useful information that addresses the issues of social justice which are central in this study.

> It establishes a complex set of inter-related mutual rights and obligations between the individual and his or her social groups, as well as between smaller and larger entities. The individual has both the right and the obligation to do what he or she can do on one's own to fulfill basic needs and satisfy the demands of human dignity. The social group has the obligation to honor and to protect individual initiative. But it also has the right and the obligation to do what individuals alone are unable to do to meet their needs and honor their dignity. The individual, for example, has both the right to an education and the obligation to seek it with diligence. But his or her community has the obligation to provide the means by which an education may be gained, e.g., a school system, libraries, teachers. It also has the corresponding right to tax individuals to support the system and to require students to attend school. More specifically, teachers should not do for students what students are able to do for themselves, but teachers may and should provide the structured setting and discipline that education requires when individuals are unable to do this.[38]

According to Hanigan, there are some things that are so essential to human life and dignity that human beings need to and ought to cooperate with each other, rather than engaging in pursuing these goals all by themselves. Thus, it is, "...a fundamental feature of our love for one another that we join together to create and to care for social bodies, social structures and social systems which help us to be more fully human."[39] This study addresses some of the issues which a given social setting could help provide for the general well-being of its citizens and those which the citizens themselves need to take up in order to bring about the mutual rights and obligations between the individual and social groups advocated by the subsidiarity principle.

Similarly, Jean - Yves Calvez and Jacques Perrin affirm that, essentially, subsidiarity does not wish to render society useless. It could not, since it is the natural means by which humans express their social characteristics. Rather, the principle does encourage that great allowance be made for individual initiative:

> ...in order to help men to realize their fundamental rights, society ought in practice to see that men have scope for free and responsible action. Society is not subsidiary in the sense of being secondary or accidental, but in the etymological sense that it ought to provide help to the person to permit the concrete realization and the guarantee of his fundamental rights.[40]

This contribution is necessary to underline the complementarities which exists, on the one hand, between the purpose of the common good to develop the indi-

---

38 Ibid; pp. 82-83.

39 Ibid, p. 83.

40 Jean - Yves Calvez and Jacques Perrin, *The Church and Social Justice: The Social Teachings of the Popes from Leo XIII to Pius XII (1878–1958)* (London: Burns & Oates, 1961), p. 122; the whole of chapter V on "Person and Society," provides critical views which explain the anthropology of the encyclicals in general and convey the degrees of relationships in society that the principle of subsidiarity took up in RN and QA.

vidual, and on the other hand, the demand that the attainment of that very common good be an open possibility for all people to exercise their personal and individual liberty in a responsible, and conscious manner:

> The Church does not oppose individual liberty to social power as two forces acting in opposite directions. What is opposed, and then only in a relative manner, is personal liberty and the common good of the society. These two concepts are put in opposition only to show that the second, the common good, is external to and above the other-personal liberty-only to the extent that the liberty of the person is the object of the care of the common good.[41]

Subsidiarity Protects Essential Rights

The principle of subsidiarity of associations encourages the bonding of the various social relationships in the whole social system. How can this role be effectively carried out in society? There are two ways of looking at the social system. On the one hand, some persons may conceive it as an external structure whose activity may or may not impact their lived experience like a solitary individualistic setup within the whole. On the other hand, one might consider the activity of the social structure to have some impact on one's life-experience and so to have integrated some essential aspects of the individual. The implication would be to challenge the internal logic of the system, which in the first instance provided room for unrelated parts of the whole, to find some form of relevance in a sociological system. In both cases, not only is an organic thought pattern lacking, it is grossly misrepresented which leads to collectivistic and universalistic tendencies. The role of subsidiarity then would be to strengthen the bonds of interrelationships existing between individual rights and the social system and vice versa. This is why QA upholds the enduring essential conditions for building up these interrelations in community by maintaining that "Man (Woman) is older than the State" and that "...the domestic household is antecedent, logically as well as in fact, to the civil community."[42] In so doing, the principle is established to both provide for the rights of the private activity of the individual and the rights of smaller communities, in contrast to the activities of larger communities, but most especially, that of the State. This means that insofar as the activity of the individual and the smaller or immediate community is sufficiently efficient and responsive to the community, it should not and ought not to be replaced by the activities of higher units within the social system. Such an intervention would be considered a violation of the rights of the smaller units to responsibly impact the social system, and should be challenged through the various organs of the social system.

41 Ibid, p. 123; words in bracket are mine.

42 QA Par. 49, p. 53.

Subsidiarity Rehabilitates State Authority

The relationship between subsidiarity and State authority is central to understanding the different levels of competencies in a given social structure. The principle of subsidiarity provides a limited role for State authority, ensuring in the process that the State does not become an absolute and domineering force without any form of control. Thus, QA advocated a process of equitable power sharing between State authorities and the other structures of civil society: "The State authorities should leave to other bodies the care and expediting of business and activities of lesser moment, which otherwise become for it a source of great distraction."[43] Rather, the State should concentrate on providing the necessary set of conditions and structures for a peaceful and harmonious ordering of society: "… a major and pressing duty of the State and of all good citizens: to get rid of conflict between 'classes' with divergent interests, and to foster and promote harmony between the various 'ranks' or groupings of society."[44] This does not in any way imply that individual and personal rights could be swallowed up by society under the guise of providing opportunities for the common good. Rather, the structures, which the society will provide, must necessarily safeguard and ensure their realization; otherwise, it would appear as if the society is the proper end of the human person, and an end in itself. Calvez and Perrin support the above position when they affirm that:

> It is in society that persons find their full development. Society is, therefore, in itself absolutely necessary. But the necessity for society is not such that it may be its own end. It remains true that society exits for the person. A simple expression of all of this teaching is to be found in the principle of the subsidiary function of society in relation to persons.[45]

The subsidiary function of the State or Society does not in any sense imply a secondary or accidental position. It is a question of society acting in some cases, as a deputy when the situation does arise as envisaged in the principle of subsidiarity to provide the desired help. In general, the exercise of this subsidiary role by the society consists:

> Primarily and above all in interventions made by society in its own right, interventions which are necessary even when there is no failure by individuals to perform their functions. Subsidiarity is the characteristic of all the functions of society, and of the common good itself, and not only of actions where the State supplements for the deficiencies of individuals in those things which they ought to be doing for themselves.[46]

43 QA Par. 80, p. 60.

44 QA Par. 81, p. 60.

45 See Calvez and Perrin, p. 121.

46 Ibid, pp. 122–123.

Here the State is envisaged to perform its subsidiary functions for the common good by providing help to other members of the society, while, at the same time, it ought to carry out its proper tasks. Hence, its subsidiary role with regard to other societies and individuals should not be subsidiary by reference to the State proper, or society as a whole. In other words, subsidiarity should not be conceived as secondary and the State thought of in the same manner. The principle of subsidiarity is about the relationship of the State with the other societies, and the nature of the State itself. Thus, everything which the State does should be a help, a support, and not forced on the citizens since the State is not an end in itself.

Pius XI stated clearly that the proper functions of the State cannot be performed by any other member of the society. The State brings help to these societies without destroying itself in the process. Rather, the role of the State is enhanced and made easier by the various roles performed by the other societies, as long as the State does not constitute a stumbling block to the lesser societies in the exercise of its subsidiary functions.

> The State authorities should leave to other bodies the care and expediting of business and activities of lesser moment, which otherwise become for it a source of great distraction. It then will perform with greater freedom, vigor and effectiveness, the tasks belonging properly to it, and which it alone can accomplish, directing, supervising, encouraging, restraining, as circumstances suggest or necessity demands.[47]

Subsidiarity and Solidarism

According to Nell-Breuning, solidarism is another major pillar of Christian social ethics next to common welfare and social justice. The central link between subsidiarity and solidarity lies in the fact that, while subsidiarity allows the community to develop itself freely without external coercion, solidarity is the dynamic principle that governs the development and creation of social structures. The word solidarity is taken from the Latin juridical term *in solidum*, which connotes that each of the persons in a group or society is responsible to the part and to the whole. It embraces the general sense of the various means of mutual dependence or belonging together.[48] Solidarity is that ethical principle that binds persons together for a common task:

> The principle of solidarity states that when the individual faces a necessary task which he cannot properly accomplish by himself, he may count upon the orderly help of others for the fulfillment of the task...this solidarity means, on the part of the community, an obligation to foster or create, within its historical possibilities, all organizations and undertakings that are necessary or useful to supply the members with the material and

47 QA Par. 80, p. 60.

48 See Walgrave, p. 150.

> spiritual goods required for the satisfaction of their individual wants and the fulfillment of their personal vocation.[49]

Thus, the principle of solidarity is a socio-ethical concept that promotes the personal and communal obligation to form proper social organs in society. These social organs serve the need for mutual assistance of the members of the community. Solidarity is the principle which helps define the social order as comprising harmonious cooperation of occupational groups and a necessary means of promoting social harmony among groups:

> But there cannot be question of any perfect cure, except this opposition be done away with, and well-ordered members of the social body come into being: functional "groups," namely, binding men together not according to the position they occupy in the labor market, but according to the diverse functions which they exercise in society. For as nature induces those who dwell in close proximity to unite into municipalities, so those who practice the same trade or profession, economic or otherwise, constitute as it were fellowships or bodies. These groupings, autonomous in character, are considered by many to be, if not essential to civil society, at least a natural accompaniment thereof.[50]

This document affirms, on the one hand, that the oppositional conflict between persons and society is destructive of the very reason for their existence, namely, the development of persons. On the other hand, it admits that the opportunities of the common good should be offered to all persons, to exercise liberty and responsibility both at the personal and community levels. Thus, there should be no opposition between individual liberty and social power.

Clearly, persons are called to higher responsibility in conscience to the common good, so that, "...personal rights and social obligations are inseparable. Social obligations find their root in personal rights and so become obligations for the person."[51] This means that the union of persons is pursued and realized in a cultural community, by coming together in solidarity to responsibly create social structures that can best serve their individual and social needs in community.

Subsidiarity and Social Justice or Social Charity

The principle of subsidiarity is related to social justice in the sense that it inspires on the one hand, the exercise of distributive justice by promoting an organic community, which allows for the participation of the different structural levels, especially smaller groups like the family, local groups, churches, and voluntary organizations. On the other hand, it gives liberty to the State's right to intervene

49 Ibid, pp. 153–154.

50 QA Par. 83, pp. 60–61.

51 Ibid.

when intervention is necessary for the common good or to protect distributive justice or the rights of members of the group, class or community. The question of the necessity for State intervention and the connection between the State and the economy was the context that moved Pius XI to appeal to subsidiarity as a guiding fundamental principle of relationship between the State and other societies or groups. The nature of the State is to seek the common good of all members and to bring about social justice. The other associations and groups which make up the State exist in their own right, but do not necessarily seek to realize the universal common good. The State should not put itself in the place of these associations or groups as regards their proper functions. Consequently, it may not seek to overrun these organs, without at the same time putting into jeopardy the freedom of persons to legitimately form self-help groups. Hence, Pius XI, points out on the one hand: "...that owing to the change in social conditions, much that was formerly done by small bodies can nowadays be accomplished only by large organizations."[52] This allows room for State intervention in some economic activity due to its size or importance in the name of the larger good of society. On the other hand, the history of human individualism is full of negative images that implicate the State itself:

> On account of the evil of individualism...things have come to such a pass that the highly developed social life, which once flourished in a variety of prosperous and interdependent institutions, has been damaged, all but ruined, leaving virtually only individuals and the State, with no little harm to the latter.[53]

Thus, it was within this context that Pius XI found it compelling to establish a principle that would coordinate the activity of the State in relation to other associations, especially with a view to the economy by saying:

> One should not withdraw from individuals and commit to the community what they can accomplish by their own enterprise and industry. So, too, it is an injustice and at the same time a grave evil and a disturbance of right order to transfer to the larger and higher collectivity functions which can be performed and provided for by lesser and subordinate bodies. Inasmuch as every social activity should, by its very nature, prove a help to members of the body social, it should never destroy or absorb them.[54]

Calvez and Perrin affirm that the principle of subsidiarity was stated here with a universal appeal to every society, and particularly to the State in its dealings with the other associations. Their articulation of the applicability of subsidiarity to the State stands out distinctively:

> The principle does not mean that the State should intervene as little as possible. To say this would be to return to a modernized version of the liberal thesis, or at least to

52 QA Par. 79, p. 60.

53 QA Par. 78, p. 60.

54 QA Par. 79, p. 60.

> conceive of the State's intervention in purely pragmatic terms, though the State were some sort of factotum. What the principle does mean is that we should so arrange matters that whenever the State does intervene, it does so to help individuals and lesser societies, which is the same as to say that it should never intervene save when the common good and distributive justice require.[55]

Furthermore, they maintain that the principle of State subsidiarity is not meant to suppress the State, but to promote the view that the State carries out the functions that are proper to it while, at the same time, allowing the other associations their proper roles. In this case, it would become clear that:

> It is quite impossible to delegate to lesser societies than the State the functions and responsibilities which belong to it. That would be to suppose that these societies also are subsidiary to the State, and this is impossible: subsidiarity looks only one way. The State brings aid (subsidium) to other societies, but they do not bring aid to the State at least, not in the same sense.[56]

What is emerging clearly is that the principle of subsidiarity does contain an intrinsic limitation on the right of State intervention. The State fulfils a subsidiary function on the basis of the common good of all and distributive justice. It does not seek to suppress them on any other account. Calvez and Perrin have warned about the attempt to exchange subsidiarity with substitution:

> Apart from such substitutive action which might be required of the State in special circumstances, subsidiarity covers all the tasks which it ought to assume for the sake of the prosperity of the community and of all its members, as well as all those which are needed to guarantee distributive justice, when one form or another of economic association endangers the lawful rights of a social class or a special group. . . If this were not so, it would be necessary to hold that State intervention is only pragmatical and is founded on no more than the de facto efficiency or inefficiency of societies which are weaker than the State and stand in need of its help. To reason in these purely pragmatic terms would be to abandon the wider view of Leo XIII and Pius XI, which sought to establish the right of the State within its own nature and that of the common good. Subsidiarity could no longer apply to the relations of this natural society, the State, with the lesser societies; the term would stand only for recourse to an instrument of general utility in those cases where lesser societies which ought to be able to look after their own affairs had failed, through some unfortunate circumstance, to do so effectively. Action would then be a matter of taking over a task, a purely empirical problem dealt with in purely empirical terms. There would no longer be any question of an authentic and natural function of the State.[57]

Thus, it is pertinent to insist that the principle of subsidiarity does not operate based only on pragmatic and empirical consequences. In other words, it is not to be subjected to the whims of social utility. Subsidiarity by nature has within it an

---

55 See Calvez and Perrin, p. 332.

56 Ibid.

57 Ibid. pp. 333–334.

inner dynamism as a principle of competencies to assign roles to the State which is proper to it and at the same time allows the State to render functions to the lesser societies that are directly aimed at protecting the universal common good and ensuring distributive justice in the process. In so doing, subsidiarity is understood as "...a fundamental principle of social philosophy, fixed and unchangeable, that one should not withdraw from individuals and commit to the community what they can accomplish by their enterprise and industry."[58]

Subsidiarity as the Principle of Social Education

John Walgrave was the one who explained the concept of subsidiarity as an important tool for social education and transformation. By education, he was not referring to the process whereby the student, not so knowledgeable, is at the receiving end of all the personal decisions of the teacher who is out flowing with knowledge. Rather, what he meant by education was the direct opposite.

> To educate means to assist another in forming his own correct judgment, and in making wise decisions for his own life. To educate is to help another in self-education, and the latter can ultimately come only from the freedom and the responsibility of the one who is being educated. If we wish to educate someone to freedom, we must also give him as much freedom of movement and initiative as possible and use coercion only when it happens to be necessary.[59]

Similarly, Paulo Freire,[60] working on the basic assumption that one's "ontological vocation" lies in being "fully human," opines that one is an active subject who is able to

> act upon and transform the world, as opposed to being a passive object that is being acted upon. Freire came to the understanding in his philosophy of education for "critical consciousness" that every human being, no matter how "ignorant" or submerged in the "culture of silence," is capable of looking critically at the world, society, community, in a dialogical participation with others. As long as the right tools for such an encounter are available, the individual is able to engage in, and to perceive his or her social reality with a new sense of self-awareness. This radical awareness of the self is considered an educational experience.

Thus, the basic principle of pedagogy is that the educator should strive toward the advancement of the student to the extent that the educator's intervention is finally

---

58 QA Par. 79, p. 60.

59 See Walgrave, p. 158.

60 Paulo Freire, *Pedagogy of the Oppressed*, rev. ed. & trans. Myra Bergman Ramos (New York: Continuum, 1997), pp. 25ff; In this book, the author makes one to realize that true education is a process of helping one to grow to help oneself. Hence, any educational encounter that seeks to take away one's sense of self in relation to others is in great danger of negating the principle of subsidiarity as a process of bringing about help to self-help.

unnecessary. This pedagogical tool is broadened into the principle of subsidiarity and made into a socio-ethical principle. Here the principle is applied to the relations of person to person, groups to persons, larger groups to smaller groups, the State to the local communities and associations, the society to the individual: do not absorb or replace, but foster free unfolding and development, promote healthy self-growth, enhance mutual participation, and intervene only to the extent that the common good of the all-embracing community, State, and persons demands it. By so doing, there is no discrepancy between the personal good of all and the good of the social groups. Together, they make up the common good of society, and encourage the growth of its members in personality: "...that is why it has as its task to help the members, according to its own nature and with its own means, to attain that degree of material freedom and of moral freedom which makes them free for the union of persons, the community of love, which is the ultimate end and the supreme common good of the community in all its members and on every level."[61]

The principle of subsidiarity is valuable as a tool for social education. Here one is concerned with an educational process that is geared toward self-formation. Thus, by providing the necessary means for self-formation, the student is given the freedom to discover critical ways of self-help. Freedom that fosters the right conditions for self-growth promotes an aspect of the absolute good. Consequently, any intervention by the higher groups in the lower, which limits the freedom of persons or associations, might be justified only on the basis of the demands of freedom itself. Since there is the human tendency to sometimes engage arbitrarily in dubious and immoral behavior like repressive and totalitarian acts against the other's freedom, which may be directed against self-development and liberty, then a higher group should and ought to intervene in the name of freedom itself in order to protect and promote it. It is in this context that the principle of subsidiarity has universal appeal with regard to the person in society.

> As much freedom as is permitted by the common good, and only as much coercion as is demanded by the common good, which, ultimately, is but the good of freedom itself. This principle is universally valid. In the first place, it applies to the State with respect to all groups and persons that live within its territory. It is also applicable to every community within the State in relation to partial groups and persons that are organic parts of the larger community.[62]

Subsidiarity as the Principle of Tolerance

The principle of tolerance in its most general formulation deals with the relationship and attitude between persons, social groups, and communities. More specifi-

61 See Walgrave, p. 159.

62 See Walgrave, p. 160.

cally, one could affirm from the outset that this principle helps maintain solidarity and subsidiarity among groups and subgroups in society, even in situations where their coexistence is hampered due to differences in opinions and convictions. Walgrave has provided the ambiance within which one can conceptualize this principle:

> Tolerance is an attitude of a person or group of persons toward another person or group insofar as these are "different." The "otherness" in question does not arise from natural differences, such as race or temperament, nor from unimportant differences in opinion, but is based on more profound differences of conviction concerning the ultimate questions of existence, concerning that which man ultimately accepts as the fundamental truth and value. From such a difference follows a different interpretation of existence, hence a divergent project of life that expresses itself in personal and social activities and conduct.[63]

This is the position from which Walgrave was able to define tolerance as "...the ethical attitude which a person must take with respect to another person who differs from him in his view of the world and of life."[64] Tolerance, understood from this perspective, connotes a secondary aspect of the attitude that should exist between persons in society. Fundamentally, it means that one allows the other to be himself or herself, which includes acting freely in his being different, not for selfish reasons, but out of respect for the other's inviolable character as a person. Here lies the primary sense in which the ethical attitude among persons is a positive one, namely, to respect the freedom of persons.

Tolerance, though, is not simply an interior disposition about one's convictions. It ought to leave some room for outward expression, especially in the form of social organizations with those who share the same opinions. Walgrave puts it succinctly:

> Tolerance means to let another act freely. Negatively it means that we abstain from any kind of coercion, physical or moral, by which we might make one who thinks differently change his conviction or prevent him, as existing in this world, from following his own way of life.[65]

In other words, one should be ready to allow the other person the freedom to lead his life in a self-responsible way, free from undue external pressure but through the dictates of one's conscience. At the same time, tolerance invites one to protect that freedom from acting out aggressively toward the other person. Thus, at the core of tolerance lies the fundamental view that the tolerant person should be open to the position that others would make an option in life that might be directed negatively toward another person. In this respect, the principle of tolerance is upheld when the tolerant one decides to speak against the violation of individual

63 Ibid. p. 164.

64 Ibid.

65 See Walgrave, p. 165.

freedom and refuses to support the ideology that justifies such acts. This concept notwithstanding, there are instances when the tolerant option might prove to be a challenge.

> Hence tolerance does not exclude every ideological battle that is fought with the weapons of force. Freedom in our earthly community of persons is a universal condition of the common good. As such, it must take away from the members of that community all freedom to combat freedom. Liberty, as belonging to the common good, excludes every action of particular freedom that is directed against freedom. Those who are responsible for the common good-this includes fundamentally all citizens and formally the bearers of authority in the community-must repress the expressions of particular freedom that are directed against the right of liberty of members, whatever might be the ideological reasons offered for those expressions.[66]

Rahner appears, on the one hand, to have challenged the above understanding of tolerance when he said that "the tolerance that lets itself be restricted by the common good is intolerant of the tolerance which free subjects demand spontaneously as their unrestricted right...Reality is not such that everything will always be harmonized."[67] On the other hand, he maintains that "...in their private and public lives, people must often be intolerant toward one another, in order to show their tolerance by securing and protecting the possibilities of freedom of others."[68] Here lies the practical difficulty with the application of tolerance. The understanding of tolerance one advocates helps to prepare the stage for it as a socio-ethical principle. Here, one is encouraged in every society to promote and practice tolerance at different levels of the community: between members of larger groups and those of smaller groups; between the State and the other social groups that make up the society. Since the family is the primary human society, it follows then that the State, which is secondary, should exist for the good of the community that has organically developed from the family.

Fitzgerald has proposed, for instance, that any form of toleration one practices should lead toward greater human solidarity. While recognizing that the human community is far from having a peaceful world because of the different levels of conflicts that abound between individuals and their distinct communities, on the one hand, and at the international levels, on the other hand, one is optimistic that "...it may be easier for rulers and people of great powers to develop a sense of human solidarity that can transcend their differences and conflicts than it is for people embedded in local conflict situations to raise their sights to broader horizons."[69]

---

66 Ibid. pp. 168–169.

67 Karl Rahner, *Theological Investigations: Humane Society and The Church of Tomorrow*, vol. XXII, trans. Joseph Donceel (New York: Crossroad, 1991), p. 23.

68 Ibid.

69 Garrett Fitzgerald, "Toleration or Solidarity?" In *The Politics of Toleration in Modern Life*, ed., Susan Mendus (Durham, NC: Duke University Press, 2000), p. 18.

In this assertion, one notices how it affirms the necessity for the levels of competencies which allows larger power groups to carry out their roles and affirms the right of smaller groups to attend to its functions so that they do not spread out beyond their capacities.

Similarly, MacIntyre proposed that one would need the right set of conditions and context to exist for any healthy conversation that might promote "effective practical decision-making." Accordingly, it would involve two subsidiary aims: "... that of enabling those who participate in it both to give voice to their own concerns and to understand those of others, and by so doing that of framing and cataloguing the best reasons for and against each alternative course of action."[70] Thus, toleration is to be extended to the different facets of life in community to ensure that different points of views are respected and that persons are not threatened in society. Hence neither the State nor persons may attempt to impose any one ideology. What is being challenged here that is central to subsidiarity is coercive violence against persons and groups in community in view of the common good of all as Keenan constructively states:

> ...tolerance (is adopted) not as a form of patience nor as a form of disapproval but rather as an admission that in the present limited situation, the obligation to protect certain values overrides the ability to recognize as right or acceptable others' decisions in conscience to live or act as they do. Thus, the tolerant attitude is one of hope that one day greater understanding will resolve the present incompatibility or threat and lead somehow to the reconciliation of which Paul calls us all to be ministers. (2 Cor 5:11–6:13)[71]

Since Pius XI, many papal social encyclicals have used the principle of subsidiarity in various ways building on the formal formulation one has examined. Thus, one could trace the major shifts and developments that have taken place in Catholic social thought on subsidiarity.

---

70 Alasdair MacIntyre, "Toleration and the Goods of Conflict," in *The Politics of Toleration in Modern Life,* p. 133. This essay offers one some understanding of John Locke's proposals concerning toleration and the State that are tied to the nature and values of the contemporary State. In particular, MacIntyre opines that tension and even conflict affect the demands of the State and the market economy on the one hand and the conditions of "rational local community," hence it is important for "...those who value rational local communal enterprise...to order their relationships with State and market so that, as far as possible, they remain able to draw upon those resources that can only be secured from State and market, while preserving their own self-sufficiency, their self-reliance, and their freedom from constraint by either," pp. 142–143.

71 James F. Keenan, "Toleration, Principle of," *The New Dictionary of Catholic Social Thought,* p. 952.

John XXIII, Mater ET Magistra (MM), 1961 and Pacem in Terris (PT), 1963

John XXIII in MM sought to apply the teachings of his predecessors to modern challenges by affirming the role of the Church as a teacher, and as a nurturing guardian of the poor and oppressed of society.

First, John XXIII articulated a pluralist vision of the world whereby different nations of the world could increase the mutuality of relations between them with an aim to providing help for the less advanced nations. MM, subsequently recognized the changed historical, technological, economic, social, and political circumstances that took place since Pius XI in the internal arrangements of individual nation States and in the mutual relations of countries. Specifically, the document stated that:

> Today, in many communities, citizens from almost all social strata participate in public life. Public authorities intervene more and more in economic and social affairs. The peoples of Asia and Africa, having set aside colonial systems, now govern themselves according to their own laws and institutions. As the mutual relationships of peoples increase, they become daily more dependent one upon the other. Throughout the world, assemblies and councils have become more common, which, being supranational in character, take into account the interests of all peoples. Such bodies are concerned with economic life, or with social affairs, or with culture and education, or, finally, with the mutual relationships of peoples.[72]

The explicit recognition of the nations of Asia and Africa in a papal social encyclical by John XXIII was a novelty. Also, the affirmation that these nations "...now govern themselves according to their own laws and institutions," was a welcomed development in the type of social and economic participation that was being envisaged. Moreover, the call for "...mutual relationship of peoples" at that point in history was itself remarkable. The following questions are evident for subsidiarity: how and why was this wonderful pluralist vision of society advocated in MM not fostered to bring about the desired cooperation and participation in the decision making process of communities? Did the "mutual relationship of peoples" advocated by MM take place in areas of economics, politics, and technology, between the advanced nations and the less advanced nations in such a way that the less advanced nations could truly say that they received *subsidium* that enabled them to help themselves? Did the less advanced nations take advantage of whatever form of *subsidium* was received or gained to improve the living conditions of their people or did they squander the opportunity?

Second, John XXIII addressed the issue of "private initiative and State intervention in economic life," which raises important consequences for subsidiarity.

72 MM Par. 49, p. 91; cf., also. Par. 150–152, p. 109.

On the one hand, he maintained the priority of "the private initiative of the individual":

> Experience, in fact, shows that where private initiative of individuals is lacking, political tyranny prevails. Moreover, much stagnation occurs in various sectors of the economy, and hence all sorts of consumer goods and services, closely connected with needs of the body and more especially of the spirit, are in short supply. Beyond doubt, the attainment of such goods and services provides remarkable opportunity and stimulus for individuals to exercise initiative and industry.[73]

On the other hand, the document maintained that where "...the appropriate activity of the State is lacking or defective, commonwealths are apt to experience incurable disorders, and there occurs exploitation of the weak by the unscrupulous strong, who flourish, unfortunately, like cockle among the wheat, in all times and places."[74] The role of the State is to follow faithfully the subsidiarity principle.[75] However, the effects of socialization, while providing the avenue for multiple social relationships, could also give room to intervention by public authorities in the personal lives of individuals.[76] Thus, the contribution of MM was to fashion a way by which the threat posed to individual initiative could be averted or minimized. This made the document to pose a pertinent question that is at the center of the principle of subsidiarity: "Will men (women) perhaps then become automatons, and cease to be personally responsible, as these social relationships multiply more and more?"[77] In response to this question, the document upheld that the provisions of the common good should be respected to enable persons to grow more fully. The common good, then, is to embrace "...the sum total of those conditions of social living, whereby men (women) are enabled more fully and more readily to achieve their own perfection."[78] Furthermore, the document indicated that the State should maintain a healthy balance between: "...(1) The freedom of individual citizens and groups of citizens to act autonomously, while cooperating one with the other; (2) The activity of the State whereby the undertakings of private individuals and groups are suitably regulated and fostered."[79] This was an important development by John XXIII, which had implications for subsidiarity and helped to explain the sense in which individual initiative could be jeopardized by the multiplicity of relationships in a commonwealth.

73 MM Par. 57, p. 93.

74 Ibid. Par. 58, p. 93.

75 See MM Par. 53, p, 92.

76 See MM Par. 59–60, pp. 93–94.

77 See MM Par. 62, p. 94; words in bracket are mine.

78 See MM Par. 65, p. 94; words in bracket are mine.

79 MM Par. 66, p. 95.

In PT, John XXIII was optimistic about the great potential for human beings to work together for peace on earth. The document focused its attention on the relations between individuals, between the individual and the community, and between nations. First, the emphasis on the rights of persons within the commonwealth was a major development in Catholic social thought that is related to subsidiarity. This teaching provided the opportunity for maintaining the centrality of the dignity of the human person as the foundation, goal, and end of all social institutions.

> Any human society, if it is to be well-ordered and productive, must lay down as a foundation this principle, namely, that every human being is a person; that is, his nature is endowed with intelligence and free will. Indeed, precisely because he is a person he has rights and obligations flowing directly and simultaneously from his very nature. And as these rights and obligations are universal and inviolable, so they cannot in any way be surrendered.[80]

In this way, PT[81] indicated the different types of rights that help promote and hold together this anthropological vision. These include personal and social rights, economic rights, rights of association, and political rights among others. In particular, PT quoted Pius XII to have upheld that: "The human individual, far from being an object and, as it were, a merely passive element in the social order, is in fact, must be and must continue to be, its subject, its foundation and its end."[82] This emphasis is critical for subsidiarity in the sense that it makes the case against unnecessary interference and coercion that might seek to overrun individual initiative. Next, PT focuses on the corresponding duties which accompany these rights such as "…the right of every man (woman) to life is correlative with the duty to preserve it; his right to a decent standard of living with the duty of living it becomingly; and his right to investigate the truth freely, with the duty of seeking it ever more completely and profoundly."[83] The document maintained that persons who fail to carry out their civic responsibilities put asunder the very rights they claim: "Those, therefore, who claim their own rights, yet altogether forget or neglect to carry out their respective duties, are people who build with one hand and destroy with the other."[84] Furthermore, mutual collaboration was encouraged on the issues of rights claims and responsibilities as integral to building a civil society. This mutuality of rights was to transcend the different facets of social life and be guided by the virtues of "truth, justice, charity and freedom."[85]

80 PT Par. 9, p. 132.

81 Cf. Par. 11–27 for details of these rights, pp. 132–135.

82 PT Par. 26, p. 135.

83 PT Par. 29, p. 135; words in bracket are mine.

84 PT Par. 30, p. 135.

85 See PT Par. 35–38, pp. 136–137.

Second, John XXIII recognized that three characteristics: the role of the working class in economic and public affairs; the role of women in domestic and public life; and the independence of many nations in social and political life;[86] make it necessary to state the relations that should exist between individuals and public authorities within a State. The central positions of this document that promote subsidiarity are the centrality of persons, the common good of all, and participation of persons in the commonwealth.[87] Consequently, the goal is to build a healthy society where rights of persons are respected and the common good of all is maintained without giving undue advantage to others in the process as the document states clearly: "It should not happen that certain individuals or social groups derive special advantage from the fact that their rights have received preferential protection. Nor should it happen that governments, in seeking to protect these rights, become obstacles to their full expression and free use."[88]

Third, John XXIII recognized another essential element of subsidiarity, namely, the protection of the rights of minorities in society. The pope considered various attempts made "…to limit the strength and numerical increase of these lesser peoples;"[89] as a violation against justice itself. In other words, civil authorities are encouraged to support rights claims of minorities particularly when it "…concerns their language, the development of their natural gifts, their ancestral customs, and their accomplishments and endeavors in the economic order."[90]

Similarly, the economic assistance that the developed countries should extend to underdeveloped countries should be the kind of *subsidium* that would lead these countries to self-help. The document affirmed that: "The wealthier states, in providing varied forms of assistance to the poorer, should respect the moral values and ethnic characteristics peculiar to each, and also that they should avoid any intention of political domination."[91]

Fourth, PT considered the role of the United Nations organization as central to the protection, promotion, and preservation of individual rights of persons especially in the international social, economic and political arenas. It upheld as a healthy development the "Universal Declaration of Human Rights" by the United Nations.[92]

86 See PT Par. 39–42, p. 137.

87 See PT Par. 46–74 for details of these positions.

88 PT Par. 65, p. 142.

89 PT Par. 95, p. 146.

90 PT Par. 96, p. 146.

91 PT Par. 125, pp. 150–151; cf. also Par. 138–141, pp. 153–154.

92 PT Par. 142–145, p. 154.

The Second Vatican Council, Gaudium ET Spes (GS), 1965

The pastoral constitution on "The Church in the Modern World" advocated for a new sense of service by the Church in a rapidly changing world, by presenting the ethical framework of the Church's commitment to pastoral work in the world. The document also emphasized the dignity of families, the uniqueness of cultures, and the importance of establishing justice in the process of development. The council also advocated for disarmament and just, peaceful international relations among nations. Significantly, the council document provided the sound basis for the promotion of culture in relation to the Gospel. This development was the key to unlocking the doors of the Church in Africa, Asia and generally in the "Third World" countries.

First, GS focused on the dignity of the human person and the claims of the person stressing individual rights over and above the claims of society. At the heart of the human person is the dignity of one's moral conscience from which flows individual capacity and initiatives:

> In the depths of his conscience, man detects a law which he does not impose upon himself, but which holds him to obedience. Always summoning him to love good and avoid evil, the voice of conscience can when necessary speak to his heart more specifically: do this, shun that. For man has in his heart a law written by God. To obey it is the very dignity of man; according to it he will be judged.
>
> Conscience is the most secret core and sanctuary of a man. There he is alone with God, whose voice echoes in his depths. In a wonderful manner conscience reveals that law which is fulfilled by love of God and neighbor. In fidelity to conscience, Christians are joined with the rest of men in the search for truth, and for the genuine solution to the numerous problems which arise in the life of individuals and from social relationships. Hence the more that a correct conscience holds sway, the more persons and groups turn aside from blind choice and strive to be guided by objective norms of morality.[93]

In order for objective norms of morality to guide people in community, it is necessary to place the human person as the foundation, goal and end of social relationships. The inner voice of conscience supports persons in their daily choices in life which help determine human interactions. The search for truth becomes a cooperative venture between persons and the social situation with which they interact. Thus, it is important for persons to form and fashion correct consciences in order that individuals and groups might objectively respond to the common good of all people.

Karl Rahner, commenting on GS 16, further articulates the freedom of conscience and of religion that distinguishes persons in community and at the same time protects the well-being of others:

93 GS Par. 16, p. 174.

> ...Through their conscience human beings are real subjects; they may not be treated like objects. Conscience must be respected by all social and ecclesiastical authorities, since their immediate function concerns the objective structures of reality. One's freedom of conscience and of religion should not infringe upon that of others because this would constitute what is usually called a violation of the common good.[94]

The implication for subsidiarity is that by forming correct consciences, persons would more truthfully make those choices that would protect their individual rights and the rights of others. Some might ask how persons could form correct consciences. Rahner offered some useful advice when he said that "...both society and the Church have the right and the duty to teach people about objective norms of morality and to exhort them to observe these norms. In other words: They teach the right way of applying conscience to concrete realities. This does not infringe upon freedom of conscience."[95] It may also be helpful in building healthy relationships that respect the dignity of persons as mutual partners without seeking to overpower them in the process. In truth, conscience protects liberty and persons act in freedom by promoting human relationships without coercion: "...man's dignity demands that he act according to a knowing and free choice. Such a choice is personally motivated and promoted from within. It does not result from blind internal impulse or from mere external pressure."[96]

Second, GS promoted the social nature of the person in human society which raises several implications for subsidiarity. The document emphasizes the fact that the promotion of communion between persons has and continues to take place at different levels in society:

> Among those social ties which man needs for his development, some, like the family and political community, relate with greater immediacy to his innermost nature. Others originate rather from his free decision. In our era, for various reasons, reciprocal ties and mutual dependencies increase day by day and give rise to a variety of associations and organizations, both public and private. This development, which is called socialization, while certainly not without its dangers, brings with it many advantages with respect to consolidating and increasing the qualities of the human person, and safeguarding his rights.[97]

Furthermore, GS challenged those who hold onto an "individualistic ethic:"

> ...Many in various places even make light of social laws and precepts, and do not hesitate to resort to various frauds and deceptions in avoiding just taxes or other debts due

94 See *Rahner, Theological Investigations,* vol. XXII, p. 11.

95 Ibid. p. 12.

96 GS Par. 17, p. 175.

97 GS Par. 25, p. 180. Note that the theme of socialization is developed in the document as it relates to the common good, the dignity of the human person, human equality, social justice, and solidarity, all which provide some implications for subsidiarity- see especially GS par. 26–32, pp. 181–185.

> to society. Others think little of certain norms of social life, for example those designated for the protection of health, or laws establishing speed limits. They do not even avert to the fact that by such indifference they imperil their own life and that of others.[98]

The persons who hold such individualistic morality are enemies to themselves and the society. Such an individualistic morality hardly promotes the cherished position of subsidiarity, which seeks to build relationships in community. In the true spirit of subsidiarity, GS stated that the obligation to build social relationships in community is paramount to persons because it promotes communal solidarity: "...the more unified the world becomes, the more plainly do the offices of men extend beyond particular groups and spread by degrees to the whole world."[99]

Third, GS articulated the role of the Church in the modern world in terms of degrees of subsidiary functions. From the onset, GS affirmed that the Church and the world are mutually related: "...everything we have said about the dignity of the human person, and about the human community and the profound meaning of human activity, lays the foundation for the relationship between the Church and the world, and provides the basis for dialogue between them."[100] The document then showed the various types of *subsidium* the Church could offer individuals, society, and human activity.[101] In the spirit of mutuality, GS showed the help the society should render to the Church. Essentially, the document acknowledged that: "...whoever promotes the human community at the family level, culturally, in its economic, social, and political dimensions, both nationally and internationally, such a one, according to God's design, is contributing greatly to the Church community as well, to the extent that it depends on things outside itself."[102]

Fourth, GS discussed the issue of the plurality of cultures and development. The document begins by acknowledging the significance of cultural values and how these are related to human values. Thus, cultural issues are pluralistic and can be found among different groups of people in different nations of the world. In fact, "...in every group or nation, there are an ever-increasing number of men and women who are conscious that they themselves are the artisans and the authors of the culture of their community."[103] Therefore, it is pertinent to advance some principles that would help promote healthy cultural development among persons in community. In truth:

98 GS Par. 30, p. 183.

99 Ibid.

100 GS Par. 40, p. 189.

101 See GS Par. 40–43, pp. 189–194.

102 See GS Par. 44, p. 194.

103 See GS Par. 55, p. 202.

> It is a duty most befitting our times that men, especially Christians, should work strenuously on behalf of certain decisions which must be made in the economic and political fields, both nationally and internationally. By these decisions universal recognition and implementation should be given to the right of all men to a human and civic culture favorable to personal dignity and free from any discrimination on the grounds of race, sex, nationality, religious or social conditions.[104]

The document hoped that cultural development would be promoted within a plural context. The implication for subsidiarity is that it supports the formation of groups and associations based on mutual needs in a community. Hence, such groups should be transparent and avoid discrimination and domination of persons based on the aforementioned elements. Its main purpose should be the service to humanity. By service to humanity "…we mean every man whatsoever and every group of men, of whatever race and from whatever part of the world."[105] Thus, GS remained faithful to the principle of subsidiarity when it stated that "…let all individuals and governments undertake a genuine sharing of their goods. Let them use these goods especially to provide individuals and nations with the means for helping and developing themselves."[106]

Fifth, GS advocated that persons participate in the life of the political community. The document made use of the principle of subsidiarity when it stated on the one hand that smaller associations be given the opportunity to contribute to the body social without unnecessary intervention from higher authorities:

> Authorities must beware of hindering family, social, or cultural groups, as well as intermediate bodies and institutions. They must not deprive them of their own lawful and effective activity, but should rather strive to promote them willingly and in an orderly fashion. For their part, citizens both as individuals and in association should be on guard against granting government too much authority and inappropriately seeking from it excessive conveniences and advantages, with a consequent weakening of the sense of responsibility on the part of individuals, families, and social groups.[107]

On the other hand, following the spirit of subsidiarity, GS acknowledged the important role that higher authorities could play in helping to coordinate the complex web of relationships that exists in society, and so allowed some limited and well defined role for the government:

> Because of the increased complexity of modern circumstances, government is more often required to intervene in social and economic affairs, by way of bringing about conditions more likely to help citizens and groups freely attain to complete human fulfillment with greater effect.[108]

104 GS Par. 60, p. 206.

105 GS Par. 64, p. 210.

106 GS Par. 69, p. 213.

107 GS Par.75, p. 217.

108 Ibid.

Paul VI, Populorum Progressio (PP), 1967 and Octogesimo Adveniens (OA), 1971

Paul VI presented the various dimensions of an integral human development and the necessary conditions for growth in the solidarity of peoples. There was also the disparity of wealth among nations which the pope identified as traceable to the heritage of colonialism, neo-colonialism, and in the imbalance of power that leads inevitably to an imbalance in contracts of trade. Hence, it was necessary to bring theological reflection to impact liberation from injustice and genuine human values that would engender true development towards a more human situation.

First, Paul VI stated that the social question had become an international issue and that in order to offer less advanced nations the means to help themselves, justice and peace was the way forward. He indicated that having visited Latin America, Africa, the Holy Land and India, it had become clear to him that development was a problem in these continents that deserved the attention of the international community.[109] Consequently, Paul VI declared that these inhuman conditions "...whose injustice cries to heaven,"[110] diminish the worth of persons and stagnate human initiative and responsibility, which are at the heart of subsidiarity. Thus, "integral development" is necessary to support developing nations to bring about the desired changes in their Communities: "Development cannot be limited to mere economic growth. In order to be authentic, it must be complete: integral, that is, it has to promote the good of every man and of the whole man."[111]

Second, Paul VI advocated that the spirit of solidarity of the human race prevail in the area of development. Thus, PP in the spirit of solidarity called for equity in trade relations between developing and developed nations. Explaining that the goal is to bring *subsidium* to the weaker nations in order to enable them to become "artisans of their destiny":

> The past has too often been characterized by relationships of violence between nations; may the day dawn when international relations will be marked with the stamp of mutual respect and friendship, of interdependence in collaboration, the betterment of all seen as the responsibility of each individual. The younger or weaker nations ask to assume their active part in the construction of a better world, one which shows deeper respect for the rights and the vocation of the individual. This is a legitimate appeal; everyone should hear it and respond to it.[112]

Furthermore, in the spirit of solidarity with the weaker nations, Paul VI challenged industrialists and multinational institutions to be socially sensitive in those developing nations where they carry out their business endeavors:

109 See PP Par. 3-5, pp. 240–241 for details.

110 PP Par. 30, p. 247.

111 PP Par. 14, p. 243.

112 PP Par. 65, p. 255.

> ...Industrialists, merchants, leaders, or representatives of larger enterprises, it happens that they are not lacking in social sensitivity in their own country; why then do they return to the inhuman principles of individualism when they operate in less-developed countries? Their advantaged situation should on the contrary move them to become the initiators of social progress and of human advancement in the area where their business calls them. Their very sense of organization should suggest to them the means for making intelligent use of the labor of the indigenous population, of forming qualified workers, of training engineers and staffs, of giving scope to their initiative, of introducing them progressively into higher positions, thus preparing them to share, in the near future, in the responsibilities of management. At least let justice always rule the relations between superiors and their subordinates. Let standard contracts with reciprocal obligations govern these relationships. Finally, let no one, whatever his status, be subjected unjustly to the arbitrariness of others.[113]

In this way, Paul VI indicated the key elements that could help persons in a weaker position gain help from one in a stronger position that would eventually lead to self-help which is promoted by subsidiarity.

Third, Paul VI linked integral development with peaceful existence and, in the spirit of subsidiarity, emphasized the need for an international body that could help establish and coordinate just political and economic environments.

> This international collaboration on a worldwide scale requires institutions that will prepare, coordinate and direct it, until finally there is established an order of justice which is universally recognized. With all our heart, we encourage these organizations which have undertaken this collaboration for the development of the peoples of the world; our wish is that they grow in prestige and authority.[114]

In OA, Paul VI set out to commemorate the 80th anniversary of RN by providing guidelines toward realizing the need for a genuine renewal in domestic and international societal structures. First, Paul VI explained that two "...fundamental aspirations: the aspiration to equality and the aspiration to participation"[115] help determine the kind of relationships which inform human dignity and freedom. However, human rights are violated and other forms of discriminations are on the increase, so much so that to legislate on such matters appears superficial. Thus, it would seem that legislation alone is not enough to build up "relationships of justice and equality." Therefore, one would turn to Gospel values where instruction is provided on how weaker persons in society should be treated: "...the more fortunate should renounce some of their rights so as to place their goods more generously at the service of others."[116] Thus, the more fortunate members of society would engage in the practice of solidarity and the common good. Furthermore, Paul VI maintained that relationships of justice and equality are enhanced through

113 PP Par. 70, p. 256.

114 See PP Par. 78, p. 258.

115 OA Par. 23, p. 273.

116 Ibid.

the building of the "political society." The political society should not be imposed on the people but should grow out of their experience as OA indicates.

> It is not for the State or even political parties, which would be closed unto themselves, to try to impose an ideology by means that would lead to a dictatorship over minds, the worst kind of all. It is for cultural and religious groupings, in the freedom of acceptance which they presume, to develop in the social body, disinterestedly and in their own ways, those ultimate convictions on the nature, origin, and end of man and society.[117]

The preference for subsidiary forms of associations to help build the political society with minimal government intervention supports the position that one should not withdraw from individuals and commit to the community what they can do for themselves.

> [Political power] While respecting the legitimate liberties of individuals, families, and subsidiary groups, it acts in such a way as to create, effectively and for the well being of all, the conditions required for attaining man's true and complete good, including his spiritual end. It acts within the limits of its competence, which can vary from people to people and from country to country. It always intervenes with care for justice and with devotion to the common good, for which it holds final responsibility. It does not, for all that, deprive individuals and intermediary bodies of the field of activity and responsibility which are proper to them and which lead them to collaborate in the attainment of this common good.[118]

Second, Paul VI realized that the realities of the political society demanded that persons have "…a greater sharing in responsibility and in decision-making,"[119] which is proper to subsidiarity. This shared responsibility should evolve out of true freedom and mutual interaction in the social, cultural, economic, religious, and political relationships that persons build in community. Moreover, shared responsibility would help promote equality and participation of persons in a more reasonable way that is humane, democratic, and dialectical:

> Admittedly, it is true that the choices proposed for a decision are more and more complex; the considerations that must be borne in mind are numerous, and the foreseeing of the consequences involves risk, even if new sciences strive to enlighten freedom at these important moments. However, although limits are sometimes called for, these obstacles must not slow down the giving of wider participation in working out decisions, making choices and putting them into practice.[120]

---

117 OA Par. 24, p. 274.

118 OA Par. 46, p. 282.

119 OA Par. 47, p. 283.

120 Ibid.

John Paul II, Laborem Exercens (LE), 1981 Sollicitudo Rei Socialis (SRS), 1987 and Centesimus Annus (CA), 1991

John Paul II, in LE, celebrated the 90th anniversary of RN by highlighting human work as the essential key to the social question. The pope recognized the value of the laborer in the process of production and subordinated the right to private property to the right of common use. Thus, he upheld the priority of labor over capital in production.

John Paul II then presented a spirituality of work with the insistence on upholding the dignity of labor. There are two main areas where subsidiarity was used in the encyclical that one needs to examine.

First, LE presented the meaning of work both in the "objective" and "subjective" sense that raises important implications for subsidiarity. The objective meaning refers to the objects produced by labor, from manufactured goods to agricultural products and technology. The subjective meaning refers to the centrality of the human person who uses his or her labor as a means for self-realization. Thus, the encyclical recognizes the pertinent position of the human person in production.

> ...A subjective being capable of acting in a planned and rational way, capable of deciding about himself and with a tendency to self-realization. As a person, man is therefore the subject of work. As a person he works, he performs various actions belonging to the work process; independently of their objective content, these actions must all serve to realize his humanity, to fulfill the calling to be a person that is his by reason of his very humanity.[121]

Evidently, LE gave priority to the human person as the measure for determining the effectiveness and quality of work: "...the basis for determining the value of human work is not primarily the kind of work being done, but the fact that the one who is doing it is a person. The sources of the dignity of work are to be sought primarily in the subjective dimension, not in the objective one."[122] Hence, one realizes that the objective dimension of work is and ought to be at the service of the subject, the human person. The manufactured goods, agricultural products, and technology are meant to help the human person and not to take over the subject.

The encyclical clearly states that "...in some instances technology can cease to be man's ally and become almost his enemy, as when the mechanization of work 'supplants' him, taking away all personal satisfaction and the incentive to creativity and responsibility..."[123] In this instance there would be a violation of the prin-

121 LE Par. 6, p. 358.

122 Ibid.

123 LE Par. 5, p. 358.

ciple of subsidiarity. Furthermore, LE maintains that "...work is 'for man' and not man 'for work'."[124] The encyclical affirms the personal worth which the human being should derive from work and the ethical meaning of work in this way.

> Work is a good thing for man-a good thing for his humanity-because through work man not only transforms nature, adapting it to his own needs, but he also achieves fulfillment as a human being and indeed in a sense becomes "more a human being."[125]

Second, John Paul II, in LE, affirms the priority of labor over capital in the process of production.

> ...We must first of all recall a principle that has always been taught by the church: the principle of the priority of labor over capital. This principle directly concerns the process of production: In this process labor is always a primary efficient cause, while capital, the whole collection of means of production, remains a mere instrument or instrumental cause. This principle is an evident truth that emerges from the whole of man's historical experience.[126]

In taking the above position, the encyclical was addressing the age-old conflict that existed between labor and capital where highly influential business people controlled the "means of production" over and against the exploited and poor majority of workers.[127] Accordingly, LE held that the conflict between labor and capital was an ethical one that had to do with the manner in which the subjects of production, namely human beings, are wrongly marginalized. Hence there was the need for solidarity with workers. The solidarity with workers was to take the form of building new partnerships that respect the majority of the persons involved in the process of production: "...proposals for joint ownership of the means of work, sharing by the workers in the management and/or profits of businesses, so-called shareholding by labor, etc."[128] One major implication for subsidiarity is that collectivist approaches in doing business that undermined the worth of the subjects of production might be minimized. Thus, LE affirms that there is the need to replace the "...system of excessive bureaucratic centralization, which makes the worker feel that he is just a cog in a huge machine moved from above, that he is for more reasons than one a mere production instrument rather than a true subject of work with an initiative of his own."[129] By so doing, the encyclical raised an important issue that is central to subsidiarity, namely, the recognition of the con-

---

124 LE Par. 5, p. 359. This is the context in which the encyclical upheld the "pre-eminence" of the subjective meaning of work over the objective dimension.

125 LE Par. 9, p. 364.

126 LE Par. 12, p. 367.

127 Cf. LE Par. 11, p. 366 for details of the conflict between labor and capital; the Marxist interpretation of this conflict for which John Paul II in LE sought to provide a new perspective.

128 LE Par. 14, p. 372.

129 LE Par. 15, p. 373.

tribution made by persons from below in the family, local workers unions, Churches, civil society groups that build various relationships to promote the dignity of persons in community.

John Paul II sets out in SRS to address the widening gap between the rich and the poor. He recognizes the universal dimension of the gap between the abundant wealth of the northern hemisphere contrasted with the dire poverty in the southern hemisphere. Accordingly, he opines that true development demands a critique of the moral dimension of development, a commitment not only from individuals, but States as well, and some recognition of the limited resources of nature. John Paul II exhorts solidarity with and a concern for the poor as motivation for reform.

First, John Paul II, while commenting on the situation in the world, opined that the right of economic initiative is one that is often relegated. According to him, economic right is related to both the initiatives of the individual and for the common good. Thus, the real threat is with "...the creative subjectivity of the citizen," which in turn affects the output of the larger society. Consequently, in the spirit of subsidiarity, the pope stated that larger organizations should not take over individual creativity since this would amount to making them "objects" rather than "subjects" of society:

> It must also be restated that no social group, for example a political party, has the right to usurp the role of sole leader, since this brings about destruction of the true subjectivity of society of the individual citizens, as happens in every form of totalitarianism. In this situation the individual and the people become "objects," in spite of all declarations to the contrary and verbal assurances.[130]

This type of situation could place in serious jeopardy the "authentic development" advocated by John Paul II which encourages the participation of individuals and poor nations in the development processes taking place in their communities.

Second, John Paul II argued that developing countries that are unable at the moment to foster authentic development could be helped through international structures and movements geared toward the fulfillment of this purpose. In this way, the key to a holistic development would be offered to these developing nations in the true spirit of solidarity. The principle of subsidiarity is respected in the sense that the aim of the pope is to bring an international collaboration to provide help that would favor "self-affirmation" of the citizens in developing nations.[131]

John Paul II sets out in CA to commemorate the centenary of RN and to examine the events of 1989 and 1990: the break-up of Eastern Europe, the weakening of oppressive regimes in Africa, Asia, and Latin America with the hope for "new things" *rerum novarum* within the social order. The pope urged all people of good will to dialogue and to cooperation for justice to overcome the alienation and poverty so extensive throughout the world. It is within this larger context of

130 SRS Par. 15, p. 403.

131 See SRS Par. 21–29; 44–45, pp. 407–414, 427–428.

the encyclical that one would sort out particular areas where the principle of subsidiarity was employed as an integral part of the Church's social thought. There are two major applications of subsidiarity that stand out in CA.

First, John Paul II used subsidiarity while carrying out some re-reading of Leo XIII's RN in the light of contemporary issues. John Paul II appealed specifically on the one hand, to the right of the State to intervene in the social order in order to bring about the needed help to promote the common good of society. On the other hand, he cautioned that the State should always protect the rights of individuals and not take them over.[132] It is from the above position that CA presents the "new things" of today in paragraph 12. Moreover, in recounting the working conditions set forth for workers and the type of relationship that should exist between workers in a union, CA thought it necessary to recall the principles of subsidiarity and solidarity as it was applied in both QA and LE to make the point for an "authentic culture of work," and the role of the State in two respects.

> The State must contribute to the achievement of these goals both directly and indirectly. Indirectly and according to the principle of subsidiarity by creating favorable conditions for the free exercise of economic activity, which will lead to abundant opportunities for employment and sources of wealth. Directly and according to the principle of solidarity, by defending the weakest, by placing certain limits on the autonomy of the parties who determine working conditions, and by ensuring in every case the necessary minimum support for the unemployed worker.[133]

The appeal to these principles, namely subsidiarity and solidarity, emphasizes the fact that they are central to building authentic human relationships and promoting integral development that respects the rights of persons in society.

Second, John Paul II, on the one hand, challenged the welfare State as frequently or often contradicting the principle of subsidiarity by intervening somewhat directly into the affairs of a lesser community and so depriving these lesser communities of their proper roles and responsibilities in society.

Accordingly, such a situation "...leads to a loss of human energies and an inordinate increase of public agencies which are dominated more by bureaucratic ways of thinking than by concern for serving their clients and which are accompanied by an enormous increase in spending."[134] On the other hand, the pope supported the principle of subsidiarity by maintaining that "...needs are best understood and satisfied by people who are closest to them and who act as neighbors to those in need."[135] In this way, the pope supported the contribution made by intermediate

---

132 See CA Par. 11, p. 447.

133 CA Par. 15, pp. 450–451.

134 CA Par. 48, pp. 475–476.

135 Ibid. p. 476.

groups and communities in creating "...networks of solidarity,"[136] that help build their social situations and encourage individual and communal initiatives.

Benedict XVI, Caritas In Veritate (CV), 2009

Benedict XVI's first social document focused on integral human development in charity and truth in the midst of world economic meltdown, ecological challenges, and the adverse effects of globalization.

First, Benedict makes the insightful connection between subsidiarity and development as a necessary path to take in countries where people are marginalized both in terms of business opportunities and exclusion from the inner cycles of the global economy.

> In these countries it is very important to move ahead with projects based on subsidiarity, suitably planned and managed, aimed at affirming rights yet also providing for the assumption of corresponding responsibilities. In development programmes, the principle of the centrality of the human person, as the subject primarily responsible for development must be preserved. The principal concern must be to improve the actual living conditions of the people in a given region, thus enabling them to carry out those duties which their poverty does not presently allow them to fulfill. Social concern must never be an abstract attitude.[137]

The pope emphasizes that any type of development which jeopardizes the personal growth of the human actors is not truly integral and is a negation of subsidiarity. Second, the pope articulates the principle of subsidiarity as constituting "the most appropriate framework for promoting fraternal collaboration between believers and non-believers in their shared commitment to working for justice and peace of the human family"[138]. In other words, the principles and positions put forward by the pope are meant to uphold the dignity of the human person and not partisan in terms of religious affiliation but relevant in all circumstances and to persons of goodwill no matter where they reside.

Third, Pope Benedict upheld that subsidiarity is the glue that can hold together the multifaceted dimensions of globalization so that it does not become a destructive force in society and end up putting asunder the global common good.

> Hence the principle of subsidiarity is particularly well-suited to managing globalization and directing it toward authentic human development. In order not to produce a dangerous universal power of tyrannical nature, the governance of globalization must be

136 Ibid. p. 477.

137 Benedict XVI, Encyclical Letter *Caritas In Veritate,* (Vaticana: Libreria Editrice, 2009), Par. 47.

138 CV, Par. 57.

> marked by subsidiarity, articulated into several layers and involving different levels that can work together.[139]

Fourth, the pope insisted that the principle of subsidiarity and the principle of solidarity are intertwined. In practical terms, the promotion of subsidiarity must necessarily have a public manifestation in community. Specifically, the question of development aid was taken up: "Aid programmes must increasingly acquire the characteristics of participation and completion from the grassroots. Indeed, the most valuable resources in countries receiving development aid are human resources: herein lies the real capital that needs to accumulate in order to guarantee a truly autonomous future for the poorest countries."[140]

Critical Comments, Implications and General Goals of Subsidiarity

Jack Mahoney raised the issue of subsidiarity in regard to the nature of the Church proper. According to Mahoney, at the heart of the debate on subsidiarity lies the question of the difference between subsidiarity and delegation.

> Delegation is the granting of power by a higher authority to a lower in terms of a carefully prescribed function and limited sphere of activity. The superior might do it better, and might prefer to do it in person. But we cannot all do everything, and so *faute de mieux,* one recruits assistants and delegates them, while keeping a careful eye on them and requiring of them a regular account of their stewardship.[141]

In contrast, subsidiarity is not a "trickle-down theory of power;" it is rather "...the acknowledgement of particular stratified competencies at each level of society. It does not impart power; it recognizes it wherever it already exists. It is an honest acknowledgment of the inherent tension in any society between particularity and universality."[142] The interpretation by Mahoney that subsidiarity seeks not to impart power, but to recognize it, was central to the formulation by Pius XI that "...inasmuch as every social activity should, by its very nature, prove a help to members of the body social, it should never destroy or absorb them."[143]

Hence, one might agree with Mahoney that it is simply accurate to restate this papal idea as a principle of "non-absorption," which implies, in the first place, that something already existed therein which ought not be taken over except in cir-

139 Op. cit., cf. Par 67.

140 Ibid. Par. 58.

141 Jack Mahoney, "Subsidiarity in the Church," *The Month* (November, 1988): 968-974. Cf. also Jack Mahoney, *The Making of Moral Theology* (Clarendon: Oxford University Press, 1987), pp. 168–172.

142 See Mahoney, "Subsidiarity in the Church," pp. 969–970.

143 QA Par. 79, p. 60.

cumstances of absolute necessity when, for instance, the common good is placed in jeopardy.

Furthermore, a pertinent ecclesiological implication was raised by Mahoney when he opined that the controversy over subsidiarity is largely a confrontation of mentalities about one's view of Church.

> Does one start from the universal Church, with a stress on its world-wide unity, and then ask how much diversity and how much initiative is permissible consonant with that unity? Such a universalistic perspective is probably more congenial to Roman curial personnel with a tradition of exercising power on a world-scale and suspicious of anything which appears to erode their power. Or does one start from the ecclesial and collegial reality of local or regional churches and their particular cultural and pastoral characteristics, then ask how much restriction or self-denying ordinance is required of them in order to maintain communion with others in the universal Church?[144]

Similarly, James D. Sangu in an address to the plenary assembly of African bishops on the theme of "Evangelization in Africa," offered some thought provoking comments on the relationship between the Church in Africa and the universal Church that support subsidiarity.

> The unity with Rome and the Holy Father is very highly valued in Africa and His authority over the Church is as yet unchallenged here. But the changing conditions, and especially the coming-of age of the Church require a re-thinking of the relations between the African Churches and the Holy See; between the African Churches and the Congregations for the Evangelization of Peoples; between Episcopal conferences and the Roman curia, so that Episcopal conferences could handle local matters which do not prejudice the universal Church; relations too between Episcopal Conferences and Papal Legates should be clearly redefined.[145]

The issue of the particular church and the universal church will take central stage in the course of this work. Suffice it now to say that the role of subsidiarity in the Church was addressed in a recent theological work by Ad Leys and other Scholars.[146] It is still an open-ended question whether the appeal to subsidiarity might help resolve the difference in basic mentalities about Church alluded to ear-

---

144 See Mahoney, p. 970.

145 James D. Sangu, "SECAM and Evangelization in Africa," *The Voice of the Symposium of Episcopal Conferences of Africa and Madagascar for the Evangelization of Africa,* (eds.), Philip O. Aguh & A. Ngindu Mushete (Accra, Ghana: SECAM Secretariat, 1987), p. 70. The views offered by Sangu, one of the bishops at the conference, were made in 1975 and it is pertinent to note how very timely and relevant they still are to this day in our experience of Church in Africa.

146 See Ad Leys, *Ecclesiological Impacts of the Principle of Subsidiarity,* Trans. A Van Santroord (Kampen, Netherlands: Kok Pharos, 1995), pp. 86–193; See also Franz-Xaver Kaufmann, "The Principle of Subsidiarity Viewed by the Sociology of Organizations," *The Nature and Future of Episcopal Conferences,* (eds.), Herve Legrand, Julio Manzanares, and Antonio Garcia y Garcia (Washington, D.C.: The Catholic University of America Press, 1988), pp. 275–291; LiLiane Voye, "Subsidiarity From A Sociologist's Point of View," *The Nature and Future of*

lier. One can only hope that it may provide an opening for addressing the issue of whether or not social categories and the principles of social justice could and should apply across the board to a body such as the Church, not withstanding its position as a divine and human institution. In fact, Leys[147] has defended the thesis that the Church as communion is an incarnate salvific reality from which follows that socio-ethical principles for human associations are, to some degree, applicable and valid for the Church. One can affirm that it is only proper that the Church as a truly human community and with a missionary obligation to practice what it preaches[148] should comply with the principles which the Church itself places on human associations, and one of those is the principle of subsidiarity.

Clifford Kossel based his argument on the fact that the Church's social teaching has always insisted that world community and the principle of subsidiarity should go together. Thus, world unity and authority should not be imposed as an imperialist project. Rather, it should arise out of the peoples' experience and need to build a viable social structure.

> Subsidiarity is simply the old principle of hierarchy viewed from the bottom up. Hierarchy looks at order from the top down. When it moved from the cosmic to the social order, it tended perhaps to see in terms of too rigid and "eternal" structures. Subsidiarity does not eliminate all hierarchy even in the social order, but it opens the way to greater flexibility and adaptability. For the human person, who is to be served by community, is the free and responsible agent who must build and adapt his forms of association to the changing conditions and to his changing awareness of his needs.[149]

The larger question that relates to subsidiarity is that of decision-making authority and leadership in the Church as some scholars have pointed out.[150] These

---

Episcopal Conferences, pp. 292–297; Joaquin Losada, "Subsidiarity From An Ecclesiologist's Point of View," *The Nature and Future of Episcopal Conferences,* pp. 350–354.

147 See Ad Leys, "Structuring Communion: The Importance of the Principle of Subsidiarity," *The Jurist* 58 (1998): 84–123. Leys argue that the principle of subsidiarity provides the framework for defining administrative structures that could mutually benefit both the universal Church and local churches. In so doing, the local churches visibly manifest and assert themselves as rooted in their own culture.

148 Richard P. McBrien, "An Ecclesiological Analysis of Catholic Social Teachings," *Catholic Social Thought and The New World Order,* ed. Oliver F. Williams and John W. Houck (Notre Dame, Indiana: University of Notre Dame Press, 1993), pp. 174–176; cf., Walter Kasper, "The Principle of Subsidiarity Within the Church," *Theology Today* 32/3 (Fall, 1985): 225–229; Joseph Fiorenza, "The Principle of Subsidiarity in the Church," *Origins* 31/19 (October, 2001): 317–320.

149 Clifford Kossel, "Global Community and Subsidiarity," *Communion* VIII (spring, 1981): 37–50.

150 John L. McKenzie, *Authority in the Church* (New York: Sheed and Ward, 1966), pp. 85ff; James Drane, *Authority and Institution: A Study in Church Crisis* (Milwaukee: Bruce, 1966), 13ff; Elisabeth Schüssler Fiorenza, *In Memory of Her: A Feminist Theological Reconstruction of Christian Origins* 10th ed. (New York: Crossroad, 1983), pp. 285–334; Leonardo Boff,

scholars have identified over the years three models of authority that have operated in the Christian community, namely: authority as hierarchical, authority as charismatic, and authority as pluralistic.[151]

Authority as Hierarchical

The term "hierarchy," is derived from two Greek words, *hiereus* (priest) and *arche* (rule, principle), which means "priest-rule." The hierarchical structure has been operative in the Roman Catholic Church down through the ages. The Second Vatican Council states the context for understanding the divine nature of the "ecclesiastical ministry" as having been "...exercised in different degrees by those who even from ancient times have been called bishops, priests and deacons."[152] According to LG 20, the hierarchical structure is grounded in sacramental ordination and the principle of apostolic succession with the divine mandate to carry on the mission of Christ until the end of the world. Thus, the hierarchical model could be said to have identified authority to a large extent with the ordained ministry and consequently the institutional Church.[153] There are two challenges that the hierarchical model of authority poses for the proper understanding of subsidiarity.

First, the hierarchical model places much emphasis on the authority of the ordained to the detriment of the other charisms and ministries in the Church. Thus, Leonardo Boff identifies this phenomenon as "...the result of the pathological view of the Church's reality."[154] Boff quotes two popes that have pursued the clericalism that is central to the hierarchical model: Gregory XVI (1831–1846) who said that: "No one can deny that the Church is an unequal society in which

---

Church: Charism and Power trans. John W. Diercksmeier (New York: Crossroad, 1985), pp. 108–124, 138–143, 154–164; Thomas P. Rausch, *Authority and Leadership in the Church: Past Directions and Future Possibilities* (Wilmington, Delaware: Michael Glazier, 1989), p. 13ff; Hans Kung and Leonard Swidler, (eds.), *The Church in Anguish: Has the Vatican Betrayed Vatican II?* (San Francisco: Harper and Row, 1987), pp. 1ff; Leonard Swidler and Piet F. Fransen, eds., *Authority in the Church and the Schillebeeckx Case* (New York: Crossroad, 1982), p. 5ff; David J. Stagaman, *Authority in the Church* (Collegeville, Minnesota: The Liturgical Press, 1999), pp. 35–63, 129–139.

151 See Rausch, *Authority and Leadership in the Church*, pp. 29–37. Most of the comments made in this section rely to a large extent on the views presented in this work which one finds very relevant and helpful.

152 *Lumen Gentium* (LG) Par. 28 *Vatican Council II: Constitutions, Decrees and Declarations*, (ed.), Austin Flannery (Northport, New York: Costello, 1996), p. 39.

153 See Avery Dulles, "Institution and Charism in the Church," *A Church to Believe In: Discipleship and the Dynamics of Freedom* (New York: Crossroad, 1983), pp. 19–40; cf., also "The Church as Institution," in *Models of the Church* (Garden City, New York: Doubleday & Company, 1974), pp. 31–42; cf., Leonardo Boff, *Church: Charism and Power*, pp. 47–64.

154 See Leonardo Boff, *Church: Charism and Power*, pp. 141–142.

God destined some to be governors and others to be servants. The latter are the laity; the former, the clergy," and Pius X who said that: "Only the college of pastors has the right and authority to lead and govern. The masses have no right or authority except that of being governed, like an obedient flock that follows its Shepherd."[155] Thus, the hierarchical model tends to take away the ontological right of the person to participate in the process of decision making in the community by relegating the person to the status of a spectator, which is a direct violation of the principle of subsidiarity.

Second, the hierarchical model tends to equate its narrow understanding of authority with power. According to Boff, the hierarchy understands itself as the primary seat of power from which the Church's teaching authority is handed out to the laity who is deprived of power. In this type of structure: "Unity is understood as conformity and uniformity. Conflict or criticism is seen as something pathological, threatening division and schism. The simplest solution is elimination of critical elements. Typical of every power structure are the court proceedings against anything or anyone not wholly part of the system."[156] This type of power structure tends to centralize all power to decide within the community in one person similar to a totalitarian State.

Authority as Charismatic

The charismatic model of authority traces its roots to the Spirit given in baptism. The word charism is derived from the Greek word *charis*-gift and is basically translated as "spiritual gift" and is found mostly in the Pauline letters, especially in 1Cor. where St. Paul stresses a variety of gifts (*charismata*) and ministries (*diakonia*) within the Church. Evidently, the spiritual gifts and ministries are not opposed to each other but work as a whole for the good of the community. According to Raymond Brown, in 1 Cor. 12 Paul used the imagery of the body.

> ...As a theological basis for rejecting jealousies about charisms. All the parts or members of the body are indispensable; and so there is no reason for the foot to be jealous of the hand, nor the ear jealous of the eye...Similarly, there is no reason for those who have one charism (apostles, prophets, teachers, workers of miracles, healers, speakers in tongues) to desire another. It would not help if all were apostles, if all were prophets, etc.; for the Church needs the diversity of members.[157]

Leonardo Boff emphasizes the charismatic structure of the primitive community, where all shared in the Spirit to develop a "laical" model of the Church. Boff argues that the Church hierarchy has imitated the tendency of ruling classes to

155 Ibid. p. 142.

156 Ibid. p. 53.

157 Raymond E. Brown, *The Churches the Apostles Left Behind* (New York/Mawah: Paulist Press, 1984), p. 90.

appropriate all power for personal use instead of for the benefit of the community. This situation has led to "...a gradual expropriation of the means of religious production from the Christian people by the clergy. In the early years, the Christian people as a whole shared in the power of the Church, in decisions, in the choosing of ministers; later they were simply consulted; finally, in terms of power, they were totally marginalized, dispossessed of their power."[158]

Similarly, Elisabeth Fiorenza has traced the roots of the Church to the "Jesus Movement" where the leadership roles of women were recognized to serve "as a renewal movement within Judaism."[159] The "Jesus Movement" also led to "Liberation from Patriarchal structures and the Discipleship of Equals."[160] Fiorenza then discusses the structure of "The Patriarchal Household of God and the *Ekklesia* of Women," emphasizing the various shifts that have taken place down through the ages that have led to the shift from the charismatic and shared authority to that of authority invested in particular authority figures.

> The shift which took place in the second century was not a shift from charismatic leadership to institutional consolidation, but from charismatic and communal authority to an authority vested in local officers, who-in time-absorb not only the teaching authority of the prophet and apostles but also the decision-making power of the community. This shift is, at the same time, a shift from alternating leadership accessible to all the baptized to patriarchal leadership restricted to male heads of households...[161]

There is no doubt that such a development would stifle individual creativity and jeopardize the contribution of the majority who are at the grassroots level of the community.

Authority as Pluralistic

Avery Dulles is the major proponent of the pluralist model of authority. Dulles advocates that any authentic authority could only teach what the whole Church believes; hence he places major emphasis on the level of participation by the faithful believers and upholds that the voices of "committed Christians should be given more weight than those of indifferent or marginal Christians," without neglecting, of course, the views of those who show less commitment.[162] Thus, Dulles describes three levels of participation that are essential to the pluralist model. These essential levels of participation are the doctoral, prophetic, and pastoral ministries.[163]

158 See Boff, *Church: Charism and Power,* pp. 112–113.

159 See Fiorenza, *In Memory of Her,* p. 105ff.

160 Ibid. pp. 140–154.

161 Ibid. pp. 286–287.

162 Avery Dulles, *The Resilient Church* (Garden City, New York: Doubleday and Company, 1977), p. 100.

163 Ibid. pp. 100–101.

In the first place, the professional theologians or doctors have an authority that is based on their scholarship and competence which calls them to offer critical perspectives that will promote the growth of the community. Second, the prophetic voices in the Church are persons who help stir it in the right path of truth. These voices should always be welcomed in the Christian community. Lastly, the bishops are called to speak in their capacity as those appointed to the Church's pastoral office with the necessary graces to help them in the task of being shepherds of their flock. Thus, one can see that the pluralist model attempts to strike a balance between the institutional and the charismatic models. The pluralist model could help promote the principle of subsidiarity by recognizing the different levels of competencies as intrinsic to the process of decision making. In this way, the pluralist model gives each of the groups mentioned above the opportunity to participate and contribute to the decision-making process.

The major setback with the pluralist model of authority is that the various groups of persons (doctoral, prophetic, and pastoral) who speak for the Church are still a select group within the community, notwithstanding its expansion. Thus, subsidiarity encourages that the voices of the majority of persons at the grassroots become an integral part of the decision-making body since most of the decisions made by the doctoral, prophetic, and pastoral groups to a large extent affect the larger Christian community.

David Hollenbach has provided some critical perspectives for understanding the principle of subsidiarity in the midst of different and differing rights claims among diverse social groups.[164] Hollenbach agrees that the classic formulation of subsidiarity contained in QA79–80, justifies government intervention when it truly provides help to persons and smaller communities which make up the society. However, smaller communities such as the family, the neighborhood, professional labor groups, and churches must be recognized as having a dynamic life of their own that needs to be respected by government, since it is out of these that their claims are rooted and structured. Accordingly, Hollenbach links the principle of subsidiarity to the claims made by people arising from the concrete experience of group life. In so doing, he makes the case for viewing society as comprised of two

164 David Hollenbach, *Claims in Conflict: Retrieving and Renewing the Catholic Human Rights Tradition* (New York/Ramsey/Toronto: Paulist Press, 1979), pp. 157–167; 187–207, what follows is an in-depth analysis of the various arguments advanced and the pertinent points made toward the healthy role of the principle of subsidiarity in the efforts made to protect human rights and address different societal "claims in conflict," by assigning the proper roles of individual persons, society and those of intermediate groups such as families, local communities, labor unions, professional associations, etc. This work is a classic text which has interpreted the meaning of the principle of subsidiarity in a pluralistic context, which relates with the type of social context one is dealing with in this study. Hence, attention is given to both the theoretical framework advanced and the policy issues addressed. See David Hollenbach, *Justice, Peace, & Human Rights: American Catholic Social Ethics in a Pluralistic Context* (New York: Crossroad, 1988), pp. 69, 81, 106.

complementary strands: individuals that are unrelated and persons who are related and active in different kinds of associations. Hollenbach makes the case that the provision for government intervention protects both the individual and the different associations to which one belongs.

> The power of government to intervene is real. It should be exercised to the extent necessary for the production of distributive and social justice...Both the scope and limits of this intervention arise not only from the claims of individual persons but also from the need to insure that multiple forms of human community are not obliterated by the power of the State.[165]

Furthermore, Hollenbach maintains that subsidiarity "...gives priority to the claims of smaller groups and intermediate associations over and against the centralizing tendencies of government."[166] However, this approach is not done in an absolute manner. It leaves some opening for government intervention when the common good is at stake. Thus, Hollenbach insists that the principle "embodies a pluralist model of social interaction," that one hopes is capable of maintaining the social balance in community relationships.

> This other face of the principle of subsidiarity emphasizes communal solidarity as a counterbalance to the disintegrative effect of competing group claims. The principle of subsidiarity, therefore, does not provide an apriori answer to the question of rights conflict. It does not assign an absolute priority to the claims of small or intermediate groups.[167]

The principle does leave open its concrete applications and implications to the nature, needs, and claims of the particular social context, which would help determine the proper action to be taken. In this way, one realizes that the principle appreciates the need for concrete human experience to serve as the governing norm, and not some abstract formulations.

The major difficulty addressed by Hollenbach concerns the issue of how the "...pluralist and organicist aspects of the Catholic tradition's model of society relates to subsidiarity."[168] According to Hollenbach, both aspects were combined to provide the possibility of a harmonious reconciliation of competing group claims under the paternal guidance of the State. This led to the downplaying of class conflict, despite appeals to pluralism. Thus, the attempt to reconcile the "plural" and the "organic" reached its apex in the "corporatist" social order advocated by Pius XI in QA 80. In the words of Hollenbach:

> As a social theory, corporatism makes the supposition that the problem of conflict will be solved by integrating the different kinds of communities and associations ("corpo-

165 See Hollenbach, *Claims in Conflict,* p. 158.

166 Ibid. p. 159.

167 Ibid. p. 160.

168 Ibid.

rations") into an organically structured social system. In effect, social conflict is to be eliminated by the creation of a functionally differentiated and hierarchically stratified social organism. The whole system is to be held together by the coordinating authority of the State. Such coordination is the help (the "subsidium") provided by government to the lower communities.[169]

In so doing, Hollenbach maintained that the "corporatist" model made a major mistake when the problem of conflict was sublimated rather than resolved.

The theory aimed at the maximum recognition of the rights claims of individuals and of communities such as families, occupational groups and neighborhoods. It also aimed at the organic harmony of society as a whole. The price paid for the denial of conflict between the claims of groups was the legitimating of unequal access to public grounds and unequal participation in the shaping of public institutions. It produced a legitimating of inequality in the sphere of instrumental rights. Institutional inequality was demanded because the relation between the plural groups in society was thought of as static. Organic harmony was identified with keeping each group in its assigned place within the whole.[170]

This is a major challenge that any healthy understanding of the principle needs to address properly: how to balance the need for pluralism with the need for communal solidarity in society as a whole? Leo XIII provided the fundamental basis for maintaining the balance between pluralism and communal solidarity by appealing to the power of governmental authority to pay attention to the proper claims of the poor, working classes and organized groups of laborers, by guaranteeing "… that these social groups had access to sufficient power to make the claims of their human dignity both known and effective."[171] Pius XI further emphasized this through appeal to social justice which has become a major contribution shaping communities and groups as one would discover in chapter three of this study. John XXIII affirmed that the achievement of equality in the concrete life of society was a major development of the "social question." The Second Vatican Council in GS took up the issue of equality especially among institutions as central and fundamental when it stated that "…with respect to the fundamental rights of the person, every type of discrimination, whether based on sex, race, color, social condition, language, or religion, is to be eradicated as contrary to God's intent."[172]

Hollenbach has provided the context for balancing the reality between the pluralism of group life with the concern for communal solidarity of society. According to him, this reality could be achieved in the midst of social conflict. This is because "…the balance between pluralism and community is not static but

169 Ibid. p. 162.

170 Ibid.

171 Ibid. p. 163.

172 GS Par. 29, pp. 182–183, See Par. 7, 8, 63, 64 and 66, pp. 169–170, 208–210 respectively.

dynamic. It is not organic but conflictual."[173] This is the vantage position from which Hollenbach advocates a positive implementation of the claims to human rights in society.

> The process of integration of group life does not occur by eliminating either pluralism or conflict. It is rather by recognizing both the positive and negative impacts of these political institutions on the plural groups of society that norms for their organization must be developed. When the "discontinuities of group life" become so great that some groups are denied access to or participation in the economic and political life of the whole community injustice is being done and human rights are being violated. Conversely the same can be said when power is so distributed that one or another privileged group is able to manipulate large economic and political institutions at will. Each of these situations indicates a breakdown of the political order itself.[174]

Furthermore, Hollenbach advocates "political responsibility" and "political solidarity" as ways of dealing with the conflict between pluralism and communal solidarity. Political responsibility "...is a kind of loyalty to the whole which does not eliminate pluralism or group conflict... Rather, political responsibility moderates the disintegrative effects of a group pluralism which is left unchecked by the notion of citizenship. Political responsibility is due to persons and groups by right."[175] Political solidarity is:

> A form of social organization which demands participation in and loyalty to the life of society as a whole. It is a form of solidarity which reaches beyond family or vocational group or class. At the same time, it is political rather than organic, for it recognizes that genuine participation of all persons and groups in the common good does not occur in a non-conflictual way. Those competing claims of persons and groups which further greater equality of access to and participation in the common life of society give concrete content to the notion of political solidarity.[176]

From this analysis of the developing social model to address the issues of pluralism and communal solidarity, one can understand how the questions of human rights claims have taken center stage. The role of subsidiarity in formulating a human rights policy cannot be overemphasized: "...the principle of subsidiarity

---

173 See Hollenbach, *Claims in Conflict,* p. 164.

174 Ibid. p. 165.

175 Ibid.

176 Ibid. p. 166. See also pp. 167–178 for the details of political solidarity and its implications for the concrete practice of "love, justice and human rights." One major implication for subsidiarity can be found on pp. 174 and 176 under the sub-title "In Quest of Political Solidarity." Here two affirmations are relevant: that "love is response to persons in their uniqueness and individuality" and that "the experience of love not only entails an affirmation of the concrete reality and worth of other persons but also leads to union between persons, for example, the interpersonal communion of friendship and the solidarity of various social and political groups" captures the priority of the human person as the origin and purpose of society which is at the heart of subsidiarity.

points out that persons are members of many different kinds of communities. They thus have rightful claims to both freedom and participation in as many different social spheres or sectors."[177]

Another significant contribution offered by Hollenbach on how the question of rights claims could be addressed that relates to subsidiarity, social and distributive justice and organizational structures in community is the relevance of "strategic morality." It is a form of social analysis "...formulated from analysis of the kinds of social activity which will lead to the protection of the rightful claims of all persons under present social conditions. It is morality because it represents a way of responding to the genuine claims of human dignity."[178] The need for "strategic morality" is to help specify the extent to which "institutional processes and instrumental rights," could be ordered toward the economic and political arena to bring about the protection of human rights. Thus, "strategic morality," understood as "...a synthesis of historical interpretation and basic value commitments,"[179] is necessary in every historical social context that seeks to uphold the protection of human rights.

Another critical interpretation took place when Michel Novak[180] followed in the direction provided by John Paul II in emphasizing the "creative subjectivity of the citizen." Some of the virtues outlined by Novak are worthy of note since they promote the dignity of the person in participation with others to bring about a new social order. Hence, the virtues of personal "initiative, enterprise, social cooperation, public spiritedness and civic responsibility," among others are at the heart of subsidiarity because they deal with the relationships that exist between persons in society at different levels and how these interrelationships could help fashion the common good of all the members. Recently, Michael Mukasa[181] followed the direction provided by Novak to put forward the theoretical and practical frameworks for the application of the principles of democratic capitalism in a given African social context in Uganda.

---

177 Ibid. p. 177.

178 Ibid. p. 188.

179 Ibid. p. 189.

180 Michael Novak, *The Catholic Ethic and the Spirit of Capitalism* (New York: The Free Press, 1993), pp. 221–237; cf. John Paul II, SRS Par. 15, p. 403; CA Par. 42–43, pp. 471–472.

181 Michael Mukasa, "Michael Novak's Vision of Democratic Capitalism: A Bridge to the Africa of the Third Millennium" (Ph.D. dissertation, Duquesne University, 2002). Mukasa agrees with Novak that the moral vision of democratic capitalism which emphasizes human creativity in union with the Divine creative Spirit could help address the issue of poverty particularly in Uganda. Moreover, this moral vision, when properly regulated by the virtue of solidarity advocated by John Paul II, would help build partnerships of cooperation especially between the developed world and the developing nations. This work is important in articulating how human initiative and creativity could be employed to encourage and promote healthy relationships in community for the common good.

The implications for subsidiarity are six-fold. First, one realizes that economic and political institutions affect the social order and consequently human relationships in the process. Hence, one needs to examine how large social institutions shape to a larger or lesser degree the actual relationships between persons in community. Thus, the content of "institutional processes and instrumental rights" should not be determined in the abstract but one need to pay attention to claims made by intermediate associations, cultural issues, family values, and religious groups, social and historical conditions.

Second, the question of the social rights of the community and the individual claims in the face of a dominating institution need to be addressed within the context of the protection of human rights. The extent to which personal rights and social rights may conflict deserves some attention that is both meaningful and respectful of human dignity. This issue is particularly a difficult one in the developing countries where economic and political arrangements are very fluid. Thus, the need to shape both individual action and institutional structures by advocating policy positions that will respect and guarantee human dignity is essential to promote healthy social interaction.

Third, the level of marginalized existence experienced by different groups in society needs to be addressed since it jeopardizes the individual creativity of the human person, which is at the heart of human dignity. The 1977 pastoral statement of the National Conference of Brazilian Bishops on the "Christian Requirements of a Political Order" capture the major elements experienced by a marginalized group of people particularly in the developing nations:

> To be marginalized...is to receive an unjust salary. It is to be deprived of education, medical attention, and credit; it is to be hungry and live in sordid huts; it is to be deprived of land by inadequate, unjust agrarian structures. To be marginalized is above all, not to be able to free oneself from these situations. To be marginalized is not to be able to take part freely in the process of creativity which forges the original culture of a people. To be marginalized is not to have effective representation to make known one's needs and aspirations in decision-making centers; it is to be seen not as a subject of rights but as an object of favors granted in the measure necessary to reduce the militancy of the common people; it is to be manipulated by propaganda. To be marginalized is not to have a chance to participate. It is to be deprived of the recognition of the dignity which God has conferred upon man.[182]

Archbishop Renato Martino appears to have taken up the challenge in a presentation of the Vatican position at the World Summit on Sustainable Development with great appeal for the application of the principle of subsidiarity to help protect the poor in society and to promote good governance.

---

182 The National Conference of Brazilian Bishops, "Christian Requirements of a Political Order," in *Latin American Bishops Discuss Human Rights LADOC Keyhole Series*, no. 16 (Washington, D.C.: 1977, Latin American Documentation), pp. 60–61.

> In keeping with the principle of subsidiarity, the poor must be heard on issues and be at the center of local, national and international programs for sustainable development. Persons living in poverty must be considered as participating subjects. Individuals and peoples cannot become tools but must be the protagonists of their future, able to be the "agents of their own development" and "in their specific economic and political circumstances, to exercise the creativity which is characteristic of the human person and on which the wealth of nations too is dependent. Mindful of the principle of subsidiarity, good governance is one of the prerequisites in the fight against poverty. It is in service of the common good. For good governance to be successful there must be new partnerships that promote investment in people and in infrastructures and that will facilitate participation of citizens in decisions that affect their lives. Valued in this context is the democratic system inasmuch as it strives to ensure the possibility of participation of citizens in making political choices and having a voice in governing.[183]

The fourth implication for subsidiarity is that a "strategic morality" in a given social context should be based on "...the three areas of need, freedom and relationship,"[184] that have led Hollenbach to propose three priority principles, which one considers are indispensable in any social arrangement of persons in community and which should provide the guidance needed toward a strategic morality that will stand the test of time. The principles are:

> The needs of the poor take priority over the wants of the rich. the freedom of the dominated takes priority over the liberty of the powerful; the participation of marginalized groups takes priority over the preservation of an order which excludes them.[185]

Fifth, the creativity of the human person should be given priority at all times and in all places insofar as it promotes the dignity of the person in community and the common good of society. This would involve, among other things, that personal rights and liberty are guaranteed, and that social justice and civil society are given allowance to thrive. Here, the "...tripartite system: the political, economic and the moral-cultural," set forth by John Paul II in CA 42 provides the key to healthy governance and subsidiarity to operate, realizing that it is necessary to maintain the balance of power in any social system.

These principles are central to subsidiarity because they emphasize the priority of human persons in social relationships who are in need of help to self-help rather than being taken over in interpersonal and group relationships. As Hollenbach puts it, "...a choice must be made between protecting privilege and guaranteeing minimum standards of living for all."[186] Moreover, Hollenbach clearly addressed the key components of the principle of subsidiarity when he affirmed

183 Renato Martino, "World Summit on Sustainable Development: Vatican Position," *Origins* 32/14 (September 12, 2002): 235–237.

184 See Hollenbach, *Claims in Conflict*, p. 203.

185 Ibid. p. 204.

186 Ibid. p. 205.

on the one hand that forming interpersonal relationships is necessary to sustain a sense of community and promote fraternity.

> Some of these relationships are highly personal and built on friendship, shared belief, and love, such as the family and the Church. Others are functional and goal oriented, such as professional and occupational groups. Still others, such as racial, ethnic and cultural groups, are the result of circumstances of birth. Participation in groups and relationships such as these is an essential condition for the preservation of personal agency as the principle of subsidiarity suggests.[187]

On the other hand, Hollenbach maintains that while respecting the importance of group life as indicated by subsidiarity, it is pertinent to realize that membership in some group's carries great social disadvantages, while membership in others brings "disproportional" advantage:

> Economic elites who control large corporations, and the intellectual elites who have major influence on the formation of policy, derive a kind of effective agency from their group memberships which is denied to persons excluded from these groups because of their race, educational level, cultural background, religion or nationality.[188]

McCormick, while articulating his ten-point vision for "Moral theology in the year 2000," maintained among other things that the principle of subsidiarity should be appropriately implemented rather than the over-centralization currently in operation, especially in the case of the roles of the individual person in society and that of national Episcopal conferences of bishops in dealing with local ecclesial issues. More specifically, McCormick opined that when it came to decision-making concerning particular circumstances, those more familiar with the local context should be given the benefit of doubt to apply the principle.

> Applications of moral principle demand expertise and knowledge of circumstances, therefore they should be entrusted above all to those who have such knowledge and expertise. When a higher authority (whether it is the Congregation for the Doctrine of the Faith, a local bishop, a pastor) attempts to assume this role, we have a violation of subsidiarity. One of the results of this is that the Church is deprived of the richness of experience and thought some of its members can contribute. Another is the promotion of a kind of moral infantilism or dependency.[189]

---

187 Ibid. p. 206.

188 Ibid.

189 Richard A. McCormick, *Corrective Vision: Explorations in Moral Theology* (Kansas City, Mo: Sheed & Ward, 1994), p. 32. See also Terence McGoldrick, "Episcopal Conferences Worldwide on Catholic Social Teaching," *Theological Studies* 59 (1998): 22-50; Thomas J. Reese, (ed.), *Episcopal Conferences: Historical, Canonical and Theological Studies* (Washington, D.C.: Georgetown University Press, 1989) for details on the roles of bishops' conferences in the history of the Church; Thomas J. Reese, *Archbishop: Inside the Power Structure of the American Catholic Church* (San Francisco: Harper and Row, 1989), pp. 349–365; Raymond E. Brown, "Episkope and Episkopos: The New Testament Evidence," *Theological Studies* 41 (1980): 325.

Thus, McCormick noted that, in allowing the subsidiarity principle to operate, the Second Vatican Council particularly sought to bring about "the toppling of the pyramidal notion of the Church wherein truth descends uniquely from above in a kind of mysterious paternalistic flow."[190] In so doing, lay people will be given more opportunities to participate in the Church in view of the different competencies they posses.

Sixth, there is the need for some urgent Canonical changes[191] in the Church in view of a better appreciation of the role of subsidiarity to address issues of global diversity and specific needs of some local Churches especially in the developing world. Thus, the application of subsidiarity would necessarily begin with the recognition of the legitimate autonomy of local Church leaders to govern themselves with the necessary powers to formulate governing principles that are relevant to their social contexts without being grand-fathered from the Vatican. Among other things, issues like the universal retirement age for the clergy worldwide with the great disparity in health care systems between the developed and developing countries would have to be addressed. Suppose every country were to fix retirement age of their clergy and religious to meet the retirement requirements of their particular country; the lack of retirement benefits for most people who work for the Church in developing countries is another major area of concern where the principle of subsidiarity might help address the near death situation people have to face after so many years of service to the Church. Another issue might be how the Church is structured to meet the needs of the extended family system which has several layers of dependents at every stage in an egalitarian and community based fashion which more often challenges the individualized Western family model and consequently Church structures. The principle of subsidiarity could be described as consisting of the following goals from our analysis of the proposals advanced by Hollenbach, McCormick, and Joseph Komonchak.[192]

1. The priority of the human person as the origin and purpose of society: *civitas propter cives, non cives propter civitatem* is at the heart of subsidiarity.

2. The human person is not a solitary individual but one that is social by nature, only able to achieve self-realization in and through social relation-

190 See McCormick, *Corrective Vision*, pp. 32–33.

191 James A. Coriden, "Necessary Canonical Reform: Urgent Issues for Action," *Louvain Studies* 26 (2001): 147–165 for details.

192 Joseph Komonchak, "Subsidiarity in the Church: The State of the Question," *The Jurist* 48 (1988): 298–302. See also Thomas C. Kohler, "In Praise of Little Platoons: Quadragesimo Anno (1931)," (eds.), George Weigel and Robert Royal *Building the Free Society: Democracy, Capitalism, and Catholic Social Teaching* (Grand Rapids, Michigan: Wm. B. Eerdmans, 1993), p. 36.

ships between persons in community-what is sometimes called the "principle of solidarity."

3. Thus, social relationships and communities exist to provide help, support and aid (*subsidium*) to individuals in their free but obligatory assumption of responsibility for their self-realization. This "subsidiary" function of society is not a matter, except in exceptional circumstances, of substituting or supplying for individual self-responsibility, but of providing the sets of conditions necessary for personal self-realization.
4. The larger, "higher," communities exist to perform the same subsidiary roles toward smaller, "lower," associations and communities.
5. The principle of subsidiarity requires positively that all communities not only permit but enable and encourage individuals to exercise their own self-responsibility, and that larger communities do the same for smaller ones.
6. The principle of subsidiarity requires negatively that communities not deprive individuals and smaller communities of their right to exercise their self-responsibility. Hence, intervention is only appropriate as "helping people to help themselves."
7. The subsidiarity principle, therefore, serves as the means by which to regulate competencies between individuals and communities, and between smaller and larger communities.
8. The principle is a formal one, needing determination in virtue of the nature of a community and of particular circumstances.
9. Since subsidiarity is grounded in the metaphysics of the person, it applies to the life of every society and has universal relevance and applicability.
10. The principle promotes the balance between pluralism and communal solidarity without sacrificing political responsibility, political solidarity, and strategic morality in the process.
11. Subsidiarity recognizes that conflict in society is real, especially class conflict. Hence, it supports the thesis that much attention be given to claims in conflict arising from the dignity and rights of the human person.
12. Subsidiarity, Solidarity, and Social justice are integral to the development and formulation of policy toward promoting civil society.
13. Subsidiarity supports the thesis that society exists for the person and not the person for the society.

Questions for Further Reflection

1. Discuss the implications for grounding subsidiarity in the dignity of the human person.
2. How might one resolve the conflict between personal rights and social rights in a given situation?
3. Given your social context, how can you promote communal solidarity that is geared toward the common good?
4. How does your experience of church sharpen or limit your understanding of subsidiarity?
5. Discuss in practical terms the understanding that society exists for the person and not the person for society.

3

THE CONCEPT OF SOCIAL JUSTICE: A THEORETICAL AND PRACTICAL FRAMEWORK FOR A JUST SOCIETY

The Biblical Meaning of Social Justice[1]

According to Donahue, "The centrality as well as the richness of the biblical statements on justice is the very reason why it is difficult to give a 'biblical definition'

1 The central scriptural text of reference is the Christian Bible in the English language and the translation one is working with is: *The Catholic Study Bible*, (eds.), Donald Senior et al. (New York/Oxford: Oxford University Press, 1990), unless otherwise stated. Thus, particular texts are examined in view of the analysis provided by the following authors to help trace one's understanding of the biblical concept of justice. John R. Donahue, "Biblical Perspectives on Justice," *The Faith That Does Justice: Examining the Christian Sources for Social Change* (ed.), John C. Haughey (New York: Paulist Press, 1977), pp. 68–112; *What Does the Lord Require? A Bibliographical Essay on the Bible and Social Justice* (Saint Louis: The Institute of Jesuit Sources, 2000), pp. 11–59; William C. Spohn, *What Are They Saying About Scripture and Ethics?* (New York/Mahwah, N.J.: Paulist Press, 1995), pp. 38-55; Michael H. Crosby, "Justice," *The New Dictionary of Catholic Spirituality* (ed.), Michael Downey (Collegeville, Minnesota: The Liturgical Press, 1993), pp. 57–583; John C. Haughey, "Jesus as the Justice of God," *The Faith That Does Justice*, pp. 264-290; Fred Kammer, *Doing Faith Justice: An*

of justice which, in the Bible, is a protean and many-faceted term."[2] Thus, our task is to trace the multi-dimensional aspects of social justice which revolve around the history and practices of the Israelites. Biblical justice has been described in the following way:

> ...The biblical idea of justice can be described as fidelity to the demands of a relationship. In contrast to modern individualism the Israelite is in a world where "to live" is to be united with others in a social context either by bonds of family or by covenant relationships. This web of relationships—king with people, judge with complainants, family with tribe and kinfolk, the community with the resident alien and suffering in their midst and all with the covenant God constitutes the world in which life is played out.[3]

The biblical notion of social justice as fidelity to the demands of a relationship challenges one to engage in some form of concrete manifestation of this relationship. Thus, I will attempt to highlight some of the concrete ways through which the different relationships that existed within the Israelite community might have informed and formed their understanding of social justice. There are, then, two tasks central to the elaboration of this biblical view of social justice: First, to describe some of the Old Testament practices that convey the meaning of social justice and the transgression of it; second, to discuss the New Testament teaching of Jesus on the practice of social justice. In this way one hopes to show that:...The contemporary realization that faith must be involved in the quest for and expression of justice, far from being foreign to biblical thought, recovers a core of the biblical heritage which, when neglected, brings the danger of reducing this heritage to a manual of personal piety.[4]

Thus, the first major elements to be identified are the various ways through which the faith of Israel found concrete expressions and how these practices inspire and challenge the practice of social justice today.

The Old Testament Teaching on Social Justice

In the book of Genesis, three key revelatory moments shed some light on the notion of social justice. The first moment of revelation is contained in Gen. 1:1ff. where the seven-day creation story conveys the true reality of how God created the world with the underlying theological intent at every stage of the process. The theological affirmation is to provide pertinent insights about God's relationship with

Introduction to Catholic Social Thought (New York/Mahwah, N.J.: Paulist Press, 1991), pp. 18–59.

2 See Donahue, "Biblical Perspectives on Justice," p. 68. The views expressed by Donahue are central to this chapter.

3 Ibid. p. 69.

4 Ibid. pp. 69–70.

humanity and the created world. In so doing, Divine intent resonates: "God looked at everything He had made, and He found it very good," (Gen. 1:31). More specifically, the fundamental substance of creation, the plants, animals, earth, water, light, and most of all, humankind are basically good in themselves.

The theological affirmation of the goodness of God's creation may not seem to be very obvious to some persons today. Kammer puts it succinctly:

> ...Many of our cultural messages and even our religious attitudes, however, are diametrically opposed to the Genesis view that God looked upon the completed creation and found it "very good" (Gen. 1:31). This opposition can be found in philosophical traditions dominated by a body/spirit dualism or religious traditions that disdain feelings and emotions...society's persistent quest for new means and measures of self-esteem betrays its profound doubt in even the fundamental worth of human persons; and too much economic development occurs with rank disregard for the basic value of the natural universe around us.[5]

The need to affirm the fundamental goodness of God's creation and the ability to appreciate this creation are at the heart of how one conceives the notion of social justice that has been passed forward. Similarly, Bergant and Stuhlmueller are of the view that "...creation in biblical thought cannot be separated from Israel's unique appreciation of God and particularly of God's action as savior in their midst."[6] The view of the goodness of God's creation is largely responsible today for the concept and practice of creation spirituality.[7] However, I am aware of the theological difficulty of theodicy[8] in affirming the goodness of creation in the face of innocent suffering of God's faithful people (1 Mac. 1:37–39). However, this issue will be addressed in the discussion on wisdom literature and social justice.

The second revelatory affirmation is contained in Gen. 2–4. This second creation story begins with God empowering human beings with the responsibility to nurture God's creation in Gen. 2:15. Kammer maintains that human beings were given dominion over the other created things but not domination or exploitation. Thus, persons are invited to be co-creators with God in caring for and giving life to the earth. Hence to destroy the resources of the earth without being conscious of its life-giving force is to engage in domination. In acknowledging the creation of men and women in the image and likeness of God one discovers an important truth that:...Explains not only the human relationship with God but also their

5 See Kammer, *Doing Faith Justice*, p. 19.

6 Dianne Bergant and Carroll Stuhlmueller, "Creation According to the Old Testament," *Evolution and Creation*, (ed.), Ernan Mcmullin (Indiana: University of Notre Dame Press, 1985), p. 153.

7 Zachary Hayes, "Creation," *The New Dictionary of Catholic Spirituality*, pp. 238-242; Anne M. Clifford, "Creation," *Systematic Theology: Roman Catholic Perspectives*, Francis Schüssler Fiorenza and John Galvin, (eds.), (Minneapolis: Fortress Press, 1991), pp. 225–240.

8 Walter Kern & Jorg Splett, "Theodicy," *Encyclopedia of Theology: The Concise Sacramentum Mundi*, (ed.), Karl Rahner (New York: Seabury Press, 1975), pp. 1664–1671.

relationship with the animals and the Lord. They are representatives of, but not identical with, the true sovereign, women and men must act as regents of the true ruler, not as absolute rulers in their own right.[9]

To have dominion over the earth is an act of justice for the earth. It shows responsibility toward the earth. However, to engage in domination over the earth is an act of injustice, which neglects its responsibility for the goodness of the earth's resources. A major challenge with this revelatory affirmation is how to understand the nature of human stewardship of creation. Today, the language of "dominion over the earth" may be perceived in some quarters, e.g., ecological groups, as pointing more toward the control and exploitation of nature than to social justice. Even so, the sense in which I have explained the meaning of the biblical text from Genesis provides room for a more holistic understanding and appreciation of the difficulty of biblical interpretation.

The third revelatory insight is contained in this covenant affirmation "I will be your God and you will be my people," (Lev. 26:12). Here one encounters the abiding relationship between Yahweh and Israel to form a covenant community of persons with shared values and common destiny. The bonding between Yahweh and Israel images the bonding between God and human beings and persons among themselves who are called to participate in a web of relationships in community.

The three revelations briefly described here help convey the meaning of reverence for the goodness of God's creation, the understanding of healthy stewardship toward the earth, and the need to build human communities that are in the image and likeness of God. Thus, I can summarize the major issues contained in the book of Genesis that have to do with faith and social justice in this way:

> ...Men and women are God's representatives and conversation partners in the world, with a fundamental dignity that must be respected and fostered. They are to exist in interdependence and mutual support and are to care for the world with respect, as for a gift received from God. Yet the human condition is flawed by a drive to overstep the limits of the human situation and to claim autonomous power. The result of this is violence (Cain and Abel) and idolatry (the Tower of Babel). The Genesis narrative functions either as a normative description of the human condition before God and a critical principle against any power that distorts or usurps the dignity of humanity or God's claim over men and women.[10]

These revelations help one to understand another important dimension of Israel's life where the issues of social justice take center stage in the Old Testament, namely, the question of the jubilee year.

---

9 See Bergant and Stuhlmueller, p. 162.

10 See Donahue, *What Does the Lord Require?* p. 17.

The Jubilee Year and Social Justice

According to Faley the jubilee derives its name from the trumpet *yobel* in Hebrew which refers to the "ram's horn" sounded to mark the beginning of the grand sabbatical year. "The year was to begin on the Day of Atonement the tenth day of *Tishri* and was a period of emancipation *deror* in which, in addition to the usual sabbatical observance, all alienated property was returned to its original owner."[11] Thus, the central tenets of the jubilee year are related to the practice of justice in the community especially to help support the most vulnerable.

The understanding that there is the need to share the resources of the earth with all the members of the community is a recurring theme that underlies the communal and social aspects of justice in the Old Testament. The following Old Testament phrases (year of the Lord, the sabbatical year, and the jubilee year) connote the reality of the interplay between the goodness of God's creation and human responsibility toward the same creation. In Lev. 25 one finds a vivid description of the major elements of the jubilee year:

1. Restoration: the jubilee shall be a period of reconciliation, when the people are restored fully to the community and engage in right order: a community of faith and fidelity, sharing the goods of the earth, with God dwelling in their midst. The restoration was not hampered by class distinctions in the community, but the sharing of the earth's resources was promoted. Property was to be returned to its original owners, and freedom given to slaves. Thus, the dignity of persons was restored to the community and their participation and integration encouraged (Lev. 25:6–7).

2. Liberty: the jubilee year shall be a period of freedom for all the inhabitants and "the land shall not be sold in perpetuity," for the land belongs to God. There shall be equitable distribution of land and its resources among the members realizing that they are all tenants of the Lord (Lev. 25:10–11, 44–46).

3. Respect for the poor: the jubilee year shall be a special time for making the poor feel they are part of the community by supporting them to help take care of their families. The poor are to be recognized as hired workers and not as slaves (Lev. 25:13–17, 23–28, 35–43).

4. Solidarity: the members of the community were continually encouraged to be their brothers' and sisters' keepers. They were to respect each other and to support the web of relationships through which they were bonded together (Lev. 25:47ff.).

---

11 Roland J. Faley, "Leviticus," *The Jerome Biblical Commentary* (eds.), Raymond E. Brown, Joseph A. Fitzmyer and Roland E. Murphy (Englewood Cliffs, New Jersey: Prentice Hall, 1968), 4:52.

The understanding of the jubilee year has led Kammer to compare its central practice with what is present today in modern times in this way:

> Even in our modern laws, then, there seems to survive a kind of jubilee year and its underpinning rationale, that the goods of the earth are meant for everybody, and that we are one human community. If people are brought so low that they cannot get up, the community helps them on their feet again and lets them start life over.[12]

We notice then, how the practices of the jubilee year support our understanding of biblical justice. In addition, the help provided by the community to the most vulnerable members to find their feet in the community was a clear indication of their attempt to give each member their due and of engaging in social justice as a means of promoting the common good. The next notion that is closely tied to faith and social justice is that of liberation to be discussed in the book of Exodus.

The Book of Exodus on Social Justice[13]

The Exodus describes the story of how Yahweh led the people of Israel out of slavery in Egypt. This event has become one of the more forceful themes of liberation in today's biblical history. Most people in dehumanizing situations find here a biblical story of hope they can identify with, and look forward to ultimate liberation from God as they pursue different avenues that might alleviate their inhuman condition. Thus, from the onset, it is pertinent to heed the advice provided by Donahue as I examine the exodus event in relation to social justice.

> The Exodus from Egypt (Exodus 1:1–15:21) has emerged as one of the most dominant biblical events for a biblical theology of liberation from evil and unjust social structures. There are two dangers here: the first, that a too generalized statement of its meaning absolves people from close attention to the rich theological dimensions of the text; the second that the exodus is considered in isolation from other biblical themes. While liberation from oppression is a fundamental aspect of the exodus narrative, it is not simply freedom from that is important, but freedom for the formation of a community that lives under the covenant.[14]

According to Fretheim, one needs to guard against three perspectives which appear to present the liberation of Israel from Egypt as "explicitly political."[15] First, it is controversial to insinuate that the people of Israel might have engaged in some

---

12 See Kammer, *Doing Faith Justice*, p. 25.

13 George V. Pixley, *On Exodus: A Liberation Perspective*, trans. Robert R. Barr (Maryknoll, New York: Orbis Books, 1987), pp. 14–80; Terence E.Fretheim, *Exodus* (Louisville: John Knox Press, 1991), pp. 18–180; Donald E. Gowan, *Theology in Exodus* (Louisville, Kentucky: Westminster John Knox Press, 1994), pp. 127–167.

14 See Donahue, *What Does the Lord Require?* p. 18.

15 See Fretheim, p. 18

form of military or violent revolution to help secure their release from Egypt. Israel's release should be seen as an act of God. Even in instances where it does appear that some form of violent encounter ensued (Ex. 2:11; 5:1–3), it was the divine activity that was in operation. Hence, the true paradigm lies in God's activity to intervene and save the Israelites.

Second, the salvific act that happened during the exodus ought not to be described in overly political tones. Rather, one should see in the exodus event some clear indication of a universal salvation that is all-embracing: "The historical redemption is real and constitutive in character because it participates in a cosmic victory. To interpret salvation in sociopolitical terms only or primarily scales down the import and effect of what happens at the Red Sea (Ex. 15:1–21)."[16]

Third, the liberation from Egypt is to be seen as the movement from freedom to responsibility for and by the people who formed the community of Israel. It involved the refusal to serve Pharaoh as a god and the turn to the service of Yahweh, because "Exodus would claim that true freedom is found only in the service of Yahweh."[17] Gowan supports the position of Fretheim here when he maintains that the central theme which ensues from the encounter between Pharaoh and Yahweh leading up to the release of the Israelites from slavery in Egypt is the issue of sovereignty.[18] Based on these three perspectives, Fretheim offers a holistic understanding of the exodus event, adopted here.

> God's salvific activity is directed not just toward internal change but toward societal change, the external conditions of life. Salvation is thus conceived in holistic terms as the work of God affecting change in all aspects of life: religious and political, social and individual. Perhaps above all, the exodus is seen to be a sign of hope that poverty and oppression are not the last word, for God is at work on behalf of a different future.[19]

The exodus event is rightly understood as embracing both the liberative and salvific aspects as two sides of the same coin. Gutierrez has interpreted the exodus event from these perspectives and asserts that they form the basis for the justice of Yahweh:

> The Exodus is the long march towards the Promised Land in which Israel can establish a society free from misery and alienation. Throughout the whole process, the religious

---

16 Ibid. p. 20.

17 Ibid.

18 See Gowan, *Theology in Exodus*, p. 137ff. In this unique work, the author has provided deep theological insights that help clarify questions about the nature of Yahweh in the context of the exodus event and general questions of theodicy. Chapter six of this work entitled "The Divine Destroyer," is essential help "…to understand some of the disturbing things the Bible says about God, in order to decide whether they represent only 'primitive' notions, or whether we may in fact discover that they are accurate reflections of the full spectrum of the Christian's experience of the love of God in Jesus Christ," p. 166.

19 Ibid. p. 18.

event is not set apart. It is placed in the context of the entire narrative, or more precisely, it is its deepest meaning. It is the root of the situation. In the last instance, it is in this event that the dislocation introduced by sin is resolved and justice and injustice, oppression and liberation, are determined.[20]

In this way, Gutierrez was able to affirm an important biblical thrust that is central to the exodus narrative on social justice, namely that "The Covenant gives full meaning to the liberation from Egypt; one makes no sense without the other"[21] Thus, the justice of the exodus event lies in recognizing that the political and religious life-giving are intertwined. This divine activity provides the paradigm for which subsequent acts of injustice might find some consideration.

In fact, Donahue[22] asserts that there are two essential elements that have emerged from Israel's covenant experience with Yahweh that relate to issues of justice: first, the covenant manifests how the people of Israel become aware of God's law and justice; second, the covenant binds together persons in community who place their trust in Yahweh and at the same time support each other in the practice of worship and social life. The unifying force for the covenant relationship between Israel and Yahweh lies precisely in Yahweh's unbreakable fidelity to the covenant promise, even when Israel deviates from this pact. Perhaps, some consideration of the role of some Prophets in Israel and how they continually challenged the people to be faithful to the covenant promises by promoting social justice in the community would be helpful.

The Prophets and the Call for Social Justice

According to Anderson:[23]

The English word "Prophet" comes to us from the Greek word *prophetes*, which literally means one who speaks for another, especially for a deity. The corresponding Hebrew term is *nabi*, which is apparently related to the Akkadian verb *nabu*, meaning "to call, to announce, to name." There is some uncertainty, however, as to whether the Hebrew form has an active meaning ("one who calls, an announcer") or a passive meaning ("one who is called"). In the former case, the emphasis would be on the role of a prophet

20 Gustavo Gutierrez, *A Theology of Liberation*, rev. ed., trans. & ed. Caridad Inda and John Eagleson (Maryknoll, New York: Orbis Books, 1988), p. 89.

21 Ibid.

22 See Donahue, *What Does the Lord Require?* p. 23.

23 Bernhard W. Anderson, *Understanding the Old Testament*, Fourth ed. (New Jersey: Prentice Hall, Englewood Cliffs, 1986), p. 247ff; cf., John L. McKenzie, *Dictionary of the Bible* (New York/London: Macmillan, 1965), pp. 694–699. These texts provide a good historical overview of Prophetic thought in Israel.

to proclaim a message; in the latter, the stress would be on the prophet's vocation to be a messenger in the service of the deity.[24]

Anderson maintains that both views are necessary for understanding Israelite prophecy. Thus, the prophet was seen as "...one who communicates the divine will...an intermediary, a spokesperson, one who acts and speaks on behalf of another."[25] The prophetic vocation in Israel embraced various concerns from cultic practices to socio-ethical living. The social message of the prophets has provided a key emphasis to the role of an Israelite prophet which Bruce Vawter has described as the "conscience of Israel."[26] In other words, the prophet provided the conscience for the people of Israel in those matters where such conscience was most needed. According to Vawter one major area that the prophets served as the conscience of Israel was their concern for "Yahweh's poor (anawim):"

> ...The socially oppressed whose redress could only come from Yahweh, and who, therefore, became virtually synonymous with the just, the faithful remnant, with the right to call upon the Lord. In this theme, too, prophetic teaching maintained its accustomed balance...The poor man was not just because he was poor, but the existential fact could not be ignored that poverty and injustice were frequent companions. It was the evil of other men that had created this situation, and the whole of prophetic effort was directed against the evil.[27]

Donahue is able to offer two important distinctions on poverty. First, etymologically speaking, poverty has not stood entirely alone as a human value but is rather an evil. Second, there is the need for a proper use of the term "spiritually poor." The term denotes those who are materially deprived and still open to God's generous love. Hence, Donahue rejects some contemporary understanding of "spiritual poverty" as embracing "...extremely wealthy people who are unhappy even amid prosperity..."[28] or those who are indifferent to riches amid wealth as not being faithful to the biblical tradition. While it is important to understand any given biblical text by looking at its literary context and *Sitz im Leben*, this is not one's goal here. There are excellent commentaries where the literary and historical contexts of prophetic texts have been critically discussed.[29]

---

24 Ibid. p. 248.

25 Ibid.

26 Bruce Vawter, *The Conscience of Israel: Pre-exilic Prophets and Prophecy* (New York: Sheed & Ward, 1961), p. 5ff; and his "Introduction to Prophetic Literature," *Jerome Biblical Commentary*, 12:20–21, p. 233.

27 See Vawter, "Introduction to Prophetic Literature," p. 233. Cf., John L. Mackenzie, *Dictionary of the Bible*, pp. 681–684; Donahue, *What Does the Lord Require?* pp. 31–32 provides some understanding of the biblical meaning of the poor.

28 See Donahue, p. 32.

29 Jon L. Berquist, "Dangerous Waters of Justice and Righteousness: Amos 5:18–27," *Biblical Theology Bulletin* 23 (1993): 54–63; James L. Mays, "Justice: Perspectives from the Prophetic

The goal here is to examine some of the prophetic messages in particular social contexts in order to identify some of their social concerns. In general, one could say that neglect of the Mosaic provisions for assistance to the poor, as well as disobedience to the Law of Moses and the prohibitions against exploiting the misfortunes of the poor were strongly and unequivocally denounced by the prophets. The Prophet Isaiah pronounced a series of woes on the legislators for their infamous laws, on those who issued tyrannical decrees, who denied justice to the unfortunate and cheated the poor, who made widows their prey and snubbed the orphan (Isaiah 10:21).

The Prophet Jeremiah showed disgust for the unjust practices against the people and demanded reform from the leaders (Jeremiah 7:5–7). Similarly, Micah carried out a mission focused on justice in the Southern Kingdom of Israel. Micah denounced the princes of the House of Israel for the evils against the poor and oppressed of their community (Micah 3:1–2). However, above all, it is the prophet Amos who has been regarded as the prophet of social justice and so I will devote some time to examine Amos' role in the prophetic tradition.

The social and political context of Amos' mission is located within the prosperous rule of Jeroboam in Israel (786–746) and King Uzziah who provided able leadership for Judah for forty years (783–742).[30] During this era, Israel experienced prosperous growth and expansion, good business and a vigorous economy (Amos 8:5); farmers raised sheep and cattle (Amos 6:4–6); planted vineyards (Amos 5:11); and erected new homes with lavish decorations in ivory (Amos 6:4–6). But while this lasted, the rich felt a sense of complete security with the resulting complacency and moral decay, particularly, the neglect of the poor who had not an adequate share in the prosperity. Thus, Amos arose from this social situation to challenge the exploitation, injustice and neglect of the poor. The message of Amos could be summarized as embracing four sections: God's punishment is coming upon the nations (Amos 1:3); the people have abandoned justice (Amos 5:12); their religion is hypocrisy (Amos 8:5–6); and consequently, the people should repent (Amos 5:14). There are some utterances and outbursts of Amos against Israel which reveal the moral and ethical corruption that existed among the different levels of society. Amos upheld that the rich degraded the poor and the helpless, and sold the debtors into slavery though they owed nothing more than the price of a pair of sandals (Amos 2:6–7).

Furthermore, Amos delivered prophetic condemnations against the court system that discriminated against the powerless. The magistrates of Israel and Judah were denounced for taking advantage of the vulnerable poor (Amos 5:7–13).

Tradition," *Prophecy in Israel*, (ed.), D. Petersen (Philadelphia: Fortress Press, 1987), pp. 144–158.

30 Eugene H. Maly, *Prophets of Salvation* (New York: Herder and Header, 1967), pp. 75ff note that a major part of the ideas expressed here are taken from this work.

Another group of people who earned Amos' wrath were the merchants because they abandoned honesty and cheated their customers (Amos 8:4). In Amos 8:5ff. the prophet analyzed how the corrupt merchants harbor in their hearts evil thoughts and plot to defraud their customers.

The flamboyant rich women of Israel did not escape Amos' harsh and scathing words because they engaged in an irresponsible lavish lifestyle which contributed toward the suffering of the poor (Amos 4:1). The leadership in Jerusalem and Samaria also earned Amos' ire for their notoriety in ease and arrogant pride (Amos 6:1).

From the above overview, what was evident in Amos' prophetic mission was the concern for social justice. The cry for fair treatment of the poor and the powerless was the central focus of the sermons he preached. Amos directed his denunciations against real human beings, such as, kings, judges, merchants, highly placed women, and the leadership of Israel in both the Northern and Southern capitals of Israel.

Wisdom Literature and Social Justice

There are five main books in the Bible that are usually classified as "wisdom literature": Job, Proverbs, Ecclesiastes, Sirach and Wisdom. Additionally, other books like Tob. 4:3–21; 12:6–13, and the poem in Bar. 3:9–4:4 are also included in the list.[31] It is beyond the scope of this project to discuss any of the above-mentioned books in detail. The task of this study is to offer some of the central elements of wisdom literature that throw some light on the concept of social justice.

Wisdom, generally {(*hokmah (Hebrew); Sophia (Greek); Sapientia (Latin)*}, deals with issues involving daily life and living. The term is used to cover a wide range of issues like the talent displayed by an artisan (Ex. 36:8), royal judgment (1Kgs. 3:28), a clever attitude (Prov. 30: 24–28), code of conduct (Prov. 2: 1–22), piety (Prov. 9:10; Job1:1).[32] Wisdom was not tied to age exclusively as in the case of King Solomon who, with great foresight cooperated with the Spirit of Yahweh in ruling God's people (1Kgs 3:28). While it is true that wisdom predates Israel, it had a specifically Israelite context in the light of Israel's faith in Yahweh. Sirach for instance affirms that "all wisdom is from the Lord and is with Him forever" (Sir. 1:1). Thus, the truly wise person will follow the commands of Yahweh, for to fear the Lord "is the beginning of wisdom" (Sir. 4:1).

Furthermore, some of the wisdom books discussed issues that deal with the problems of life, of good and evil, and of human suffering. The books of Job and Ecclesiastes for example, question the justice of human experience, the failure of righteousness and the success of wickedness. Wisdom Literature categorizes human

31 Roland E. Murphy, "Introduction to Wisdom Literature," *The New Jerome Biblical Commentary*, 27:3 for details.

32 Ibid.

beings into two main divisions: the wise and the foolish. The wise ones accept correction and good counsel (Prov. 9:8ff; 21:11) while the foolish ones refuse to learn and that accounts for their unhappiness. Wisdom is therefore both a moral and practical norm for life.[33]

Specifically, there are two interrelated theological principles in wisdom literature that are central to social justice, namely: the principle of retribution and of deeds and destiny on the one hand, and on the other hand, the principle of divine reversal of human fortune.[34]

The principle of retribution affirms that the attitude and actions of wise persons bring them prosperity and happiness, while those who take the path of folly end up in disaster and unhappiness. This was the central idea supported by the biblical doctrine of divine retribution (Deut. 28, 30). Therefore, the doctrine of divine retribution had two implications. The first was the consequence of deeds: "Thus the good or evil deed produces of itself a good or evil consequence (Prov. 26:27; Ps 7:16). This is supposedly a 'deed-consequence' order of things established in creation and watched over by God."[35]

The second implication was the consequence of destiny. Since one's actions determined their situation in life, it directly affected their destiny in life. According to (Prov. 28:1) the faithful member of the community dwells in safety, will have a goodly inheritance (28:10), will prolong life (28:16), and will obtain honor (29:23). "But whoever digs a pit will fall into it and stone will come back on the one who starts it rolling" (26:27). What is stressed in these verses is that the one who acts in a particular way either 'good' or 'bad' is going to experience the consequences of his or her actions. This is seen as divine justice at work. Thus, the role of God is to complete the process by seeing to it that human "deeds and destiny" correspond. But there are clear instances where the principle of "deeds and destiny" has been challenged in biblical history as one would point out.

The "deeds and destiny" doctrine has suffered many setbacks in the midst of individual and community experiences of the people of Israel which contradicted it. The events of 587 B.C.E. were the turning point. In 587 B.C.E. Nebuchadnezzar took over Jerusalem, destroyed the temple, and exiled the nobles and leaders of the people. Thus, it clearly appeared as though God was using Nebuchadnezzar and the Babylonians as the "rod of anger" against Israel. The result was that some Jews wondered why God would allow his temple to be destroyed at all. Did the

---

33 John L. McKenzie, *Dictionary of the Bible* (New York: MacMillan, 1973), pp. 929–932 for details.

34 See Roland E. Murphy, "Introduction to Wisdom Literature," 27:12–13 for details of the position advanced here; Klaus Kock, "Is There a Doctrine of Retribution in the Old Testament?," *Theodicy in the Old Testament*, (ed.), James L. Crenshaw (Philadelphia: Fortress, 1983), pp. 79, 57–87; Joseph Blenkinsopp, "Deuteronomy," *The New Jerome Biblical Commentary*, 6:46, 50.

35 See Murphy, 27:12.

punishment fit their crime? Was their suffering so enormous that God appeared to some to be a malevolent deity who inflicts suffering on the innocent (Lam. 3:1–19)?

At the individual level, the principle of "deeds and destiny" was challenged in the Book of Job. Though Job was "blameless and upright" (Job 1:1), God appeared to have disregarded Job's actions and allowed disaster to fall upon him (Job 1:6–2:10). This meant that the good deeds and righteousness of Job never counted. In the same tradition, Qohelet could not square his own experiences with the traditional doctrine of "deeds and destiny": "Another thing I have observed about man's life in this world is that where justice should be found, there wickedness is; and where the just man should be, there is an evildoer" (Eccl. 3:16; 4:1).

Thus, both Job and Qohelet seem to suggest a major failure of the "deeds and destiny" principle. To them, there is no divine justice on earth but rather a divine reversal of their human fortune in spite of their good deeds. They seem caught up in a situation where the righteous suffer while evildoers prosper. Perhaps that is why, in order to vindicate divine justice, the Book of Daniel moved God's justice to the next life: "Many of those who sleep in the dust of the earth shall awake, some to everlasting life, and some to shame and everlasting contempt" (Dan. 12:2).

The major implication to the understanding of social justice is how to respond on the one hand to the reality of innocent suffering of individuals and groups, and on the other hand to explain the reality of the goodness of God in creating the world good. This question is the age-old problem of theodicy alluded to earlier. There are several complex questions that are implicated in the issue of theodicy in the face of injustice in the world. How does one justify the viewpoint, for instance, that some persons who find themselves in situations of desperate poverty are paying the price for their bad actions? Human experience informs us that, while this might be true in some cases, there are instances when this argument is very untrue. How does one explain natural phenomena like drought, earthquakes, tornadoes, and hurricanes that bring unbearable hardship on people? While it is true that there are some phenomena in the world that transcend human understanding, which are attributed to the divine, one may and must not absolve human beings of their responsibility to be co-creators with God. In this way, the challenge to take up the task of providing social justice in the world remains very much a partnership of cooperation between persons among themselves and between them and God. Thus, the principle of "deeds and destiny" and that of divine reversal of human fortune appear somewhat inadequate to determine the nature and cause of injustice in the world and by implication are insufficient for articulating the necessary path to social justice.

The New Testament Teaching on Social Justice

The goal is to utilize the different insights provided in New Testament studies, which offer some of the major critical perspectives that scholars[36] have developed over the years as indicators to the theme of justice in the message and mission of Jesus.

The Kingdom of God and Social Justice

The central event around which cohere the New Testament writings is the message and mission of Jesus on the fulfillment of the kingdom of God (Mk. 1:15ff.). Jesus expanded the prophetic tradition by identifying with the plight of the poor, the oppressed, and the afflicted in proclaiming the coming of God's kingdom in their favor, and offering humanity new hope for liberation from the sins of injustice.

Jesus' preaching centered on the coming of the kingdom as a historical reality to challenge the existing unjust social order. His preaching indicated that human coexistence in the socio-political and religious context of Israel did not reflect that the will of God was being done adequately on earth as in heaven, as stated in Jesus' prayer: "Your Kingdom come, your will be done, on earth as in heaven" (Matt. 6:10). The coming kingdom in the context of this prayer has historical and social implications. The historicity of the coming reality could be determined by the fact that Jesus preached and demanded from different groups who were apparently in conflict with each other, a change of heart or conversion. Jesus proclaimed the poor blessed, for the coming kingdom was theirs (LK. 6:20–21).

---

36 The following works will provide the major insights from which one would appropriate to discuss the theme of justice in the New Testament. Raymond E. Brown, *An Introduction to the New Testament* (New York: Doubleday, 1997), pp. 55–93, 817–830; Pheme Perkings, *Reading the New Testament* (New York/Mahwah, New Jersey: Paulist Press, 1988), pp. 51–89, 160–189; Gerhard Lohfink, *Jesus and Community: The Social Dimension of Christian Faith* (Philadelphia: Fortress Press, 1982), pp. 75-147; John P. Meier, "Jesus," *he New Jerome Biblical Commentary*, (eds.), Raymond E. Brown, Joseph A. Fitzmyer, and Roland E. Murphy (Englewood Cliffs, New Jersey: Prentice Hall, 1990), 1319–1328; Albert Nolan, *Jesus Before Christianity* (Maryknoll, New York: Orbis Books, 1978), pp. 21–72; Juan Luis Segundo, *The Historical Jesus of the Synoptics*, trans. John Drury (Maryknoll, New York: Orbis Books, 1985), p. 13ff.; Nicholas T. Wright, *Jesus and the Victory of God* (Minneapolis: Fortress Press, 1996), pp. 204 ff.; James P. Mackey, *Jesus: The Man and The Myth* (New York/Ramsey: Paulist Press, 1979), p.54ff.; Mark A Powell, *W hat Are They Saying About Luke?* (New York/Mahwah: Paulist Press, 1990), p. 94ff; Mark A. Powell, *What Are They Saying About Acts?* (New York/Mahwah: Paulist Press, 1991), pp. 67–72; Elisabeth Schussler Fiorenza, *In Memory of Her 10th ed.* (New York: Crossroad, 1998), p. 97ff; Justin S. Ukpong, *Proclaiming The Kingdom: Essays in Contextual New Testament Studies* (Port Harcourt, Nigeria: Catholic Institute of West Africa Press, 1993), pp. 149–158.

Jesus addressed the rich and the powerful whom he challenged to change their ways or they might be made wretched by the kingdom which was at hand (LK. 6:24–25). Jesus also challenged those who, because of their position in the socio-religious structure, felt the kingdom which was being proclaimed was not designed to overturn the values around which they had organized their lives. There were also those who enjoyed a certain level of socioeconomic security because of the wealth they had accumulated (LK. 12:16–22; 16:1–9).

Michael Cook[37] has identified three fundamental emphases associated with the teaching of Jesus with regard to the fulfillment of the 'kingdom of God.' This perspective helps point out some of the healthy tension that exists in the message proclaimed by Jesus between the 'already' and 'not yet' dimensions of Christian hope. First, the kingdom is by nature eschatological. It symbolizes the end of history and the definitive act of God for the people. However, one does not visualize the kingdom as distinct from the concrete and particular activity of God here and now. Thus, the symbolic reality of the kingdom is described more in prophetic terms. It is a call which challenges the people to a deeper appreciation of their worth and the hope of future possibilities in God.

Second, the 'kingdom of God' for Jesus is another way of pointing out the countless blessings of salvation. The reality of the kingdom was and continues to be realized in and through the words and deeds of Jesus and at the same time is moving toward definitive fulfillment. Third, the tension between the present realization of the kingdom and its future consummation is an integral part of the dynamic unfolding of the kingdom. According to Cook, the tension is a healthy one because it affirms the understanding that "... the message of Jesus proclaims the prophetic presence of the future kingdom of God...Jesus does not offer teaching about the future, but enforces the decisiveness of the present for the future."[38]

Similarly, Wright has offered some insights on the teaching of Jesus on the kingdom in terms of a political reality, which might help specify one's perception of justice. Wright placed side by side the teaching of Jesus with the political movements of first-century Palestine and compared it to the sayings found in the Aramaic Targums. In the former, Jesus is associated with the zealot revolutionary party while the latter seems to identify Jesus as blending both the future and present realities of the kingdom in His message:

> God's kingdom, to the Jew-in-the-village in the first century, meant the coming vindication of Israel, victory over the pagans, the eventual gift of peace, justice and prosperity. It is scarcely surprising that, when a prophet appeared announcing that this kingdom was dawning and that Israel's god was at last becoming king, he found an eager audi-

37 Michael I. Cook, *The Jesus of Faith: A Study in Christology* (New York: Paulist Press, 1981), pp. 42–45 for detailed analysis of these views.

38 Ibid. p. 43.

> ence. This was the story they were waiting to hear; or, better, this was the proper and fitting conclusion to the story in which they were already living.[39]

Duling offered some words of caution against an extreme interpretation of Jesus' message which might seem to suggest that "... the kingdom of Heaven was a code word for God's political restoration of the Davidic kingdom with Jesus as king and his followers as his chief counselors."[40] Thus, while not denying the reality that some of Jesus' message on the 'kingdom' might have political implications, there is the tendency that an overly political presentation might deviate attention from Jesus' teaching on the love of enemies for instance in Matt. 5:44. One might suggest then some way of understanding the kingdom of God in relation to concrete historical activity.

In the context of the argument so far, there is little room to doubt that the Jewish hope was concrete, specific, and focused on the people as a whole. In this sense, one can appreciate the emphasis made by the evangelists with regard to Jesus' kingdom message. In the words of Wright: "...they were not simply reading their own communities' preaching back into an imagined 'history'; recent studies have shown that part of what they wanted to convey, as their message to their own communities, was the fact that in the unique and unrepeatable career of Jesus, Israel's history had reached its climactic moment."[41] The climactic moment in Jesus' teaching on the kingdom is best captured in the Sermon on the Mount (Matt. 5:1–7:29).

According to Raymond Brown, the Sermon on the Mount in the Gospel of Matthew represents "...a harmonious masterpiece of ethical and religious teaching...the Matthean Jesus teaches with *exousia*, i.e., divine power and authority, and by this empowerment makes possible a new existence."[42] Similarly, Benedict T. Viviano maintains that "The dominant themes of the sermon are the kingdom of God and justice...The sermon is fairly systematic, covering the main areas of ethical and religious life as understood in Israel."[43] Thus, the beatitudes (Matt. 5:3–12), which are central to the sermon provide the major building blocks which hold together the values which Jesus emphasized in preaching the kingdom of God. The beatitudes demand a deeper observance of God's command, not simply for

---

39 Nicholas T. Wright, *Jesus and the Victory of God*, p. 204.

40 Dennis C. Duling, "Kingdom of God, Kingdom of Heaven," *The Anchor Bible Dictionary vol. 1.* (ed.), David Noel Freedman (New York: Doubleday, 1992), p. 63.

41 See Wright, p. 227.

42 See Brown, *An Introduction to the New Testament*, p. 178.

43 Benedict T. Viviano, "The Gospel According to Matthew," *The New Jerome Biblical Commentary*, 42:23, p. 640 for details on the major aspects of the Sermon on the Mount which reveal the ethical implications of the kingdom of God.

the sake of the law but by penetrating the root of these commands to see in them the means for God's countless blessings and justice.[44]

Crosby's presentation offers some pertinent insights on the ecclesial and economic implications in the meaning of justice advanced in Matthew. First, the centrality of the virtue of justice in the keeping of "house-order" is explained. The process of housekeeping, whether it is in the ecclesial, social, economic, or political life should consist of the right ordering of relationships at the personal, social or community, and international levels. Thus, such a process would allow room for mutual respect and build structures that would respect equitable distribution of the resources of the community. Second, Crosby identifies in the sermon the principle for Christian commitment to social justice. The beatitudes (5:3–12) describe the practices that one ought to engage in toward promoting proper housekeeping. Proper housekeeping includes fidelity to the elements of salvific and economic justice, and participation through concrete actions in the households of God in and through the community. While Crosby's position may appear to have outlined very general issues in the practice of social justice, the specific issues of social engagement will have to depend on need, social context, availability of resources, and public policy formulations.

Another major teaching of Jesus that is often quoted in the promotion of social justice concerns is the parable of the sheep and the goats (Matt. 25:31–46). In this apocalyptic judgment scene, the Son of Man will return as king and bring all the nations of the world to judgment. Thus, women and men will be separated one from the other like sheep and goats, the sheep to eternal joy and the goats to eternal punishment. The measure for judgment would be how they treated the king (Son of Man) when he was hungry, thirsty, a stranger, naked, sick, or in prison. But the radical nature of the demand for justice lies in the fact that the moment of recognition or non recognition of the elect and the condemned is in this practical and shocking response of the king: "Whatever you did to the least of my brothers and sisters, you did it to me; what you did not do for one of these least ones, you did not do for me" (Matt. 25:40, 45).

John R. Donahue has offered an important contribution to understanding the parable of the sheep and goats.[45] Essentially, Donahue argued for the position that recognizes both the universal and particular implications of the parable. Thus, the Christian missionary challenge and witness to the world should transcend the social, religious, and economic boundaries to embrace all peoples. The key issue

44 Michael Crosby, *House of Disciples: Church, Economics and Justice in Matthew* (Maryknoll, New York: Orbis Books, 1988), pp. 99–182; Lisa Cahill, "The Ethical Implications of the Sermon on the Mount," *Interpretation* 38 (1984): 380–397; Warren Carter, *What Are They Saying About Matthew's Sermon on the Mount?* (New York/Mahwah, New Jersey: Paulist Press, 1994), pp. 113–120.

45 John R. Donahue, "The Parable of the Sheep and the Goats: A Challenge to Christian Ethics." *Theological Studies* 47 (1986): 3–31.

here is that the mandate to practice social justice has no limits and does not pay attention to the societal barriers which sometimes serve as stumbling blocks to Christian faith commitment in the world.

The Letter of James has been identified as a Jewish-Christian message,[46] and so its message would be appropriate here. James offers one some practical principles toward the living out of social justice ideals in community. The first of these principles is that members of the community ought to "Be doers of the word and not hearers only, deluding yourselves" (Jas. 1:22). The challenge here is to strike a balance between what one hears and the deed one is able to carry out as a result of the message one has received. The demand of James is made concrete when the true nature of religion is specified to include: "Religion that is pure and undefiled before God and the Father is this: to care for orphans and widows in their affliction and to keep oneself unstained by the world" (Jas. 1:27).

Furthermore, James challenges the community to refrain from the "sin of partiality" (Jas. 2:1–7) particularly the manner they have made an issue of class distinctions in the community, by favoring the rich who oppress them and neglecting the poor who have been called to be "heirs of the kingdom." More specifically, James categorically states a principle that has stood the test of time in fashioning the commitment of the Christian, namely, that faith without works is useless and works without faith is dead (Jas. 2:14–26). Notice that James declares that faith and works are intertwined. Some of the works mentioned that are the result of genuine faith include clothing and feeding the poor brother or sister (Jas. 2:14–17). Lastly, James offers in (5:1–6) devastating denunciations of the impending threat to the unchecked lifestyle of the rich who continually oppress the poor.

Social Justice in Luke's Gospel and the Acts of the Apostles

According to Donahue,

> The Lucan writings constitute about one quarter of the whole NT. With the exception of James, these writings contain the most explicit statements on wealth, poverty, and the use of resources...Luke-Acts has also been that NT work most often invoked on issues of social justice and concern for the marginal.[47]

The present aim is to highlight areas where concerns for those disadvantaged in the Luke-Acts communities are given special attention. The list of such persons

46 Massey Shephard, "The Epistle of James and the Gospel of Matthew," *Journal of Biblical Literature 75* (1956): 40–51; John R. Donahue, *What Does the Lord Require?* p. 48; Thomas W. Leahy, "The Epistle of James," *The New Jerome Biblical Commentary*, 58:1, p. 909.

47 See Donahue, *What Does the Lord Require?* p. 50. Note that some of the major points advanced by Donahue will be presented here as they prove invaluable to this research.

includes the poor, the sick, the handicapped, lepers, slaves, prostitutes, tax collectors, Samaritans, Gentiles, foreigners, refugees, children, the elderly, widows, and women in general. While the needs of such people vary greatly, they are generally considered as those whom society neglects and despises.

The infancy narratives convey a special message to the *anawim*, the poor of Yahweh. In her prayer of gratitude to God, Mary's "Magnificat" celebrates the God who brings down the mighty from their thrones and lifts up the lowly, fills the hungry with good things, and sends the rich away empty (Luke 1:52f.). The birth of Jesus is first proclaimed to those on the margin of society, "shepherds," and Jesus is born in the most humble circumstances in "a manger," because there was no room for them in the inn (Luke 2:7–14); the gifts offered at Jesus' birth convey the offering of poor people (Luke 2:24); Simeon and Anna (a widow) who were present at his dedication in the temple are ordinary faithful representatives of their communities (Luke 2:25–38).

The starting point for the public ministry of Jesus in Luke emphasizes the need for proclaiming the kingdom message as "the good news to the poor" (Luke 4:17–19). The call to discipleship in Luke is typified by Levi who "leaves everything" in order to follow Jesus (Luke 5:28). The "poor" receive blessings while the rich and powerful receive woes (Luke 6:20, 24–26). The parables of the Rich Fool (Luke 12: 13–21), that of the Unjust Steward (Luke 16:1–8), and of the Rich Man and Lazarus (Luke 16:19–31) teach particular messages about how to relate to people on the underside of society.

Furthermore, it is in Luke that the "great banquet" is to be celebrated with the poor, the maimed, the lame, and the blind (14:13, 21). The story of Zaccheus, the "chief tax collector," who received God's mercy and dedicated his wealth to the well-being of the poor (19:8) is another masterpiece on the theme of social justice. The issue of the mercy of God challenges the type of justice administered here when compared to existential justice. It evidently suggests that existential forms of justice are only one side of the story, and that ultimately, true justice and mercy lies with God.

There is a special place for the contribution made by women in Luke's Gospel. Powell maintains that in Luke one finds "...an affinity for parallel references to men and women."[48] In the parables where the kingdom of God is compared to a man planting a seed (13:18–19), there is the corollary of a woman working with leaven (13:20–21), the annunciations to Zechariah (1:5–25) and to Mary (1:26–38), the prophecies of Simeon (2:25–35) and Anna (2:36–38), the Sabbath healings of a woman (13:10–17) and a man (14:1–6), the stories about a man who lost a sheep

48 Mark Allan Powell, *What Are They Saying About Luke?* (New York/Mahwah: Paulist Press, 1990), p. 94; See also Jane Kopas, "Jesus and Women: Luke's Gospel," *Theology Today* 42 (1986): 192–202; Jane Schaberg, "Luke," *The Women's Bible Commentary*, (eds.), Carol A. Newsom and Sharon H. Ringe (Louisville, Kentucky: Westminster/John Knox, 1992), pp. 275–292.

(15:3-7) and a woman who lost a coin (15:8–10), and the references to two men in bed (17:34) and two women at the mill (17:35), are all peculiar to Luke's Gospel. There is also an important balancing in the list of Jesus' male disciples (6:12–16) with a list of women who were Jesus' faithful followers (8:1–3).

In the Acts of the Apostles, one is challenged by the communal lifestyle of the early Christian community. The early community shared their goods and services ensuring that there is no needy person in their midst (AA 2:41–47, 4:32–37). Thus, Ananias and Sapphira by withholding the "proceeds of the land," are guilty of deceit before God and the community (AA 5:1–11). Though it was left up to their conscience and freewill to contribute to the common fund, their possessions revealed the true nature of their commitment to God and the community.

Furthermore, one discovers in Luke's account of the death of Judas (AA 1:18–20), in comparison to Matt. 27:3–10, that Judas did not return the ill-gotten money, but "buys a farm" (AA 4:32) with the "payment of his injustice" and appears to die accidentally and the farm is deserted. Similarly, Simon tries to use money to buy power (AA 8:9–24). On a positive note, Lydia, "the seller of purple," gives a good example of faithful discipleship by showing hospitality to Paul (AA 16:16–24), while the silversmiths of Ephesus feel challenged by Paul's preaching (AA 19:23–41).

Powell agrees with Jacques Dupont that the mission to the Gentiles is central to the existence of the Acts of the Apostles.[49] The Gentile mission which was prompted by God rather than the rejection of the Gospel by the Jewish community raises a pertinent implication for social justice. The "Mission to the Gentiles replaces the mission to Israel," especially in view of AA 10:35 with the statement that "in every nation, anyone who fears God and does what is right is acceptable to him." The universality of the Gospel is affirmed without any ties to a particular ethnic grouping and would appear to prepare the way for the resolution passed in the Council of Jerusalem on the acceptance of non-Jews in the Christian Assembly (AA 15).

There is a strong indication in Acts that the relations between the Church and the State appear to be in harmony from Luke's perspective.[50] Christians are presented as law-abiding citizens who do not threaten the peaceful existence of the social order (AA 18:14–15). Paul is not seen as the real threat to the community but to the lawbreakers (AA 19:40; 25:18–19; 26: 31–32). Luke is also said to present the Roman Empire as supportive to Christians (AA 18:12–16; 19:35–41; 23:10).

49 Mark Allan Powell, *What Are They Saying About Acts?* (New York/Mahwah, New Jersey: Paulist Press, 1991), pp. 67–72.

50 See Powell, pp. 72–74.

Social Justice in the Johannine Community[51]

Raymond E. Brown has offered the most compelling reading of the Johannine community by tracing "the life, loves, and hates of an individual Church in New Testament times."[52] There are two major issues that deserve one's attention: the relationship between the Johannine community and the outside world; and the role of women in the Johannine community.

1. The relationship between the Johannine community and the outside world involved a complex web of relationships. Brown maintains that one need not rule out the universality of the Johannine community especially in view of John 3:16–17: "For God so loved the world that he gave his only son, so that everyone who believes in him might not perish but might have eternal life..." Yet, John 3:18–21 would seem to challenge the claim to universalism in the Johannine community. According to Brown:

   > The human race is divided into non-believers and believers, into those who prefer darkness and those who prefer light, into those who are condemned and those who already have eternal life. Since the Johannine community identifies itself with the believers, it is no surprise that most of those outside the community are looked upon as more or less shadowed by darkness. No other Gospel so lends itself to a diagnosis of community relationships in terms of opposition. Yet...the reader must not forget the light which shines within the Johannine community of faith and which is the main emphasis of the Gospel.[53]

   Thus, Brown upholds that it is on the basis of the above thesis that the commandment of love becomes the central tenet of the Johannine community (John 13:34; 15:12). But the real challenge for social justice lies in the reception that was given "...to various shades of non-believers and

---

51 The views presented in this section are largely adapted from the major insights offered in the following works that have critically reflected on the question of social justice in relation to the Gospel of John. Joseph A. Grassi, *Informing the Future: Social Justice in the New Testament* (New York/Mahwah, New Jersey: Paulist Press, 2002), pp.208-226; Bruno Barnhart, *The Good Vine: Reading John from the Center* (New York/Mahwah, New Jersey: Paulist Press, 1993), pp. 143–190; Raymond E. Brown, *The Community of the Beloved Disciple* (New York/Mahwah: Paulist Press, 1979), pp. 51–91,123–135, 183–198; Pheme Perkins, "The Gospel According to John," *The New Jerome Biblical Commentary*, pp. 942-985;Teresa Okure, *The Johannine Approach to Mission: A Contextual Study of John* 4:1-42 (Tübingen: J.C.B. Mohr/Paul Siebeck, 1988), pp. 160–168ff.

52 This is the sub-title to Brown's celebrated book *The Community of the Beloved Disciple*. What follows is an attempt to highlight some major issues from this work that support the theme of social justice.

53 Ibid. p. 60.

other believers"[54] by the Johannine community. Brown identified six major areas of conflict between the Johannine community and other groups generally called nonbelievers: the world, "the Jews," the adherents of John the Baptist, the Crypto-Christians (Christian Jews within the Synagogues), the Jewish Christian churches of inadequate faith, and the Christians of Apostolic churches.[55]

The point of bringing these issues here is to show the deep hostility and sense of superiority that the Johannine community had toward other groups in the larger community whom they considered as not reflecting their ideological positions. Thus, some of these issues offer a critical perspective at the reality of fellowship both within the Christian community and outside the community. Brown raises two relevant questions for addressing social injustice in the community. In the first place, when someone or a group of persons are rejected in a community, is it better to break ranks with the entire community or to remain within it and seek to provide the needed change at the risk of further rejection? "In subsequent Christianity there have been many times when it was not easy to decide whether for the sake of the Gospel one should split from the establishment or should stay and work stubbornly within it, striving for change. On the long road which position really exhibits more courage?"[56] In the second instance, Brown challenges those who are comfortable within their parochial world and find it difficult to let in fresh air from the outside for fear of heretical positions that might derail their claim to orthodoxy.

> When the charge of heresy is raised in Christian communities today, there is the tendency to associate that stigma with wild - eyed radicals proposing new ideas. In Christian history, however, some of the most significant heresies have been conservative rather than radical-the tendency to hold on to old theological answers when new questions have caused the main body of Christians to move on to new answers..."Orthodoxy," then, is not always the possession of those who try to hold on to the past. One may find a truer criterion in the direction toward which Christian thought has been tending, even if that direction suggests that past formulations of truth have to be considered inadequate to answer new questions.[57]

54 Ibid. p. 62.

55 Ibid. pp. 62–88 provides an in-depth discussion on the areas of conflict between the Johannine community and each group.

56 Ibid., p. 73.

57 Ibid. pp. 80–81.

2. The role of women in the Johannine community is another key social justice issue discussed by Brown.[58] Brown chose to discuss the role of women in John's Gospel "...because of the perceptive corrective that the evangelist offers to some ecclesiastical attitudes of his time - his should be a voice heard and reflected upon when we are discussing new roles for women in the Church today."[59] Brown emphasized that the important role played by the Samaritan woman (John 4:25–26, 29) in recognizing that Jesus is the Christ was significant for helping Nichodemus to have a better understanding of the Christ. Moreover, the dialogue between Jesus and his male disciples would indicate that the Samaritan woman had a "missionary function" (John 4:35–37). The Samaritans come out to meet with Jesus in response to what the woman has told them about Jesus.

   Similarly, the role of a woman, Mary Magdalene (John 20:17–18), as a witness to the resurrection of Jesus stands in contrast to the other male disciples who had gone to the tomb earlier but did not see anyone (John 20: 2–10). Thus, Brown summarized his findings in this way:

   > In researching the evidence of the Fourth Gospel, one is still surprised to see to what extent in the Johannine community women and men were already on an equal level in the fold of the Good Shepherd. This seems to have been a community where in the things that really mattered in the following of Christ there was no difference between male and female—a Pauline dream (Gal 3:28) that was not completely realized in the Pauline communities. But even John has left us with one curious note of incompleteness: the disciples, surprised at Jesus' openness with a woman, still did not dare to ask him, "What do you want of a woman?" (John 4:27). That may well be a question whose time has come in the church of Jesus Christ.[60]

   This study affirms that the role of women in both the Church and society is central to building relationships for self-help that recognize the human dignity of all persons.

Pauline Teaching on Social Justice

John Donahue offers one a clear presentation on this theme and one hopes to follow in that direction.[61] Donahue poses the challenge before anyone who attempts to relate the message of Paul to the social question as a paradox:

---

58 Ibid. pp. 183–198.

59 Ibid. p. 186.

60 Ibid. p. 198.

61 See Donahue, *What Does the Lord Require?* pp. 54–61 for details.

> On the one hand, no NT author uses the term *dikaiosyne* (justice) more than Paul, nor does any other author link it so explicitly with issues of faith. Yet the contemporary concern for social justice has been most often based on OT considerations (Exodus, the Prophetic concern for the poor) or on the teaching of Jesus.[62]

The above dilemma is explained in view of the theological debate over "faith and good works," which seems to offer an individualistic perspective to Pauline theology in terms of how the individual sinner relates to God. The practical applications of Paul's message on issues confronting the communities and their relations to the theological content are not adequately digested: the charge is that Paul teaches only an "interim ethic" in view of his imminent eschatological expectations. The question then is how to make Paul's ethical teaching relevant "…for Christians settling in for the long haul of history."[63]

Donahue, following Fitzmyer, offers some resources for the faith that does justice in Pauline theology and pastoral engagement in the context of the significance of the "Christ event."[64] First, the Christ event is presented as the foundation of Christian faith, which demands responsibility for the world. In addition, "newness of life" is offered to the Christian who is called to participate in the Lordship of Christ over evil.

> The Christian is to be a witness in mission of the victory over death and the transforming power of the resurrection. To pursue the quest for justice in faith means that the Christian walks in confidence that evil is not the Lord of life and that even death for the sake of others cannot separate a person from the love of God (Rom. 8:28–39).[65]

Second, "Justification of the sinner by God's grace through faith results in a personal and communal liberation that enables people to live for others rather than for themselves."[66]The emphasis here is that, on the one hand, the Christ event provides the Christian with "freedom from" sin, law, and death (Gal. 5:1). On the other hand, the Christ event provides "freedom for" the Christian to face up to their responsibilities to each other in the community (Gal. 5:13, 16–21; 6:2; Rom. 8:21–23).

Third, "Paul's eschatology does not warrant an 'interim ethic,' but rather summons Christians to responsibility for life in the world."[67] The Christian is between and betwixt the "already" and the "not yet." In this atmosphere, the challenge is "to walk in the newness of life and not let sin reign in their mortal bodies (Rom.

---

62 Ibid. p. 54.

63 Ibid. p. 55.

64 See Donahue, pp. 55–59; Joseph A Fitzmyer, "Pauline Theology," *The New Jerome Biblical Commentary*, p. 1389ff.

65 See Donahue, pp. 55–56.

66 Ibid. p. 56.

67 Ibid.

6:12). They should yield themselves to God, so that they might become instruments and servants of justice (Rom. 6:13, 18)."[68]

Donahue offers two major practical and pastoral directives from Paul's message. They include the raising of funds for the poor churches in Judea to help facilitate Paul's missionary work and show solidarity between the Greek churches and the Jerusalem church (Rom. 15: 25–29; 1Cor. 16:1–4, 2Cor. 8f.). The challenge of bridging the gap between the rich and the poor today is a central issue of social justice which different societies will continue to face and pursue in their different social contexts.

The second pastoral concern is "the dispute over the celebration of the Lord's Supper."[69] The central concern of Paul would seem to be that the Christian community should not let the social distinctions between the different classes of people impact the celebration of their liturgy (1Cor. 11:17–33). In this case, Paul maintains the position of integrating the community as evidenced in Gal. 3:28 "in Christ there is neither Jew nor Greek, slave nor free, male nor female." As Donahue clearly puts it:

> Paul's directives here show that issues of justice and concern for the more vulnerable members of the community enter into the most central act of Christian community, the celebration of the Lord's Supper. They also show Paul's constant concern for the weaker members of the community and for the creation of a community in which economic and social divisions do not invalidate the faith of the community as a whole process.[70]

So far, the central biblical thrust for social justice is respect for the dignity of the human person who is created in the image and likeness of God. Thus, wherever and whenever that dignity is marginalized, the demands of social justice come into operation to restore and fashion the human person toward his or her God-giving dignity. Furthermore, the mission and message of Jesus affirm the revelation of God and make ethical demands centered on the commandment to love God and neighbor as primary to participation in God's kingdom. Hence, the kingdom of God has social, economic, political, and religious consequences that the followers of Christ would have to deal with on a day-to-day basis as they encounter the present, imminent, and eschatological dimensions of the kingdom.

The Philosophy of Social Justice

There are two reasons why examining the philosophy of social justice is pertinent: to show that there is a correlation between the understanding associated with the

68 Ibid. p. 57.

69 Ibid. p. 58.

70 Ibid. p. 59.

Thomistic philosophy of law and morals and the papal term of social justice; to identify the component parts of social justice which make it such an important theoretical framework for a just society.

Justice According to St. Thomas Aquinas[71]

The Thomistic theory of justice sets out to make a major distinction between "general" justice or "legal" justice as the objective rule protecting social relationships among persons in community, and "particular" justice as the subjective rule which is further divided into two parts, namely, "commutative" justice and "distributive" justice. Thus, the "particular" kinds of justice have binding force only in as much as they are tied to the general objective of justice.

In considering the issue of justice, Aquinas specified the relationship between "right" and "justice" by indicating that it is central to the virtue of justice to help direct the right relations of persons in the community.

> Accordingly that which is right in the works of the other virtues, and to which the intention of the virtue tends as to its proper object, depends on its relation to the agent only, whereas the right in a work of justice, besides its relation to the agent, is set up by its relation to others. Because a man's work is said to be just when it is related to some other by way of some kind of equality, for instance the payment of the wage due for a service rendered. And so a thing is said to be just, as having the rectitude of justice, when it is the term of an act of justice, without taking into account the way in which it is done by the agent: whereas in the other virtues nothing is declared to be right unless it is done in a certain way by the agent. For this reason justice has its own special proper object over and above the other virtues, and this object is called the just, which is the same as right. Hence it is evident that right is the object of justice.[72]

---

71 St. Thomas Aquinas, *The Summa Theologica, 3 vols. trans. Fathers of the English Dominican Province* (New York: Benziger Brothers, 1947), IIa IIae, q. 58, art. 1–12; q. 61, art.1–4 note that all quotations are taken from this work unless otherwise stated. Other important works consulted are: Paul J. Glenn, *A Tour of the Summa* (Rockford, Illinois: Tan Books, 1978), pp. 222–237; Jean-Yves Calvez and Jacques Perrin, *The Church and Social Justice: The Social Teaching of the Popes from Leo XIII to Pius XII , trans. J. R. Kirwan* (London: Burns & Oates, 1961), pp. 133–173; Emile Guerry, *Social Doctrine of the Catholic Church* (New York: St Paul, 1961), pp. 112–201; William F. Drummond, *Social Justice* (Milwaukee: Bruce Company, 1955), pp. 19–118; Oswald von Nell-Breuning, "Social Movements," *Encyclopedia of Theology: The Concise Sacramentum Mundi,* (ed.), Karl Rahner (New York: Seabury Press, 1975), pp. 1594–1608; Jonathan Westphal, (ed.), *Justice* (Indianapolis/Cambridge: Hackett, 1996), pp. 95–114; Leo W. Shields, "*The History and Meaning of the Term Social Justice,*" Ph.D. Dissertation. University of Notre Dame, Indiana, 1941, pp. 5–72; J. Brian Benestad, "The Catholic Concept of Social Justice: A Historical Perspective," *Commonweal* 11/4 (Winter 1984): 364–381; James P. Hanigan, "Militant Nonviolence: A Spirituality for the Pursuit of Social Justice," *Horizons* 9/1 (1982): 7–32; Daniel P. Moynihan, "Social Justice in the Next Century," *America* 165/6 (September 14, 1991): 132–137.

72 Thomas Aquinas, *The Summa Theologica*, IIa IIae, q. 57, art. 1.

Similarly, Aquinas maintains that the object of the other virtues depends on an important quality in the agent, namely, "...in the other virtues nothing is declared to be right unless it is done in a certain way by the agent."[73] In this way, justice relates to the other virtues by way of equality in the relationship among persons in community and not by an already determinate quality in the agent. Thus, the distinctive mark of justice as a special virtue from the others lies in the fact that: "For this reason justice has its own special proper object over and above the other virtues, and this object is called the just, which is the same as right."[74] In reality, there are many virtues that are linked to day-to-day human relationships and there are several reasons why human acts may be considered to be right and just in themselves. Therefore, "justice, as such, is independent of these motivations. It exists whenever the norm of equality or of proportion is effectively respected in one man's dealings with the other."[75]

Aquinas then proceeded to address the question "Of Justice," in twelve articles. In the first article, justice is defined as "a habit whereby a man renders to each one his due by a constant and perpetual will."[76] This definition of justice underscores its unique position as a special virtue with a distinct objective from the other virtues. Thus, the distinction is made here between what Aquinas refers to as a "general" virtue of justice in relation to the "particular" virtues of justice.

> Justice directs man in his relations with other men. Now this may happen in two ways: first as regards his relation with individuals, secondly as regards his relations with others in general, in so far as a man, who serves a community, serves all those who are included in that community. Accordingly justice in its proper acceptation can be directed to another in both these senses. Now it is evident that all who are included in a community, stand in relation to that community as parts to a whole; while a part, as such, belongs to a whole, so that whatever is the good of a part can be directed to the good of the whole. It follows therefore that the good of any virtue, whether such virtue direct man in relation to himself, or in relation to certain other individual persons, is referable to the common good, to which justice directs: so that all acts of virtue can pertain to justice, in so far as it directs man to the common good. It is in this sense that justice is called a general virtue. And since it belongs to the law to direct to the common good...it follows that the justice which is in this way styled general, is called legal justice, because thereby man is in harmony with the law which directs the acts of all the virtues to the common good.[77]

There are two major implications arising from the understanding of "general" justice. First, the term "general" justice applies to the essence and object of justice. It is that which is proper to itself and which gives signification to justice in rela-

73 Ibid.

74 Ibid.

75 See Calvez and Perrin, *The Church and Social Justice*, p. 140.

76 See *Summa Theologica*, IIa IIae, q. 58, art. 1.

77 Ibid. q. 58, art. 5.

tion to the other virtues. Hence, one can also say that from it the "special" virtue of justice flows in connection with the other virtues. Conversely, the other virtues may be regarded as just to the degree that they are geared toward or away from the common good, which is the goal and end of all the virtues: "Just as charity which regards the Divine good as its proper object, is a special virtue in respect of its essence, so too legal justice is a special virtue in respect of its essence, in so far as it regards the common good as its proper object".[78]

In the second place, "general justice" refers to the extent to which the virtue of particular justice is subordinated in the general justice, and how the right relationship with individuals is determined in view of the common good. Calvez and Perrin express this point clearly when they declare:

> In practice, given the relationships which exist between the whole and the parts according to the Thomist system, the direction of conduct to the common good is made actual in the particular dealings of men with each other, considered as individuals. General Justice regulates conduct with respect to the common good; but this is never expressed by any specific acts, but in all particular dealings in which justice is concerned...It is from the righteousness of all these dealings that there results, in a certain sense, the righteousness of the whole, that conformity to the common good which is general justice.[79]

Next, one may focus attention on the specific attributes of "particular justice" in Aquinas. The passage where there is a clear indication of the establishment of the term "particular justice" states:

> Legal justice is not essentially the same as every virtue, and besides legal justice which directs man immediately to the common good, there is a need for other virtues to direct him immediately in matters relating to particular goods: and these virtues may be relative to himself or to another individual person. Accordingly, just as in addition to legal justice there is a need for particular virtues to direct man in relation to himself, such as temperance and fortitude, so too besides legal justice there is need for particular justice to direct man in his relations to other individuals.[80]

While general or legal justice is the object of the virtue of justice, it is not absolutely an end in itself but a means to an end. Justice is able to regulate relations between individual persons in mediate manner by pointing them toward the common good.

Hence, Legal justice does indeed direct man sufficiently in his relations towards others. As regards the common good it does so immediately, but as to the good of the individual, it does so mediately. Wherefore there is need for particular justice to direct a man immediately to the good of another individual.[81]

---

78 Ibid. q. 58, art. 6.

79 See Calvez and Perrin, p. 142.

80 See *The Summa Theologica*, q. 58, art. 7.

81 Ibid.

The question may be raised whether in assigning such a role to particular justice, one does end up making it a self-sufficient entity. In other words, since particular justice assumes the position of individual personal relationships, could it be said that general justice is brought about merely as a result of particular justice?

According to St. Thomas, the common good does not result simply from particular goods or from an accumulation of these goods. Therefore, one is not just dealing with a quantitative phenomenon but rather with realities that are mutually supportive of the end of the other.The common good of the realm and the particular good of the individual differ not only in respect of many and the few, but also under a formal aspect. For the aspect of the common good differs from the aspect of the individual good, even as the aspect of the whole differs from that of the part.[82]

It is pertinent to realize that general justice and particular justice are essentially two sides of the same coin. The practice of particular justice is based on the standard set by general justice, through which it is mediated in the particular human relationships.

> Particular justice is directed to the private individual, who is compared to the community as a part to the whole. Now a twofold order may be considered in relation to a part. In the first place, there is the order of one part to another, to which corresponds the order of one private individual to another. This order is directed by commutative justice, which is concerned about the mutual dealings between two persons. In the second place, there is the order of the whole towards the parts, to which corresponds the order of that which belongs to the community in relation to each single person. This order is directed by distributive justice, which distributes common goods proportionately. Hence there are two species of justice, distributive and commutative.[83]

The subject of the acts of the virtue of justice could be either an individual member of society or one who holds social power in the community and acts as such to enable persons toward the realization of the common good. Commutative justice and distributive justice as "subjective parts" of particular justice appear to be distinct from general justice. However, this is not completely true since general justice is the first determinant of justice, which cuts across all types of social relationships between the whole and the parts and the parts amongst themselves. What has happened is that "all the requirements of general justice are resolved in practice into rights and duties, either of individual towards individual, or of the wielder of social power to the subjects of that power, but the determination of all these rights and duties is subordinated to general justice."[84]

---

82 Ibid.

83 IIa IIae, q. 61, art. 1.

84 See Calvez and Perrin, p. 144.

Having stated the major points that reflect the concept of justice in Aquinas especially the interrelationship between general justice or legal justice and particular justice and the parts of particular justice, namely, commutative justice and distributive justice, one wonders why Pius XI did not speak of general or legal justice and a particular justice but preferred to use the phrase "social justice" to formulate his social, economic, and moral philosophy. Perhaps, history will provide the best answer to this puzzle.

The History of the Term Social Justice[85]

The major historical development that ensued as a result of the meaning of justice articulated by St. Thomas Aquinas was the confusion that existed among the different schools that sought to expound the positions of traditional Thomism.[86] The first school recognized the inherent distinctions between "general or legal justice" and "particular justice" by creating room for the understanding which appeared to reduce all justice to the obligations of commutative justice. The State was seen as being capable, as a result of justice, to impose obligations upon the citizens who are obliged in virtue of justice to perform certain duties. But this was conceived as an extension of distributive justice. Their attempt was to entrench "legal justice" to embrace the practical roles of both commutative and distributive justice which would be a far cry from what Aquinas had intended. The difficulty of some traditional Thomists to be relevant in the same categories put forward by St. Thomas Aquinas to formulate an objective norm that would take into consideration the "whole" community and its common good was its greatest undoing.

The second school of Thomism spearheaded by the work of A. Tapparelli in Italy began from 1880 onwards to formulate the concept of social justice in relation to the right of persons. They hoped to offer some precise interpretation that would be faithful to Aquinas by providing an objective norm capable of holding together social relations in community.[87] The views of this school of thought spread to France where scholars like Antoine, Albert *de Mun* and *La Tour du Pin* became strong proponents of the social justice agenda. Antoine for instance offered an important understanding of social justice which freed it from the subjective obligations of commutative and distributive justice. In his *Cours d' Economie Sociale* there appears to be some indication of an objective social justice, that is related to

85 To offer a detailed history of social justice is very much beyond the scope of this project. Thus what is presented is a brief history that is consistent with the argument of the work namely to show the correlation between the Thomistic concept of justice and the development of the term social justice. For a detailed history of social justice, see- Leo W. Shields, "The History and Meaning of the Term Social Justice," pp. 26–46.

86 See Calvez and Perrin, *The Church and Social Justice*, pp. 145–146.

87 Ibid.

the meaning attached to "general or legal justice" in Aquinas. Antoine is quoted as saying that social justice is only legal justice: "that justice which has for its object the social good and the common good to all."[88]

In Germany, Pesch is considered to have formulated the phrase *soziale Gerechtigkeit* after 1905 when most of the German writers leading up to Oswald von Nell-Breuning, who was a major collaborator of Pius XI in the drafting of QA, promoted the understanding of the term social justice as synonymous to legal justice.[89] In so doing, they were being faithful to the traditional Thomistic concepts of justice under another nomenclature. It is pertinent to state that while the term social justice was already in use, it was in the papal social encyclical QA that a normative definition and understanding of social justice was offered. Ferree points out the fact that: "The only reasonable place to study either notion (Catholic Action or Social justice) is in the work of Pius XI and in works inspired by his teaching; for it is only here that the words are surely used with a definite and precise signification."[90]

Social Justice and Society in Quadragesimo Anno

Pius XI used the term social justice in relation to social charity as governing principles of society in QA in several major contexts. These governing principles deal with how wealth is generated and distributed; the setting up of wages and, how they affect the common good as is evident in subsequent discussion.

Social Justice and the Distribution of Wealth

The context where social justice first appears in QA is when the pope examined the relationship between capital and labor. More precisely, the subject matter under review was that of the "Guiding Principle of Just Distribution." The pope introduced a prelude to the principle of social justice by stating that: "This principle

---

88 Ibid. p. 147.

89 See Leo W. Shields, who, after an elaborate history of the term of social justice, affirms on the one hand that "our conclusion must be that the commonest opinion is the right one and that social justice as a scientific term must be a new name for legal justice" pp. 45–46. On the other hand, he observed rightly that social justice as formulated in the papal encyclicals is not limited to a scientific use, it embraces doctrinal and moral values which challenge individualistic and totalitarian thoughts: "The Catholic message of social justice is written in sharp relief against this background of individualist thought in all its forms—romantic, rationalistic, humanitarian, and totalitarian. It is the key to the reintegration of social life that must be inspired by Christian faith and charity and supported by grace" p. 71.

90 William Ferree, *The Act of Social Justice* (Dayton, Ohio: Marianist Publications, 1951), p. 95.

must be constantly borne in mind if we would not wander from the path of truth."[91] Then, social justice as the guiding principle of distribution is offered. Now, not every kind of distribution of wealth and property among men is such that it can satisfactorily, still less adequately, attain the end intended by God. Wealth, therefore, which is constantly being augmented by social and economic progress, must be so distributed among the various individuals and classes of society that the common good of all, of which Leo XIII spoke, be thereby promoted. In other words, the good of the whole community must be safeguarded. By these principles of social justice one class is forbidden to exclude the other from a share in the profits. This law is violated by an irresponsible wealthy class who, in their good fortune, deem it a just state of things that they should receive everything and the laborer nothing. It is violated also by the property-less class, when, strongly aroused because justice is ignored and too prone to vindicate improperly the one right well known to them, they demand for themselves all the fruits of production. They are wrong in thus attacking and seeking the abolition of ownership and all profits deriving from sources other than labor, whatever is their nature or significance in human society, for the sole reason that they were not obtained by toil. In this connection it must be noted that the appeal made by some to the words of the Apostle: "If any man will not work, neither let him eat" is as inept as it is unfounded. The Apostle is here passing judgment on those who refuse to work though they could and ought to do so: he admonishes us to use diligently our time and our powers of body and mind, and not to become burdensome to others as long as we are able to provide for ourselves. In no sense does he teach that labor is the sole title which gives a right to a living or to profits.[92]

> Each class, then, must receive its due share, and the distribution of created goods must be brought into conformity with the demands of the common good and social justice. For every sincere observer realizes that the vast differences between the few who hold excessive wealth and the many that live in destitution constitute a grave evil in modern society.[93]

From this initial presentation of the guiding role of social justice in the "just distribution" of the resources of the earth among persons in community, emerges an important implication that specifies the role of social justice toward promoting the common economic good of persons in community.

---

91 QA Par. 56, p. 55.

92 QA Par. 57, pp. 55–56

93 QA Par. 58, p. 56.

Social Justice and the Common Good

The connection between social justice and the common good provided here appears to be somewhat limited to the socio-economic sphere. While there is a clear indication that the goal and end of social justice is the common good, the type of good that is commonly desired in this context is specific, namely: "Wealth, therefore, which is constantly being augmented by social and economic progress, must be so distributed among the various individuals and classes of society."[94] Similarly, the persons who are to share in these virtues appear to be those who belong to the socio-economic world of capital and labor. Hence, those who go contrary to the principle of social justice are: "the wealthy class who…receive everything and the laborer nothing; the property-less class (who)…demand for themselves all the fruits of production."[95] Thus, the role of the virtue of social justice in this circumstance is to ensure and enhance the just distribution of economic goods in order that the bridge between the economically wealthy and economically poor would be narrowed. In so doing, the economic conditions which threaten the life of some persons in society might be nonexistent.

The pope offered also the condition in which the principle of social justice might be wrongly utilized. Social justice does not mean, for instance, that all goods in society are to be equally distributed among the members without recognizing the just contribution of the different members and their peculiar circumstance. Neither does social justice deny individual members of their personal right to own property. Consequently, social justice would have to allow some degree of inequality in society, while at the same time working towards the "harmonization" of the respective rights of capital and labor.

Lastly, the pope offers a classic interpretation of the second letter of St. Paul to the Thessalonians, 3:10: "If anyone was unwilling to work, neither should that one eat." There are two pertinent issues worthy of note: first, to state the saying of St. Paul as "He who does not work shall not eat," is to wrongly apply the biblical text. In this case, one will be saying that only those who work and earn a living by their labors are entitled to subsistence. However, it is clear that, in reality, if one were to apply this saying completely, then what will become of very young people, sick people, the elderly, the physically and mentally challenged, and of course the jobless who are able to and ought to work but cannot find a job? Moreover, it is part of our humanity as ordained by God that one is capable of working only during a certain period of one's life. Thus, in order to do away with these intractable difficulties the pope stated his position unequivocally; the appeal to St. Paul "is as inept as it is unfounded." Second, the pope states the true thought of St. Paul by saying that the Apostle did not teach the doctrine that "labor is the

94 QA Par. 58, p. 56.

95 Op. cit.

sole title which gives a right to a living or to profits." Rather, what St. Paul wants Christians to know is this: "He who is too lazy to work does not deserve, in other words, is not worthy to have daily bread. Whoever is capable of supporting himself shall not live at another person's expense. Whoever received abilities and powers from God shall not permit them to rust, but shall employ them usefully."[96] Thus, the concrete application of St. Paul's injunction would depend on one's situation in life which is multifaceted. It is also a clear case of an interpretation which appeals to both the letter and spirit of the law.

Social Justice and Wages

The other major instance where social justice appears in QA is in connection with the wage system. First, the human person who is ready and willing to work deserves to receive a "living family wage" according to the demands of social justice.

> In the first place, the wage paid to the workingman should be sufficient for the support of himself and of his family...If in the present state of society this is not always feasible, social justice demands that reforms be introduced without delay which will guarantee every adult workingman just such a wage. In this connection we might utter a word of praise for various systems devised and attempted in practice, by which an increased wage is paid in view of increased family burdens, and a special provision is made for special needs.[97]

The second condition is that there should and ought to be purposeful dialogue between the employer and the employee. In so doing, the true nature of the business including benefits and burdens are fraternally discussed. Thus, decisions that are taken as a result of such a dialogical process are more beneficial to both parties: "The guiding spirit in this crucial decision should be one of mutual understanding and Christian harmony between employers and workers."[98]

The third condition deals with the "requirements of the common good." The intrinsic connection between social justice and the common good is again brought to one's attention. In other words, social justice does not only demand and guarantee a living family wage but it also demands a wage policy that respects, enables and ensures the proper working conditions of the working members of the society.

> Finally, the wage level should be arrived at with the public economic welfare in mind... All are aware that a scale of wages too low, no less than a scale excessively high, causes unemployment. Now unemployment, particularly if widespread and of long duration, as we have been forced to experience it during our pontificate, is a dreadful scourge; it causes misery and temptation to the laborer, ruins the prosperity of nations, and endan-

96 See Nell-Breuning, *Reorganization of Social Economy*, p. 146.

97 QA Par. 71, p. 58.

98 QA Par. 73, pp. 58–59.

> gers public order, peace and tranquility the world over. To lower or raise wages unduly, with a view to private profit, and with no consideration for the common good, is contrary to social justice. This latter requires that by combining effort and good will to the extent possible, wages is so determined as to offer to the greatest number opportunities of employment and of securing for themselves suitable means of livelihood.[99]

The concern expressed by the pope on the relationship between wage fluctuation and unemployment is noteworthy. The pope states cautiously that a one-sided application of an economic purchasing power or cost theory of wages might result in unemployment. Consequently, the emphasis on the public economic good is the logical result of a good understanding of the common good and social justice.

Social Justice as the Guiding Principle of Socio-Economic Life

The pope had indicated that in order to effectively carry out the agenda set forth in QA, two conditions were indispensable: the reform of institutions and the correction of morals.[100] The reform of institutions was carried out chiefly through the principle of subsidiarity, which was discussed in chapter two.

The serious challenge to human solidarity that the pope notices is the free competition that individualism has accepted as the guiding principle for the economy. In order to curtail the aspirations of "rugged competition" the pope advanced new guiding principles for economic life: social justice and social charity.

> It is therefore very necessary that economic affairs be once more subjected to and governed by a true and effective guiding principle. Still less can this function be exercised by the economic supremacy which within recent times has taken the place of free competition: for this is a headstrong and vehement power, which, if it is to prove beneficial to mankind, needs to be curbed and governed by itself. More lofty and noble principles must therefore be sought in order to regulate this supremacy firmly and honestly: to wit, social justice and social charity. To that end all the institutions of public and social life must be imbued with the spirit of justice, and this justice must above all be truly operative. It must build up a juridical and social order able to pervade all economic activity. [Society charity] should be, as it were, the soul of this order. It is the duty of the State to safeguard effectively and to vindicate promptly this order, a task it will perform the more readily if it frees itself from those burdens which, as we stated above, are not properly its own.[101]

The question might be asked today: why was it necessary for the Church to set a guiding principle for economic life? Nell-Breuning, more than any other commentator on QA has provided the significance of a "principle" that is worthy of

99 QA Par. 74, p. 59.

100 QA Par. 77, p. 60.

101 QA Par. 88, p. 62.

note. According to him, the Latin word *principium* provides the key for understanding the concept of a guiding principle. Since *principium* recognizes the "autonomy or self-sufficiency of the principles proper to each department of culture...It means that the various cultural spheres stand, so to speak, on their own feet, are based on their own intrinsic nature, and follow the laws emanating from this foundation."[102] In essence, "economic science and moral science have each their own intrinsic principles."[103] Furthermore, Nell-Breuning indicated that the clearest use of *principium* that has stood the test of time was advanced by the Second Vatican Council to explain the relation between faith and reason as both possessing their own intrinsic proper principles without jeopardizing the role of the other.[104] Thus, the different spheres of culture ought not to oppose one another but should mutually support them in building the common good of society.

By advancing social justice and social charity as the new guiding principles of economic life, the pope brought about a restoration of the socio-economic lifestyle of society. There are two critical comments that are necessary at this stage: first, it should be pointed out that while social justice and social charity serve as guiding principles to socio-economic life, these principles may not be used interchangeably to mean economic justice; second, social justice and social charity are not meant to replace the important roles played by distributive justice and commutative justice in society.

Social Justice, Capitalism, Commutative Justice, and the Common Good

The pope examined the many changes that had taken place in economic life since Leo XIII. Thus, with the understanding that social justice is geared toward the common good, a pertinent distinction is made between capitalism as a system and the unfortunate consequences which result from its wrongful application.

> Leo XIII's whole endeavor was to adjust this economic system to the norms of right order. It is clear then that the system as such is not to be condemned. Surely it is not vicious of its very nature; but it violates right order whenever capital so employs the working or wage-earning classes as to divert business and economic activity entirely to its own arbitrary will and advantage without any regard to the human dignity of the workers, the social character of economic life, social justice, and the common good.[105]

Therefore, the arbitrary use of capital is described as negating the right order of the social economy. Leo XIII had declared very correctly that capital and labor

---

102 See Nell-Breuning, *Reorganization of Social Economy*, p. 81; cf. also p. 246.

103 Ibid. cf. also CA Par. 42, p. 51.

104 See Nell-Breuning, *Reorganization of Social Economy*, p. 82, note 1.

105 QA Par. 101, p. 64.

are intertwined: "Capital cannot do without labor, nor labor without capital."[106] The pope warned that the lack of balance between capital and labor leads to domination instead of free competition in three ways: "First, there is the struggle for dictatorship in the economic sphere itself; then, the fierce battle to acquire control of the State, so that its resources and authority may be abused in the economic struggles..."[107] This situation has led to different forms of "unfortunate consequences" which the pope believed lead to imperialism and human alienation. Nell-Breuning captures this point succinctly:

> The utter lack of conscientious scruples in this respect the pope characterizes by applying to international capital the Latin proverb: *ubi bene, ibi patria*, 'where a man's fortune is, there is his country.' In other words, a disposition of purest egotism completely lacking every interest in, and responsibility for, the fate of one's native land.[108]

Similarly, the connection between social justice and the common good is advanced without sacrificing in the process the important role played by commutative justice in the socio-economic life of the society toward promoting the common good of all members.

> The mutual relations between capital and labor must be regulated according to the laws of strict justice, called commutative justice, supported however by Christian charity. Free competition, and especially economic domination, must be kept within definite and proper bounds, and must be brought under effective control of the public authority; in matters pertaining to the latter's competence. The public institutions of the nations should be such as to make all human society conform to the requirements of the common good, that is, the norm of social justice. If this is done, that very important part of social life, the economic system, will of necessity be restored to sanity and right order.[109]

Oswald von Nell-Breuning has offered an interpretation that reflects the letter and spirit of the right relationship between commutative justice and social justice in relation to wages which should serve as a general principle since every case of commutative justice should posses this intrinsic relationship to social justice.

> According to *Quadragesimo Anno* the demand for a family wage is justified. In an economic system in which vast numbers of the population are forced to live on income from wages, this demand is absolute, as a demand of social justice. The public order in such a community contradicts social justice until conditions have been changed so that a family wage can be paid, not only to those workers who have a family, and must support these families solely from their wage income, but to every adult worker. As a demand of commutative justice, however, it is conditional; as soon as the demands of social justice have been fulfilled, and work has actually attained the value to which it

106 QA Par. 100, p. 64.

107 QA Par. 108, p. 65.

108 See Nell-Breuning, *Reorganization of Social Economy*, pp. 276–277.

109 QA Par. 110, p. 66.

> is entitled according to economic conditions, it automatically becomes the employer's duty to pay family wages.[110]

This means that the goal and end of social justice is the common good. It is the common good that is the measure of social justice. That is why it is possible to argue for restrictions on commutative and distributive justice in the name of the common good.

Social Justice and Social Charity

In QA Pius XI recognized social justice as the universal standard of all social relationships which leads them to the common good. However, the pope also considered the place of charity, that supernatural love which has as its foundation the infinite love of God for his people and would appear to have the last say over any socio-economic and political union expressed in justice alone. Having recognized social justice as the objective norm of all human social relationships, how can it be said at the same time that social charity has primacy over social justice?

In order to answer the above question, one will first trace the context in which Pius XI sought to make a distinction between the exercise and practice of charity on the one hand, and social charity as a virtue and norm of socio-economic organization. On the other hand, the pope made it clear that the works of charity alone could not adequately address the societal ills brought about by social distinctions in society, so the pope made this passionate appeal to the wealthy class who were satisfied with their charitable gestures:

> This state of things was quite satisfactory to the wealthy, who looked upon it as the consequence of inevitable and natural economic laws, and who, therefore, were content to abandon to charity alone the full care of relieving the unfortunate, as though it were the task of charity to make amends for the open violation of justice, a violation not merely tolerated, but sanctioned by legislators.[111]

Evidently, it was the goal of the pope to determine properly the roles of social charity and social justice in the socio-economic process. Both Calvez and Perrin declared that "Charity is the fundamental standard for the whole of social life, while justice is the objective universal standard for all the relationships which arise there. It follows that the connections between the two must be described in a manner which takes away nothing from either of them."[112] This is precisely what the pope did when he specified the role of charity in dealing with the institutional framework of justice in this way:

---

110 See Nell-Breuning, *Reorganization of the Social Economy*, p.178.

111 QA Par. 4, pp. 42–43.

112 See Calvez and Perrin, p. 163. Note that the discussion here borrows to some extent the views advanced in chapter VII of this work especially pp. 164–173.

> Now, in effecting this reform, charity "which is the bond of perfection," must play a leading part. How completely deceived are those inconsiderate reformers, who, zealous only for commutative justice, proudly disdain the help of charity. Charity cannot take the place of justice unfairly withheld, but, even though a state of things be pictured in which every man receives at last all that is his due, a wide field will nevertheless remain open for charity. For, justice alone, even though most faithfully observed, can remove indeed the cause of social strife, but can never bring about a union of hearts and minds. Yet this union, binding men together, is the main principle of stability in all institutions, no matter how perfect they may seem, which aim at establishing social peace and promoting mutual aid. In its absence, as repeated experience proves, the wisest regulations come to nothing...[113]

Perhaps, some analysis of the above papal statement will help one answer the question of the relationship between social charity and social justice alluded to earlier. From the onset, the pope said that while acts of charity are necessary and should be encouraged, there are some conditions when the duty of charity ought to become the requirement of justice. Nell-Breuning's pragmatic comments are relevant here when he said that the pope was in essence declaring that: "justice first, charity always."[114] This means that: "To withhold from a man what is legally his, and, instead of it, to donate to him out of open-handed benevolence something else, usually inferior, is self-contradictory."[115] In other words, the intentions to do justice and to engage in charitable deeds are not opposed to each other. The opposition lies in the direct withdrawal of what is due the person as a matter of justice, but not as a social gesture. Thus, the pope declares that "charity cannot take the place of justice unfairly withheld."[116]

Next, the pope affirms the proper place of charity, noting in the process that there is a universal primacy of the law of charity which is different from particular charitable acts. The primacy of the law of charity over justice is not meant to place charity and justice in an oppositional relationship. Rather, it is meant to place charity on a higher level transforming the work of justice. Charity does not take away anything from the specific requirements of justice but fashions it to completion. However, one does not in any way imply that the norm of justice is insufficient or incomplete. The real question lies with the practical applications of justice by persons in community which ought to and should be connected to charity because as the pope says: "justice alone, even though most faithfully observed, can remove indeed the cause of social strife, but can never bring about a union of hearts and minds."[117] Calvez and Perrin captured this fact clearly when they stated:

113 QA Par. 137, p. 74.

114 See Nell-Breuning, *Reorganization of the Social Economy*, p. 337.

115 Ibid.

116 Ibid.

117 Ibid.

> Charity goes beyond justice, but not beyond the sphere of social relations, which is governed as much by justice as by charity. It inspires actions more disinterested than any which look only to the remedying of the consequences of injustice. Quite apart from this, men ought to set no limit to the services they will do for each other. Charity incites men to do more for each other than justice demands. The Church demands no less, when it speaks of charity. Nor are the requirements of social justice in any way diminished: on the contrary, they are heightened, transformed from within, raised to the dignity of being "commandments" of charity.[118]

Since social justice and charity were advanced by Pope Pius XI to provide the guidance to individuals and groups in society, in order to help bring about reorganization of the social order, it is proper to briefly examine the relationship between social justice, and the principle which was at the heart of the reform of institutions, namely, the principle of subsidiarity.

Social Justice and Subsidiarity

The two guiding principles of socio-economic life (social justice and social charity) offered by Pius XI were meant to help fashion a just society that is neither individualistic nor collectivistic in nature. Thus, they were to help build an organic society that recognizes the contributions of the individual and the various occupational, social, economic and political groups or organs of the social body. In this way, the relationship between the parts and the whole is essentially that of promoting cooperation, social pluralism and the philosophy which Pesch called solidarism.

In QA, Pius XI described the new social order[119] he was advocating as embracing among other things "solidarism," "pluralism," and "organic" society. The emphasis here was to promote unity in diversity by encouraging autonomous persons and organs of society to forge cooperative ventures of self-help. The principle of subsidiarity ensures that the lesser organs or groups within the society are given their particular and proper responsibility, and that this shared responsibility by various social groups, is geared toward the personal dignity and common good of all members.

Thus, one could affirm that both social justice and subsidiarity are in solidarity in bringing about harmonious socio-economic activities toward the common good without engaging in collectivist tendencies in the process. Some of these tendencies include rugged competition in economic and political life and the ever-growing size of government. While healthy competition is recognized by QA as necessary for any proper socio-economic growth,[120] unlimited competition which

118 See Calvez and Perrin, p. 173.

119 QA Par. 84, p. 61.

120 QA Par. 88, p. 62.

seeks to reduce human beings to economic objects is considered an aberration. Moreover, the situation where citizens turn to the government for an answer to every aspect of their socio-economic life, largely brought about by uncontrolled free competition, simply and smoothly ushers in the totalitarian State by dominating individual creativity and liberty.

Consequently, subsidiarity serves as a check and balance in the social order. In this regard, QA was able to distinguish between "state" control and "social" control as part of the process of harmonization in society to help restore the disbanded organic structure.

> ...As we called it, things have come to such a pass that the highly developed social life, which once flourished in a variety of prosperous and interdependent institutions, has been damaged and all but ruined, leaving virtually only individuals and the State, with no little harm to the latter. But the State, deprived of a supporting social structure, and now encumbered with all the burdens once borne by the disbanded associations, is in consequence overwhelmed and submerged by endless affairs and responsibilities.[121]

Furthermore, it is evident that the subsidiary nature of social activity is grounded in the self-responsible and self-determining nature of the human person which was discussed at great length in chapter two. Suffice it now to say that persons in society seek to cooperate in social activity that is complementary and life-giving. They seek ways that would mutually support them toward the common good and not activities that would annihilate them. The pursuit of social justice rightly understood will embrace what Messner described as a "socially integrated democracy," which sets the ethical framework for socio-economic life ordered by the principles of solidarity, social justice and subsidiarity in this way:

> A social system in which freedom and order, individual interest and general interest, individual and community, are so correlated that the individual can make profit only if he is also promoting the general interest, and the community can benefit only so long as it respects and promotes the freedom of the individual. In such a correlation lies the essence of the social order.[122]

Social Justice in a Multiethnic and Pluralistic Society

The next question to be discussed is how to apply the theoretical framework for social justice in a pluralistic society with many diverse ethnic, cultural, religious, and political affiliations?

---

121 QA Par. 78, p. 60.

122 See Drummond, *Social Justice*, p. 116.

Building Community through Social Justice

The most basic structure that gives some stability and order to the social body in society is the common sense of the laws and values of a people, which are grounded in the day-to-day interrelationships in terms of their beliefs, market arrangements, family setup, politics, and generally accepted social practices. The norms by which a society governs itself, therefore, may be codified or unwritten. In different circumstances, such norms have some degree of binding force, though the codified norms such as the constitution of a State always receive much attention as the rule of law. To the extent that most people live by the acceptable norms of society and see them as useful and true, social order is maintained. However, to the extent that social norms are grossly violated, there exists generally social disorder. Thus, there needs to be a healthy interaction between social order and cultural values because culture is developed over long periods of struggle, exchange and interchange. Consequently, when the culture of a people is disconnected, the building process might be overwhelming because naïve and unconstructive arrangements which fail to recognize the cultural make-up are bound to collapse. T. S. Eliot made this point clearly when he said that when culture erodes "you must start painfully again, and you cannot put on a new culture readymade. You must wait for the grass to grow to feed the sheep to give wool out of which your new coat will be made."[123] In chapter four, I will show that the task of rebuilding a multiethnic and plural society such as Nigeria is more daunting and that some of the arrangements made so far by the successive governments in Nigeria reveal a gross underestimation of the enormous task involved in building a vibrant community. The study will propose how healthy partnership with civil society, decentralization of some major institutions and dedication on the part of the State might promote a society where citizens can have a fair say on how their culture and social order might interact for the common good of all members.

Another key issue that is central to the building of community is moral responsibility of the citizens. While to some degree morality springs out of the cultural experience of a community, it is not limited to human individual choices, lifestyles, values, and interpretations. Morality, as one has investigated, is also revealed and is grounded in nature and the Creator of the Universe whom we call God. In essence, the divine law envisions a moral order that promotes the common good and respects all human life and is able to serve as corrective to the moral order of society. The attempt to build a prosperous socio-economic and political community without moral standards may be likened to building a house without a solid foundation. The challenge then is how to develop social policy that is sensitive to human culture and at the same time transcendent of nature? T. William Boxx raised this question in similar fashion when he said that: "Our human nature is

123 T.S. Eliot, *Christianity and Culture: The Idea of a Christian Society and Notes Towards the Definition of Culture* (New York & London: Harcourt Brace Jovanovich, 1948), p. 157.

such that cultural arrangements cannot be subject to limitless reconstructions which might, for example, present a false dichotomy between the individual and society or which would tend to blur the distinctions or which would diminish the validity of moral life."[124] The concept of altruism is central to building a community that respects the personal interest of individuals and the common interest of society since they ought not to oppose each other in a healthy socio-political setup that is morally grounded.

Altruism and the Common Good

Andrew Reeve has offered a concise understanding of altruism that connotes both particular and universal human relationships in community that I intend to adopt as a working definition. It is worth quoting in detail.

> Benefiting other persons or interest-bearers. The common contrast with selfishness reveals some variations in the understanding of altruism, which may refer to a disposition, to an intention, or to behavior. Hence an altruistic person might intend to benefit others, but fail to do so when executing that intention. Altruism is sometimes understood as giving more consideration to others than oneself, and sometimes as giving equal consideration to oneself and others. Since there are commonly more 'others' than the decision-maker, the distinction usually lacks practical importance, but it may be significant in two-person cases. In discussions informed by game theory, a contrast is drawn between reciprocal altruism and universal altruism. Reciprocal altruists display that behavior towards those from whom they received it, or from whom they expect to receive it. Universal altruism, often seen as the central ethical prescription of Christianity, is unconditional. In socio-biological applications, it can be shown that the survival chances of individuals and groups depend not only on the incidence of selfishness and altruism, but also on the type of altruism in question.[125]

The above understanding takes into consideration three attitudes that individuals and groups are encouraged to cultivate in order that selfishness may be curtailed and thus enhance their survival in the community. These are: giving more consideration to others than oneself in a way that might be reciprocal; giving equal consideration to oneself and others; and the unconditional ethical self-giving of

124 T. William Boxx, "Building the Well-Ordered Society: Subsidiarity and Mediating Structures," *Building A Community of Citizens: Civil Society in the 21st Century*, (ed.), Don E. Eberly (Lanham, Maryland: University Press of America, 1994), p. 254. This work contains useful material for addressing the issues of nation building in a pluralistic society.

125 Andrew Reeve, "Altruism," *The Concise Oxford Dictionary of Politics*, (ed.), Iain Mclean (Oxford: Oxford University Press, 1996), p. 8. Some of the philosophical debate on altruism in relation to ethics can be found in these works by: Alasdair MacIntyre, "Egoism and Altruism," *The Encyclopedia of Philosophy, Vol. II*, (ed.), Paul Edwards (New York: Macmillan & Free Press, 1967), pp. 462–466. See his *After Virtue* 2nd ed. (Notre Dame, Indiana: University of Notre Dame Press, 1984), p. 229; also his *Whose Justice? Which Rationality?* (London: Duckworth, 1988), pp. 290ff.

oneself to others. How then might one combine self-interest and the interest of others in order to build one's community for the common good of all?

Patrick Riordan[126] has addressed the above question at some length, and I will borrow his analysis to a certain extent. According to Riordan, the desire and quest for an alternative way of dealing with the challenge that self-interest poses several questions to human solidarity[127] has led to much discussion about altruism as the desired alternative. Indeed, Riordan poses several questions that altruism is supposed to confront and wonders why anyone might embark on such a task in the face of the pope's prescription about the need for human solidarity.

> Why should anyone take responsibility for others, and bear extra costs and burdens which benefit them, not herself? Why should I have to pay to support people who do nothing for me? Translate this prescription into the debates on contemporary problems: world hunger, the destruction of the rainforests, the environment, the North-South divide, unemployment, and the burden of debt. Can the pope seriously expect all involved to take responsibility for everyone else? Hasn't each person enough to do to look out for herself, and hasn't each State enough to do in safeguarding its own interests?[128]

Thus, Riordan believes that the challenge of the common good is to "perform both descriptive and prescriptive functions, and that it can be of use in the thinking of social participants and in the analysis of scientific observers."[129] This is the context in which he addresses the concept of altruism as a moral philosophy that may be an essential component of the common good. However, Riordan departs from an understanding of altruism that is caught up in the "disjunction egoism-altruism," on two grounds. First, it does not provide an adequate model for explaining the role of the altruist agent and the beneficiary as involved in a communal project but rather as involved in a separate one.[130] Second, there is the risk of reducing the language of the common good to a fantasy world where one is encouraged to suppress self-interest while the interest of others becomes the determinant force for the common good. In such a situation, there could be the danger of irrelevance by some organs in society like the Churches who present themselves as champions of the common good that respects the interest of others, but self-interest appears to be at the core of the social fabric of both private and public discourse. Thus,

Riordan warns that:

126 Patrick Riordan, A *Politics of the Common Good* (Dublin, Ireland: The Institute of Public Administration, 1996), pp. 44–49 for details on the relationship of altruism to the Common Good.

127 Ibid. p. 28 where Riordan quotes John Paul II's social encyclical SRS Par. 38, p. 421.

128 Ibid. p. 29.

129 Ibid. p. 43.

130 Ibid. pp. 44–45.

> Rather than contributing to social and cultural cohesion, pursuit of a solution in terms of altruism may lead to further disintegration of the social fabric. The danger is that institutions in society like churches and educational bodies will be asked to train people in altruism, when the message communicated by the market, including competition for university places and jobs, is that self-interest is the only rational stance. Teachers and preachers would increasingly find themselves on the margins and outside the mainstream of serious business of society.[131]

In order to avert this danger, the need for a proper understanding of altruism that is devoid of the "disjunction egoism-altruism," is posited. Thus, our task is to offer a language of the common good that takes into consideration the self-interest of individuals and at the same time the interest of others in society. According to Riordan this means that:

> The political rhetoric which is required not only to make sense of people's willingness to cooperate but also to offer persuasive arguments to encourage greater efforts in common ventures...However, cooperation, common ventures, whether on the small scale or on the large scale in politics and society, require shared convictions on the interests at stake...We need a language for talking about our common interests, and a way of evaluating them. A vocabulary for speaking of the good and of the good life is the appropriate alternative to the language of interest, whether of self or another.[132]

Developing a language of shared interests and values in a pluralistic and multiethnic society would involve among other things developing a culture of human cooperation at different levels of society.

Social Justice, Social Groups, and Solidarity

The task of developing and maintaining a language of human cooperation among social groups is a difficult one but not impossible. There are several necessary levels of communication and interaction that may promote the recognition of shared values and interests in a community. In some circumstances, there might even be some clash of beliefs and cultures as a necessary state of purification in order to discover the necessary adjustment needed toward building a more socially cohesive community. John Gardner[133] has identified some of the critical stages for building a responsible community which will prove helpful in this research. According to Gardner the traditional community is bound to undergo some necessary adjustments in order to be responsive to the contemporary society.

131 Ibid. p. 49.

132 Ibid.

133 John Gardner, "Building a Responsive Community," *Rights and the Common Good: The Communitarian Perspective*, (ed.), Amitai Etzioni (New York: St. Martin's Press, 1995), pp. 167–178. This work is a useful resource which contains many articles on building communities.

The traditional community was homogeneous. Today most of us live with heterogeneity, and it will inevitably affect the design of our communities. Some of the homogeneity of traditional communities was based on exclusionary practices we cannot accept today. The traditional community experienced relatively little change from one year to the next. The vital contemporary community will not only survive change but, when necessary, seek it. The traditional community commonly demanded a high degree of conformity. Because of the nature of our world, the best of our contemporary communities today are pluralistic and adaptive, fostering individual freedom and responsibility within a framework of group obligation. The traditional community was often unwelcoming to strangers, and all too ready to reduce its communication with the external world. Hard realities require that present-day communities be in continuous and effective touch with the outside world, and our values require that they be inclusive.[134]

Thus, the traditional community will have to continually undergo a process of rebuilding and reformulating its shared values, beliefs and cultural practices. Some of the most cherished values will be passed on to the next generation with renewed vigor and meaning. Other beliefs and cultural practices will become obsolete and irrelevant, losing their meaning in view of new realities. In the midst of these challenges, the role of the extended family system and the levels of support it provided or did not provide for the social structuring of the community would play a vital role in reshaping new models of social groups.

Another important stage of community rebuilding is the identification by Gardner of the "ingredients of community."[135] First, the type of community envisaged by Gardner which we support is "...a set of attributes that may appear in diverse settings - a school, a congregation, a town, a suburb, a work place, a neighborhood."[136] We will expand our understanding of community for the sake of relevance to include a clan, a mono-tribal village, a multi-tribal village, a mono-religious town, or a multi-religious town. These categorizations will become helpful in chapter four when we deal with the Nigerian social structure.

Gardner proposes that "wholeness incorporating diversity" is necessary to promote and maintain the different and constantly interacting system of multiple cultures. The goal of social justice would be to ensure that the common good of all is upheld within the law by recognizing and accepting the individuality of the different social groups, while at the same time allowing some room for the social fabric of society to be governable and relatively peaceful.

> The play of conflicting interests in a framework of shared purposes is the drama of a free society. It is a robust exercise and a noisy one, not for the fainthearted or the tidy-minded. Diversity is not simply "good" in that it implies breadth of tolerance and sym-

---

134 Ibid. p. 167.

135 Ibid. pp. 168–177 for detailed explanation of these themes.

136 Ibid. p. 168.

pathy. A community of diverse elements has greater capacity to adapt and renew itself in a swiftly changing world.[137]

Thus, a philosophy of pluralism is the key to maintaining the balance between diversity and wholeness. Such a philosophy will make allowance for open dissent and critical comments without sacrificing one's identity in the process. This would mean allowing minority groups to present their vision within the setting of larger groups. Here, concrete grassroots arrangements for groups to dialogue with one another are fundamental to community rebuilding. The emergence of a new crop of leaders both in government and within civil society that will engage in broad based initiatives rather than engage in divisiveness by exploiting diversity cannot be overemphasized.

Furthermore, Gardner opines that there is the need for "a reasonable base of shared values," to help build a responsible community. To expect that members of the community agree on everything is a direct violation of the diversity required. Therefore, the community ought to promote its cherished values by not only talking about them but, most especially, by living and practicing them. The community where respect, rights, equality, freedom of speech, education, are taught and promoted will embrace them. However, the community that constantly lives in fear of armed bandits, bribery, corruption, nepotism, tribalism, and violence will find it difficult to be a healthy community. The role of social justice is to encourage that we teach the truth by living it. Let the diverse social groups recognize and put together their shared values be they religious, cultural or political as long as they promote the common good of all in community.

The need for caring, trust, and teamwork is encouraged as necessary steps toward responsible community building. We examined in chapter one how an African community engaged in the process of self-government,[138] and was able to provide for themselves the essentials of life as dictated by the circumstances of lived experience. Today, some of these duties and responsibilities have been taken over by local, state, and federal governments. Even so, there are still some functions that remain that government alone cannot adequately provide. These include building trust, care of the community, and teamwork.

Social Justice, Civil Society, and Development

The goal of the analysis is to ensure that some of the shared cultural values, beliefs, and practices will be respected by the government of their choosing and not by some oligarchy or unrepresentative group of despots. To ensure effective participation of the majority of the people, one will have to look at the role of civil society groups as trusted partners in the process of governance. Thus, recognizing smaller

137 Ibid. p. 169.

138 See chapter one, p. 23ff.

organizations at the grassroots level such as Churches, ethnic and tribal group associations, labor unions, traditional councils, local school systems, and market associations, where intimate relationships are central to authentic human existence, is crucial to upholding social justice, law and order and promoting participation and social development.

Wogaman has suggested that it is essential to have these "mediating structures" because they help to link people with one another, link people with sources of meaning, and link people with power centers.[139] Such a linkage is important because it is not enough to look at the humanizing role of these mediating structures. It is necessary for these structures to understand how governments work so that they may be able to guide against manipulation by government for its ends. In the case of Church organizations, for instance, one agrees with Wogaman that "The Churches' best contributions as mediating institutions are nurturing interpersonal relationships, transmitting traditions, and providing avenues of access to power, not implementing the State's purpose."[140] Thus, there is no need to draw an absolute dichotomy between the Church and the State because they are both aspects of the one society. However, they need to both uphold and maintain their respective roles even though, in some cases, cooperative ventures might become inevitable and necessary.

The role of organized labor in the form of unions and workers' associations that are free from government control also supports the civic responsibility and participation of the citizens. That is why one needs to pay attention to the position of Tom Kahn who opined that for most people in some communities and societies, "unions are schools of democracy":

> They are the place where workers, many of them with relatively little formal schooling, learn how to raise their hands, be recognized, get up, say something, and sit down. They learn how to organize and run a meeting; and they learn about parliamentary procedure, which is important as a formalization of the rules of where your rights stop and someone else's begin. That is, parliamentary procedure teaches us that the other person has rights, too: no one has the right to talk all night without giving others a chance to speak, and a speaker cannot be hooted off the platform or out of the hall by those who disagree...Trade union democracy is imperfect, like other forms of democracy, but it is the only place many people ever have a chance to learn about democracy at all.[141]

---

139 J. Philip Wogaman, "The Church as Mediating Institution: Theological and Philosophical Perspective," *Democracy and Mediating Structures: A Theological Inquiry*, (ed.), Michael Novak (Washington, D.C.: American Enterprise Institute for Public Policy Research, 1980), pp. 70–74 for details.

140 Ibid. p. 81.

141 Tom Kahn, "Organized Labor as a Mediating Structure," *Democracy and Mediating Structures*, pp. 129–130.

Thus, from trade union democracy emerges a decentralized structure of governance where local leadership is selected by the people and for the people to act as their representatives. The local leadership organize themselves at ward, state, regional and national levels. In so doing, trade unions respect the principle of subsidiarity by acting as support to their members in order that they may help themselves. Moreover, local leaders are not sidelined by those at the State or national levels but mutually work together for the common good of the members.

Another key mediating structure that promotes civil society is the Family.[142] The family is the oldest institution known to human beings. While there may be variations in family setup due to cultural, social, environmental, and religious influences, human values of respect and honor for the integrity of the human person as an individual being with social obligations appear to be universal. Thus, the extent to which families are nurtured in communities determines to a larger degree the type of society one is developing.

In Africa, the theme: "The Church as Family," has been one concrete way of promoting the role of the family in society. Having identified the different ways in which the model of Church as family is relevant to its social context, the bishops offered critical comments that show the centrality of the family in relation to social justice.

> The family is indeed the first school of justice. By the Creator's will it is the basic cell of society within which the young take their first steps in the exercise of social justice, solidarity and fraternity. Nothing can take the place of this natural environment where so many young Africans have learned the rules of life in society, respect for other people and social responsibility. Alas, the profound social and cultural changes we are experiencing have shaken the very structure of the family which is finding it more and more difficult to carry out its role as it is plagued by a whole arsenal of false human values...We must do all in our power to ensure that the next generation on our continent will be able to enjoy the protection, security and love of a family. If each child is able to grow up within a healthy family, a great step will have been taken along the road to education for justice.[143]

In this connection, one is able to re-echo the affirmation made by the 1971 Synod of Catholic bishops in their document *Justice in the World* (JW), while reflecting on the meaning of justice as a tool for promoting positive and concrete action in socio-political life and relations between Church and State.

> Action on behalf of justice and participation in the transformation of the world fully appear to us as a constitutive dimension of the preaching of the Gospel, or, in other

142 See Brigitte Berger, "The Family as a Mediating Structure," *Democracy and Mediating Structures*, pp. 144–179 for details on this topic.

143 "Justice and Evangelization in Africa," *Justice, Marriage and Evangelization in Africa Today* (Accra, Ghana: SECAM, 1981), Par. 21, p.9. This declaration was made over two decades ago but the task, namely, to provide education for social justice to the family for the common good of society is still relevant today.

words, of the Church's mission for the redemption of the human race and its liberation from every oppressive situation.[144]

The above statement has and continues to greatly influence social responsibility based on Gospel values to promote the common good of members of the society.

Questions for Further Reflection

1. Does the biblical perspective clarify your notion of social justice? Explain.
2. What is the relationship between social justice and the common good in terms of human work, wages, and welfare in your community?
3. Discuss the reasons why the attainment of social justice in your community is possible or not possible.
4. Can you offer any ideas, practical ways, and suggestions, as to how social justice can become an important tool for your community to make positive change in people's lives?
5. What can you do to make your community oriented toward social justice? How might others join you in the process?

144 JW "Introduction," *Catholic Social Thought: The Documentary Heritage*, (eds.), David J. O'Brien and Thomas A. Shannon, p. 289. See Charles M. Murphy, "Action for Justice as Constitutive of the Preaching of the Gospel: What Did the 1971 Synod Mean?" *Readings in Moral Theology: Official Catholic Social Teaching* (eds.), Charles E. Curran and Richard A. McCormick (Mahwah, New Jersey: Paulist Press, 1986), pp. 150–166 for a critical commentary on this subject.

4

THE NIGERIAN SOCIAL CONTEXT: A CRITICAL ANALYSIS

A Critical and Analytical History of the Nigerian State: 1914 to the Present[1]

The analysis of the historical development of the Nigerian State has its origins in 1914 and revolves around four major issues: the social context of the Nigerian State; the State and Citizenship in Nigeria; the Political and Administrative Structures in Nigeria, and the state of Labor and Capital in Nigeria.

The year 1914 is significant in Nigeria because it is the official birthday of the nation. January 1, 1914, the day when Lord Lugard effected the amalgamation of the Protectorate of Northern Nigeria Colony and Protectorate of Southern Nigeria which were previously administered as separate though related territories, is generally regarded as the

---

1 The historical analysis of Nigeria was informed largely by the following important works. Eghosa E. Osaghae, *Crippled Giant: Nigerian Since Independence* (Bloomington and Indianapolis: Indiana University Press, 1998), pp. 1–30; Rotimi T. Suberu, *Federalism and Ethnic Conflict in Nigeria* (Washington, DC: United States Institute of Peace Press, 2001), pp. 19–46; Paul E. Lovejoy, "Historical Setting," *Nigeria: A Country Study*, (ed.), Helen Chapin Metz (Washington, DC: Library of Congress, 1992), pp. 3–83. In these works, some of the structural classifications that have shaped the historical developments in Nigeria are evaluated as the basis for Nigerian politics.

> birth date of the Nigerian State. Before it—indeed, before the advent of colonial conquest and rule—there was no Nigeria and the likelihood that a State like it could have evolved was quite remote. What existed in the period before the establishment of colonial rule was a motley of diverse groups whose histories and interactions, interlaced as they were by external influences—principally trade with Europeans and with the Arab world—had nevertheless crystallized in three clearly discernible regional formations by the end of the nineteenth century.[2]

Thus, it is pertinent to trace the consequences of the emergence of Nigeria and to show how some of the structural imbalances that existed at its birth have continued to manifest as birthmark scars. Hence, some understanding of the structural setup of the major regional groupings is inevitable in the attempt to put into perspective the events that led to the amalgamation of Nigeria and the challenges thereafter.

In Northern Nigeria the Islamic influence was widespread due largely to prolonged trade relations established along the trans-Saharan route and migrations which brought the Hausa States, the Kanem Bornu Empire and the Fulanis mainly to North Africa, the Mediterranean, and the larger section of the Islamic world together. Another major influence of Islamic push in the North was the event of 1804 during which the Fulanis launched a jihad in order to bring the peoples of the Middle Belt region under a theocratic and centralized system of rule by the Sokoto Caliphate. The Islamic incursion, while it proved successful in the far north of Nigeria, met fierce opposition around the Benue and Plateau regions where groups like the Tiv, Idoma, and the Ngas and Berom refused to embrace the Islamic religion. However, the Islamic surge brought its challenges. According to Osaghae, this Islamic incursion had two major consequences "...which received reinforcement and elaboration under colonial rule and shaped inter-group relations in Nigeria in the post-independence period."[3] First, the Muslim groups and their followers were presented and accepted as the major group in the North by the colonial power. This made non-Islamic groups virtually powerless in the face of the numerical strength of the Muslims. Moreover, the British policy of indirect rule ensured that "appointees of the Caliphate and Emirates were imposed as rulers on the non-Muslim groups,"[4] to enhance the political agenda of the colonial power. Second, the colonizers accepted the Sokoto Caliphate's political and social organization as the ideal to spread and enforce near and far in what was emerging as Nigeria.

In the West, the Oyo and Benin kingdoms were formidable and provided the political, social, and religious climate that would shape this region of Nigeria. The major tribal groups that formed the Oyo kingdom were the Yorubas; they were

2 See Osaghae, *Crippled Giant*, p. 2.

3 Ibid.

4 Ibid.

made up of several sub-groups and were linked to a common ancestry traced to the legendary Oduduwa (the creator of the earth and ancestor of the Yoruba kings). The Benin kingdom consisted of different ethnic communities like the Edo speaking people made up of the Urhobo, Isoko, and some Igbos with no common ancestry, who were forged into the kingdom. Both the Oyo and Benin Kingdoms witnessed several communal wars in the late nineteenth century that gradually led to their decline and, consequently, the emergence of new regional powers and political arrangements. According to Osaghae the reorganization of political loyalties in the Western region was orchestrated by the Northern political figures in alliance with the Colonialists for both economic and religious interests.

> The wars and crises in the West were instigated and fuelled by the meddling of Fulani jihadists whose sphere of influence spread to Oyo and other northernmost parts of the West, and European traders and colonialists who, particularly since the era of the slave trade, pursued manipulative and divisionist strategies to gain trade advantages and retain political-cum-military control in the region.[5]

Finally, in the Eastern region there were many ethnic groups like the Igbo, Ijaw, Efik, Annang, Kalabari, and others who organized their village settlements in a non-centralized fashion. The largest group was the Igbo speaking people who occupied most of the land in the eastern region. While upholding the identity of the sub group, the Igbos were united by Arochukwu, an Igbo clan of mixed Igbo and Ibibio origins who had entered into various alliances and treaties with Igbo clans. These groups had some political and religious power in many of the areas of their jurisdiction. Some scholars have wrongly argued that these societies were "stateless"[6] because they had no centralized government. In fact, though, they were organized around local tribal rule in an autonomous manner, which maintained some degree of independence and limited power structure within the ethnic group.

The emergence of the Nigerian State was the creation of the British colonial power that brought their political might as an empire to bear on the independent city-states in the West-African region. They were able, through collaboration with local chiefs, to effect in-direct rule and to fashion a nation that would serve its needs and, hopefully, the needs of those who would live in the State. Following the amalgamation and the evolution of the Nigerian federation, the British ruled Nigeria as a unitary State under the guidance of the Macpherson constitution of 1951 as a quasi-federal unit.

> Through a piecemeal and combined process of trade monopoly, military superiority, 'divide and rule' and outright conquest, the various groups were brought together under the aegis of colonial authority. The nature of this bringing together requires elaboration because of the far-reaching implications it had for state and nation-building. British acquisition of territory in Nigeria had three different strands which roughly approxi-

---

5 Ibid. p. 3; cf. also Paul E. Lovejoy, *Nigeria: A Country Study*, pp. 6–9.

6 See Lovejoy, pp. 9–10.

mated to the regional formations described above: the colony of Lagos and hinterland (Western) protectorate; the oil rivers and later Niger Delta protectorate (Eastern); and the Northern protectorate.[7]

Rotimi Suberu[8] has shown how the colonial federal legacy that sought to bring harmony within Nigeria's major ethnic groups was flawed by a system of centralization of power that encouraged corruption and political fragmentation on ethnic grounds. He proposed a decentralized system that would bring about constitutional reform in Nigerian federal character that would face the challenges posed by the ethno-political complexity of the State.

The Lyttelton Constitution of 1954 formally established Nigeria as a three-region federation. The constitution provided the framework for Nigeria's three large, but unequal, regional groups that control the internal and administrative arrangements of the nation, while the central government held on to external affairs and inter-regional matters. According to Suberu, one can trace three interrelated factors that brought about a substantial change to the federal form of government adopted in Nigeria in 1954.

1. The staggering diversity and sheer strength of ethno-linguistic forces in the federation.
2. The differential regional impact of colonial administration, modernization, and mobilization.
3. The enormous attraction that federalist guarantees of sub-national autonomy had for the emergent, regionally based Nigerian successor elites.[9]

The combined force of the above mentioned factors supported by British power produced Nigeria as "one of the most ethnically diverse countries in the world" and probably the one most deeply divided amongst all the countries created during the European occupation of Africa.[10] Therefore, "within Nigeria's borders were to be found, some 380 linguistic modes of communication, as many as twenty distinct geographical regions, and such divergent forms of political organization as clan communities, villages, republics, city-states, chiefdoms, kingdoms, and a Caliphate."[11]

Furthermore, the political stratification of the nation on ethnic affiliations prepared the ground on which the nation may be placed in perpetual tension as

---

7 See Osaghae, *Crippled Giant*, p. 4.

8 Rotimi T. Suberu, *Federalism and Ethnic Conflict in Nigeria* (Washington, D.C.: United States Institute of Peace Press, 2001), pp. 19–46, 171–206.

9 Ibid. p. 19.

10 See Suberu, p. 20; cf. John P. Mackintosh, "Federalism in Nigeria," *Political Studies*, 10/3 (1962): 223–224; and Eghosa E. Osaghae, "The Status of State Governments in Nigeria's Federalism," *Publius: The Journal of Federalism*, 22/3 (1992): 181–200.

11 See Suberu, p. 20.

each ethnic group sought power to protect its turf. Suberu captured this situation more clearly:

> The most politically salient feature of Nigeria's ethnic diversity, however, was the distribution of ethnic groups into a relatively centralized ethnic structure, with the Hausa-Fulani, Yoruba, and Igbo formations predominating. As the rivalries among these three groups crystallized into bitter political struggles during the late colonial era (under the combined impact of economic competition and electoral mobilization), it became increasingly clear to all interested observers that only by some form of highly decentralized political arrangements could the major groups be accommodated within a single country. Nigeria's federalism, therefore, developed as an institutional response both to the federal character of the society (with its sharp territorial ethno-linguistic divisions), and to the explosive demographic configuration of the ethnic structure, which pitted three major nationalities in fierce competition with one another.[12]

However, one may equally make a case for some positive role by the British colonial power to establish a federal government in Nigeria, which they hoped would serve as a uniting factor for a nation whose people are deeply multi-national, multi-religious, multicultural, multiethnic, multi-regional, and multi-structural. Thus, the argument was made that the British served "...as a force for both integration and differentiation in Nigeria."[13] According to Suberu, one needs to examine three major British colonial policies in order to make a balanced assessment of their role in Nigeria.

The first policy was that of indirect rule, which administered the Nigerian people through their existing political and social institutions. In Northern Nigeria, particularly, the emirates wielded much power and used this to enforce the system of taxation that was welcomed by the colonial power and which ensured submission by the subjects. In so doing, the position of the emirs was assured and re-enforced. In some parts of the country where such hierarchical system of traditional governance was lacking, the indirect rule that operated gave prominence to tribal political institutions. Accordingly, the policy of indirect rule in Nigeria served "to reinforce the most conservative features of local political institutions, perpetuate communal consciousness, and scuttle the forces that had been pushing toward inter-ethnic integration or assimilation in the pre-colonial era."[14]

The second colonial policy adopted by the British was to isolate the emirs of Northern Nigeria from engaging in the process of modernization that was taking place and having effective change in most of the North central region known as the "Middle Belt" of Nigeria. There was some treaty between the British and Fulani emirs to maintain and uphold the system of indirect rule as long as the British remained in power. Christian missionaries were prevented from carrying

12 Ibid.

13 Ibid. p. 21.

14 See Mackintosh, "Federalism in Nigeria," p. 223.

out their activities in Northern Nigeria, and any form of contact with Southern Nigeria was viewed with disdain because of the imagined threat to the theocratic position of the emirs. Suberu made this case concretely:

> Thus, despite the amalgamation of 1914, direct official political intercourse between northerners and southerners did not take place until 1946, when the former were invited to participate for the first time in the advisory central legislative council in Lagos. This insularity ultimately engendered a combustible North-South duality. The most poignant expression of this dichotomy was the huge historical Southern head start over the North in virtually every aspect of modernization, including education, per capita income, urbanization, wage employment, commerce, and industrialization.[15]

The uneven development between northern and southern Nigeria, coupled with the quest for political and economic security, especially by the Hausa-Fulani in the North, and the fear of domination by the south on the north, were at the roots of much of the political instability in Nigeria during the fifties and sixties; this continues to plague Nigerian politics and society today.

The third British colonial policy was that of administrative regionalism.[16]

In 1939, the plan to divide Nigeria into three regional groups was carried out. The regions were Northern, Eastern, and Western provinces, which eventually became administrative regions under the Richards Constitution of 1946, and were regarded by the British as the "natural" regions of the emerging Nigerian federation. How "natural" these regions where could be traced to the Benue and Niger Rivers which coincided with the main trade routes through which the British entered Nigeria via Lagos in 1856, and which also became the major stronghold of each of the major ethnic groups. Therefore, one can decipher that the 'natural' regions were determined by the extent to which they served British interests, at least via their policy of indirect rule. The British turned down most of the agitations by minority groups for self rule, in order to move away from the oppressive rule by the majority tribe in a region. The British remained unperturbed with their commitment to the three-fold regional structure in Nigeria. The creation of new regions for the minority groups was to take effect only as a last resort.[17] Suberu argues that the British were prepared to listen to agitations put forward by ethnic minority groups only if it meant shifting the proposed date for Nigeria's independence. Since this was too much of a concession to make, ethnic minorities were coerced into the tripartite regional system as a basis for Nigeria's federalism which became the bane of Nigeria's self-rule.

---

15 See Suberu, pp. 22–23.

16 Ibid. p. 23.

17 Crawford Young, "Patterns of Social Conflict: State, Class and Ethnicity," *Daedalus* 3/2 (1982): 73; Larry Diamond, "Issues in the Constitutional Design of a Third Nigerian Republic," *African Affairs* 86/343 (1987): 212.

> Any hope for the satisfaction of ethnic minority autonomist pressures was finally dashed at the 1958 London Constitutional Conference when the Colonial Office explained that any proposals for immediate territorial reforms could only mean the postponement of the agreed 1960 date for the granting of independence. Thus, although the conference agreed on constitutional provisions for creating new regions in the future, it inevitably endorsed the tripartite regional structure that was to become a source of great instability after independence.[18]

So far, as indicated above, there have been several factors that have led to the creation of Nigeria's federalism. The British colonial policies set the tone for maintaining the three-tier regional grouping of the country following the three major ethnic majority tribes. In so doing, the ethnic minorities were unwittingly grouped to serve both the colonial policy and the ethnic majority tribes, and so the smaller tribes were immersed in the larger ones, thereby losing their identity. The rise in ethnic tensions in post-independence Nigeria is a direct consequence of the failure to recognize the identity of minority groups and the important role that these groups of people will play in the Nigerian federation.

Similarly, Nigeria's nationalist leaders supported the British colonial policies and collaborated significantly to fashion the type of constitutional self-government that emerged in Nigeria. In hindsight, it appears that these leaders were each promoting their regional base and only discussed the Nigerian question in so far as it served their purpose of being at the federal level of government with the aim of advancing their regional cause. Suberu supports this position by advancing two complementary perspectives.

> As Ladipo Adamolekun and Bamindele Ayo have argued, Nigerian federalism "resulted from a consensus decision reached between Nigeria's nationalist leaders and the British colonial authorities." Beginning with the landmark Ibadan General Constitutional Conference of 1950, the Nigerian political class collaborated with the British to fashion the basic outlines of a constitution for a self-governing Nigeria. At the conference, and in subsequent constitutional deliberations, the majority of Nigeria's leaders increasingly and persistently emphasized the need to grant the fullest autonomy to the country's component groups or regions. Indeed, as Eme Awa has shown, these leaders behaved as if "original sovereignty" lay with the regions, which could, therefore, appropriately allocate functions to the center and reserve the residue to themselves.[19]

Furthermore, the agitation for regional self-government reached its peak in 1957 when each of the regions was granted their autonomy. The direct consequence of this was the emergence of regional political parties. In Northern Nigeria, the Northern People's Congress (NPC) was the overseer of that region with Abubakar Tafawa Balewa as leader of the legislature. In Western Nigeria, the Action Group (AG) was in charge of the regional government and its prominent leader was Obafemi Awolowo. In Eastern Nigeria, the National Council for Nigeria and the

---

18 See Suberu, *Federalism and Ethnic Conflict in Nigeria*, p. 24.

19 Ibid. pp. 24–25.

Cameroons (NCNC) was the regional party which took charge of governance and its undisputed leader was Nnamdi Azikiwe. Each regional party sought to have a stake in the emerging Nigerian federation and so loyalty to regional issues became a major yardstick for aspiring leaders to engage in politics, electioneering and party coalition leading up to the formation of the first republic when Nigeria gained its independence from Britain on October 1, 1960.

Nigeria's First Republic, 1960–1966

The period in Nigeria's history referred to as the first republic covers the five years and three months span from October 1, 1960, to January, 1966, following its independence. The major characteristics of the 1954 Federal Constitution and those of the 1960 Independence Constitution were merged to form the first Nigerian post-independence civilian administration. The Prime Minister was Sir Abubakar Tafawa Balewa, and the President in 1963 when Nigeria formally became a Republic was Nnamdi Azikiwe.

According to Suberu, the main constitutional features that provided the governing framework during the early stages of independence gave much power to the federal government.

The Independence Constitution gave the federal government exclusive control of external affairs, defense, currency, mines and minerals, and the major forms of communication and transportation. The constitution's list of concurrent central and regional powers included higher education, industrial and water-power development, the judiciary, the police, and the regulation of labor, including the medical and legal professions. Unenumerated residual powers, including responsibility for a wide range of expensive socioeconomic programs in health, education, and agriculture, were left to the regions.[20]

The challenge of the First Republic was how to balance the power of the growing federal government with the growth of a regional party system. The pre-independence policy of granting governing status to the regions was now overshadowed with the emergence of a Nigerian federation as the seat of governmental power. There were instances when the regional autonomy and the federal autonomy conflicted in matters of statecraft, particularly in areas of revenue allocations and development loans. In fact, "the growing subordination of the regions to the center in economic development matters was reinforced by the inelastic nature of regional tax revenues, especially personal income taxes, and the downturn in international prices for regionally controlled primary commodities."[21] There were some political developments that indicated the subordination of the regions in favor of the federal government. In the Western region, a rift in the Action Group party

20 Ibid. p. 26.

21 Ibid. p. 27.

provided the opportunity for the NCNC federal coalition government to step in after declaring a state of emergency and take control of both the legislative and executive arms of government and to divide the Mid-Western region under new leadership.[22]

Moreover, the large size of the Northern region in comparison to the other regions ensured its dominance in political and economic activities. Since the Northern People's Congress and the NCNC were in coalition at the federal level, it was inevitable that the population size of the NPC would come to bear on a federal structure of government. Billy Dudley affirms: "with political power shifting to the center, the real levers of power [was] actually to be found in the North. Federal super ordination…in practice turned out to be Northern dominance."[23]

Similarly, the federal structure aided and abetted conflicts between majority and minority ethnic groups between regions. The Tiv crisis of February and November 1964 was a case in point where the attempt by the Tiv to be excised from the North turned into a blood bath that led to the death of about 326 civilians and eleven policemen.[24]

Badru's perspective presents one with some understanding of the challenges that existed prior to Nigerian's independence and the consequences that befell the First Republic.

The complex pattern of antagonistic relationships within the class of the nationalist elite that fought for independence is intersected by class and ethnicity. The majority of the nationalists who were at the forefront of the struggle for independence were themselves representatives of hidden social classes who, because of some traditional or religious reasons, did not partake directly in the struggle for the control of the colonial state. In essence we have, after independence, at least on the surface, a state structure that reflected the economic interests of the feudal oligarchy, particularly from the North and the Lagos based comprador elite. The defining characteristic of the neocolonial state shortly after independence was the struggle between the feudal and the comprador elite in terms of the sort of alliance each would form with metropolitan capital.[25]

Thus, it seems reasonable to suggest that the major challenge before the first Nigerian administration was how to balance power between the central federal government and the regions. The government favored centralization without making adequate provision for the regions. Henceforth, the challenge of those who

---

22 Ibid. 28.

23 Billy Dudley, "Federalism and the Balance of Political Power in Nigeria," *Journal of Commonwealth Political Studies* 4/1 (1966): 21.

24 Kenneth Post, and Michael Vickers, *Structure and Conflict in Nigeria*, 1950–1966 (London: Heinemann, 1973), p. 200.

25 Pade Badru, *Imperialism and Ethnic Politics in Nigeria* (Trenton: Africa World Press, 1998), pp. 27–28.

serve as representatives of the regions will be how to draw resources from the center to the regions. This process has sometimes led to unhealthy tension among the different regional groupings in the Country as they attempt to seek recognition from the federal government. At times, the perception of neglect, domination, and control by one region over the other has led to grave consequences as one discusses next the emergence of military rule in Nigeria.

Federalism and Military Rule, 1966–1979

On January 15, 1966, the First Republic was overthrown in a bloody coup d'etat organized by a group of young officers mostly from the Eastern region of Nigeria and masterminded by Major Kaduna Nzeogwu. Since most of the regional leaders were executed, a vacuum of political leadership was created and the general officer commanding the Nigerian army, Major General J.T.U. Aguiyi-Ironsi,[26] an Igbo by tribe, became the first military head of State and ruled Nigeria for six months.

The promulgation of Decree Number 34 of 1966, which dismantled the federal system of government and replaced it with a unitary system, was seen by the Northerners as an attempt by the Igbo's to control both the political and economic goods of Nigeria.

One major consequence of a unitary structure was the abolition of regional public services and the establishment of one public service for the nation. Since Northern Nigeria was less developed than the South, the north felt threatened both by the decree which repealed the "federal character principle that sought to give each area some parity of representation,"[27] and by the imbalance which followed the prosecution of those who were involved in the January, 1966 coup d'etat. As one northern observer puts it "It was the height of northern opposition to unitarism that the countercoup of July 1966 took place. Most top-ranking Igbo officers, including Ironsi, lost their lives; the 'status quo' of northern dominance was restored."[28]

In July, 1966, a second bloody coup d'etat took place and was headed mostly by officers from the north including Major Murtala Mohammed and Captain T.Y. Danjuma. This coup was seen by the South as a revenge mission by the North to avenge the death of Northern officers in the January, 1966, coup. The North saw

26 Eghosa E. Osaghae, *Crippled Giant*, p. 56. It is an open-ended question as to the extent of Ironsi's involvement in the 1966 coup. He embarked on sweeping changes that would bring unity to Nigeria but his political naïveté, the perception from the North that he was promoting an Igbo agenda and the abrogation of Nigeria's federal character by Decree no. 34 among other things led to a countercoup mostly by officers from Northern Nigeria, who saw his agenda as a major threat to their well-being. See Osaghae, pp. 57–61.

27 See Osaghae, "Government and Politics," *Nigeria: A Country Study*, p. 215.

28 Ibid. p. 216.

it as an attempt to maintain a balance of political power and to restore the true federal character of Nigeria. On August 1, 1966, Lt. Col. Yakubu Gowon, a Christian consensus candidate from the *Ngas* minority tribe in the Middle Belt region of Northern Nigeria, became the second military head of State in the midst of growing opposition from the Eastern and Southern parts of Nigeria.

The Gowon administration was ushered into office at the height of deep national crises. The first major policy act by the administration was to restore the federal and regional systems of government; this action of government would trigger the deep sentiments of animosity that the Eastern region perceived were directed to it by the new administration because of the number of killed during and after the Northern led countercoup which brought Gowon to power. At an ad hoc meeting summoned by Gowon to discuss the issue of constitutional reform for Nigeria's future, Colonel Chukwuemeka Odumegwu Ojukwu, military governor of the Eastern region, insisted that any region that wished to secede from the federation be allowed to do so. The other regions were mostly in favor of confederate type system of government to replace the federal government. The conference produced no tangible results and ended in a stalemate.

In January, 1967, at a summit of military leaders in Aburi, Ghana, some attempt was made to resolve the growing tension between the Eastern region and the federal government. The military officers recommended the creation of a loose confederation of regions as the mid-way between regional and federal governments. The Gowon regime, anticipating that the growing desire by the Eastern region to secede might be realized, directed the creation of twelve States to replace the four regions. This move by Gowon was meant to achieve two results: a response to the call by minority groups for creation of States; and a diffusing of tension between the East and the federal government. In reality, neither goal was achieved; instead, the Eastern region declared the State of Biafra, independent of Nigeria. This situation would result in the Nigerian civil war between the federal troops and the Eastern region supported Biafran army for almost three years.

The Nigerian Civil War, July 1967 to January 1970

The announcement of the "Republic of Biafra" was made by the military governor of the Eastern region, Col. Ojukwu on May 27, 1967. The Gowon administration responded by declaring a state of emergency on the Nigerian federation and called Ojukwu's actions illegal, rebellious, and unconstitutional. However, the actual fighting between the federal troops and Biafran army started on July 6, 1967. Initially, the Gowon regime called on the police to take action with the hope that the uprising would not last long. But foreign involvement changed it to a protracted civil war.

> Stremlau (1977) reminds us that with only 10 million pounds in foreign reserve, Ojukwu could not have waged a war for as long as he did without external support. French sup-

> plies of arms, which averaged 300 tons per week in September-October 1968, gave the life-line to a practically defeated Biafra. External support also neutralized the devastating effect of the decision by the federal government to change currency notes at the height of the war in January 1968.[29]

Another form of foreign support received by Biafra was by whipping up religious sympathy. Osaghae has pointed out the systematic fashion in which the religious propaganda was organized in this way.

> The external support and sympathy obtained by Biafra was partly the result of campaigns by relief organizations like Oxfam, the Red Cross and Caritas, which had pro-Biafran sympathies. But it was more the result of well organized and effective propaganda machinery which was handled internally by the 'Biafra Directorate of Propaganda' headed by Uche Chukwumerije...and coordinated externally by the Geneva-based Mark Press. The war was presented as a genocidal one waged by the Muslims of Northern Nigeria who had declared a jihad to exterminate Igbos from the face of the earth...In Italy, for example, pro-Biafra sympathies were strong, and Ojukwu protested in letters to the pope and prime minister over the sale of arms by 'Catholic' Italy to Muslim Northern Nigeria to be used in killing the 'Catholic' Igbos of Eastern Nigeria.[30]

The Catholic Bishops Conference of Nigeria (CBCN) in their 1968 Pastoral Letter[31] denied any connection between the civil war and the Vatican in no uncertain terms though this document is not often quoted by those who wish to make the religious case for the civil war in Nigeria. According to the bishops:

> Patriotic Nigerian Catholics have been greatly distressed and acutely embarrassed by the recent attitude of the Press, Radio and Television towards the Church. Allegations, without sufficient evidence, of political and military involvement in the civil war have been made against the Church. We protest and emphatically deny these charges.[32]

The bishops proceeded to explain why there may have been the wrong perception that the Church was somehow involved in the civil war.

> We reject the suggestion that Pope Paul VI is involved in this war, directly or indirectly, in any capacity except that of bringing peace and reconciliation. His personal efforts for peace are well known. Equally well known is the Holy Father's concern for the poor and suffering. Wherever they may be, he sends help to them through Caritas Internationalis because this is an organization dedicated exclusively to bringing aid to victims of war, famine and disaster.[33]

---

29 See Osaghae, *Crippled Giant*, pp. 65–66.

30 Ibid. p.66.

31 "Statement on the Nigerian Crisis, December 1968," *The Voice of the Voiceless: Pastoral Letters and Communiqués of the Catholic Bishops' Conference of Nigeria* 1960–2002, (ed.), Peter Schineller (Ibadan: Daily Graphics, 2002), pp. 53–54.

32 Ibid. p. 53.

33 Ibid.

The religious implications for the civil war should be placed in the context of the North–South divide which polarized the nation on ethnic, social, economic, and political grounds. Thus, the perception from both parties in the conflict about each section of the nation receiving support from their religious affiliations was obvious. The South regarded the North as Moslem and receiving support from other Moslem Countries, while the North saw the South as Christian and as receiving support from Christian nations. Perhaps, one may argue from this position that both sides were blaming each other and trying to win a political advantage in the process.

Post-Nigerian Civil War Developments and the Gowon Regime

Pade Badru[34] has discussed some of the class conflicts that were responsible for the civil war and the role played by the Gowon administration. However, it is indispensable to state that in the Nigerian situation, class and ethnic consciousness are intertwined. The quest for political power, economic security, and social status are all tied to one's ethnic affiliation or geographical location. Okwudiba Nnoli has captured this unfortunate state of affairs.

> In-group out-group boundaries emerged with (ethnicity) and, in time, become marked, more distinct than before, and jealously guarded by the various ethnic groups. Acceptance and rejection on linguistic-cultural grounds characterize social relations. These are expressed inevitably through interethnic discrimination in jobs, housing, and admission into educational institutions, marriages, business transaction or the distribution of social welfare services. The factor of exclusiveness is usually accompanied by nepotism and corruption.[35]

Badru further argued that the economic class distinction that existed between the Northern Hausa-Fulani merchants and nobles and the Igbos in the East and the Yoruba's in the West was a major factor in the civil war that engulfed Nigeria. Since the Northern commercial class was supported by the ruling British colonial administration, a new class of local administrators was emerging that would implement the policies of the colonial power. The new elite group would emerge as the main actors during Nigeria's first Republic, and their failure to engage in responsible stewardship would plunge Nigeria into a bloody civil war.

In response to the question: "Whose war was it?" Badru said: "The answer is simple; it was the elites' war of greed fought over the private distribution of petrodollars."[36] How did the elite manipulate the war to their advantage? According to

34 Pade Badru, *Imperialism and Ethnic Politics in Nigeria*, pp. 79–90.

35 Okwudiba Nnoli, *Ethnic Politics in Nigeria* (Enugu: Fourth Dimension, 1978), p. 7.

36 Ibid. p. 85.

Badru the contest was between the civilian administrators appointed to serve in the Gowon military regime and the civil servants, who ushered in new state bureaucrats that would determine the economic power base of Nigeria.

> The council of civil commissioners that was set up during the early phase of the war by Gowon played an important role in the prosecution of the war...By consolidating the power of the civil commissioners, General Gowon had displaced the economic power of state bureaucrats and senior civil servants. The civil servants, in particular, played a significant role during the first fifteen months of the crisis. As the war progressed, the civil servants were replaced by another set of social actors who had strong connections to international capital.[37]

The result was that the war became a money making venture for those who were at the corridors of power. The civilian administrators engaged in mismanagement of the foreign capital that was meant to help the war torn nation develop by diverting these funds to personal enrichment. Some of the corrupt military officers were involved in the sharing of war booty and the collection of pay checks of dead soldiers in their command. The elite class that benefited from the war, both in the military and the civil service, succeeded in entrenching corruption as a way of life in the Nigerian political system that would have far-reaching implications beyond the civil war and the Gowon administration.

Another major crisis that the Gowon regime had to deal with was the effect of the civil war on the production of crude oil. Since the war had adversely affected oil production, there was some drop in revenue and the war was sponsored on foreign loans. However, the real crisis was with the senior civil administrators and military officers who became major beneficiaries of the oil cartel. By this time, it was evident that the Gowon regime had become very corrupt, especially in view of the despicable role played by some of the major actors in the government of the day.

In fairness, the Gowon administration embarked on a nine-point reconstruction program that would culminate in the transition to a civilian government on October 1, 1976. Some of the laudable programs included the National Youth Service Crops (NYSC) instituted in 1973, a community-based service program that required one year of service of each Nigerian immediately after graduation from the university or institution of higher learning. The interesting aspect about this requirement was that each member of the corps had to serve in a State other than his or her home State in order to help diffuse ethnic tension and encourage solidarity among Nigerians across ethnic, religious, cultural, and social boundaries. The creation of the twelve states was another major accomplishment of the regime that sought to bring the different ethnic groups together and to protect the minority groups. Gowon defended his policy of State creation several years after he was ousted in these words:

37 Ibid.

> In May 1967, when my government created twelve states out of the existing four, it was to restructure the federation such that no one state or group of states could threaten the corporate existence of the country or hold the country to ransom. The creation of states by my government was to make for justice and fairness as the new states would now start on equal footing. There was also the fact that the twelve states structure was established to ensure the protection of the minority elements in the regions dominated by the major ethnic groups. This way we believe that the principle of self determination would be allowed to flourish.[38]

Gowon engaged also in the building of federal roads to link the different states, reconstruction of bridges and factories to provide jobs and enhance the social mobility of the citizens across the nation. Murtala Mohammed came to power according to Badru the class struggle by the elite reached the apex of personal greed by Nigerian government officials.

> The fall of General Gowon reflects the contradictions and intra-class struggles between the comprador elements and the rising national bourgeoisie. The economic dominance of the national bourgeoisie was affirmed during the brief rule of the slain populist soldier, General Murtala Mohammed.[39]

The civil war in Nigeria shook the fragile political ground on which the country was built. Apart from the political fragmentation, it heightened ethnic tensions and created a wide gulf between Northerners and Southerners that had deep religious implications. In fact, the war was presented, at one point, as a religious strife between Christians and Muslims. During the same period, the elites who had become an integral part of the civil service and the hope of a better future, engaged in reckless corruption thereby placing the moral and economic fabric of the nation in jeopardy. The various attempts made by the Gowon administration to heal the wounds of the war did not completely do away with the feelings of deep animosity and betrayal by some parts of the country.

The Murtala Mohammed/Olusegun Obasanjo Regime—1975–1979[40]

The Mohammed/Obasanjo regime had two heads of states, Mohammed (July, 1975 to February, 1976) and Obasanjo (February, 1976 to October, 1979). They are considered one continuous regime in the sense that Obasanjo was Mohammed's dep-

38 Yakubu Gowon, "Federalism and Nigerian Unity: Problems and Prospects," *Federalism and Nation Building in Nigeria: The Challenges of the 21st Century*, (eds.), J. Isawa Elaigwu, P.C. Logams, and H.S. Galadima (Abuja: National Council on Intergovernmental Relations, 1994), p. 27.

39 See Badru, p. 87.

40 The details of the Mohammed/Obasanjo regime are found in Eghosa E. Osaghae, *Crippled Giant: Nigeria Since Independence*, pp. 79–96.

uty when Mohammed was head of State. After Mohammed's assassination in an abortive coup in February 1976, Obasanjo became head of State and maintained the key officers of Mohammed's administration including its structural makeup and policies.

General Mohammed was able through the Armed Forces Ruling Council (AFRC) to implement the Indigenization Decree of 1975, which nationalized British interests in BP-Shell, the crude oil group of companies. He also set forth the program to move Nigeria's capital from Lagos to Abuja, a more central location in the country, and the Aguda Panel was set up to undertake the study. The issue of the creation of States was also on the table, and the Irikefe panel was to study the proposals and make recommendations to the government. The regime then aimed at ridding the civil service, public sector, and society of corruption through massive retrenchment of corrupt civil servants. The regime set in motion a four year time table to a civilian government transition that began on October 1, 1975 and was to continue until October 1, 1979. At the inauguration of the members of the Constitution Drafting Committee (CDC), who were to fashion and determine the nature of the civilian administration, Mohammed outlined among, in addition to other aspects, six important guidelines:

1. elimination of 'cut-throat' political competition based on a system of winner-takes-all;
2. discouragement of institutionalized opposition to the government in power, and encouragement of consensus politics and government based on a community of interests;
3. decentralization of power;
4. establishment of the principle of public accountability;
5. free and fair elections; and
6. depoliticization of the census.[41]

The above guidelines were meant to help in the drafting of the constitution that after several years of military rule, would usher in the second civilian administration.

The assassination of General Murtala Mohammed in an abortive coup on February 13, 1976, was widely condemned in Nigeria. His short reign as head of State was noted by many Nigerians as worthwhile. General Obasanjo, Mohammed's deputy, became head of State and vowed to continue with Mohammed's policies. Obasanjo launched an agricultural program called 'Operation Feed the Nation' (OFN) to boost agricultural productivity and diversify Nigeria's oil economy. However, this undertaking ended up to be another white elephant project, serving the needs of the rich and not having any impact at the grassroots level.

41 Ibid. p. 87.

Nevertheless, the time-table of transition to civilian rule continued without any major modification and a smooth hand over to the civilian administration of Alhaji Shehu Shagari took place on October 1, 1979.

The military regimes wielded power and governed Nigeria by military fiat and decrees. The military continued to centralize power through government appointees who were answerable to the supreme military ruling council as the final arbiter of political power, and not the supreme court of the nation. Thus, in order to have absolute control over the nation, the centralization policy weakened the organs of the federal structure that made the task of the civilian government a major problem.

Federalism and the Second Republic, 1979 to 1983[42]

Nigeria's Second Republic was ushered in on October 1, 1979. Alhaji Shehu Shagari was elected president after a much disputed decision by the Nigerian Federal Electoral Commission. Since this administration was the second one after decades of military rule, it was necessary to re-orient the citizens toward participatory democracy rather than military decrees. Moreover, since the elections had caused much antagonism among the different political parties, it was inevitable that some form of reconciliatory measures would prove beneficial.

The Shagari government followed the recommendation of the Constitution Drafting Committee (CDC) by promoting the 'Federal Character Principle.' This principle was meant to bring about a balance of political and economic power between the 'North' and 'South' of Nigeria. By way of definition, this approach meant:

> The federal character principle is a variant of the consociational principle of proportional representation or quota system where the main objective was to ensure that the kaleidoscope of the country's diversity was reflected in composition of government at all levels.[43]

The government hoped that by applying this principle to ministerial appointments, government agencies, the armed forces and other public services, somehow the issue of national unity and integration would take a positive shape. However, the falsity of achieving political stability in this manner was glaring to critical political analysts. How does one deal justly with ethnic groups that have more States or are in the majority without at the same time encouraging the marginalization of minority groups? The other question that arose was the use of representation in executive bodies as a mechanism for power sharing. While representation in executive bodies may be considered a legitimate way of power sharing, State

42 Ibid. pp. 110–162 for details.

43 Ibid. p. 115.

power sharing will have to go beyond a cosmetic dressing in the form of appointment in executive positions. Consequently, more often than not, the political office holders often came to office with a personal agenda that might be different from that of the State they are representing.

The attempt to implement the 'federal character' principle and the implications arising thereto during the Shagari administration permeated the different levels of political, social, and economic life of the nation. The administration became very corrupt, substituting State power sharing with personal power sharing, and State representation for patronage representation. The consequence was another military take over:

> On the night of December 31, 1983, the military struck once again to overthrow the young Republic. The chaos that followed the 1983 elections provided only the last straw for this, if justification had to be found. More powerful underlying reasons were the massive corruption, economic mismanagement and authoritarian tendencies that characterized the Republic. Panels instituted to probe governors and other officials after its overthrow found evidence of widespread abuse and embezzlement of public funds, for which they were sentenced to various jail terms and/or asked to refund their misappropriations to the State...[44]

Consequently, another military government was imposed on Nigeria due largely to the failure of politicians to live up to their oath of allegiance.

The Return of the Military: The Buhari (1983–85); Babangida (1985–93); Abacha (1993–98); Abubakar (1998–99) Regimes[45]

The return of the military to political power in Nigeria revealed a major centralization of political and administrative power. These regimes were characterized by sweeping institutional and structural changes, the eruption of violent tensions due to military, sectional, minority, and religious agitations. It became clear that the military had placed the Nigerian federal structure as a unit within and under military command. "This subordination of the federal institutional structure to the military organizational superstructure was not significantly reversed by the introduction of the elaborate, but eventually aborted, program of transition to the

44 Ibid. p. 154.

45 To read more about the second phase of military rule in Nigeria, these works are relevant: Pade Badru, *Imperialism and Ethnic Politics in Nigeria*, pp. 115–39; Mojubaolu Okome, *A Sapped Democracy: The Political Economy of Structural Adjustment Program and the Political Transition in Nigeria* (1983–93) (Lanham: University Press of America, 1998), p.83ff; Karl Maier, *This House Has Fallen: Midnight in Nigeria* (New York: Public Affairs, 2000), pp. 1–110; Eghosa E. Osaghae, *Crippled Giant: Nigeria Since Independence*, pp. 163–310.

Third Republic in January, 1986, and the subsequent election of civilian State governors in December, 1991."[46]

Between December 1991, and November 1993, civilian governors ruled their States under the military who dominated the central government. According to Suberu, "The political vulnerability of the democratically elected State governments was clearly dramatized in June, 1993, when the federal government shut down several State-owned media organizations that had criticized the military's annulment of that month's elections to the Third Republic's inaugural presidency."[47] Moreover, the decentralization initiatives proposed and implemented by the military regimes at the local government level were aimed at promoting "...a uniform national system of local government and to further constrain the scope for autonomous intervention by the States in the affairs of the localities."[48] Some of the sweeping local government reforms included:

1. A doubling (from 10 percent in the Second Republic to 20 percent in 1992) in the proportion of the Federation Account allocated to the localities, an increase that was implemented primarily at the expense of the states whose allocations fell from 30 to 24 percent.
2. The announcement of formal provisions for the direct, as distinct from indirect (that is, State-channeled), transfer of central statutory allocations to the localities.
3. The abolition of State-controlled Local Government Ministries and Service Commissions as part of the move to eliminate or reduce intervention by the states in the local government system.
4. The establishment of an approved national scheme of service for local government employees.
5. The establishment of provisions and regulations in the federal constitution regarding the areas, structure, composition, jurisdictions, and election of local councils.
6. The extension of the presidential system of government to the local government level.
7. The realignment of local government boundaries with federal and State legislative boundaries.

46 See Suberu, *Federalism and Ethnic Conflict in Nigeria*, p. 39.

47 Ibid.

48 Ibid. p. 40.

8. The devolution of increased responsibilities to the localities for primary education, health care, and local infrastructural improvements.[49]

The above mentioned reforms at the local government level ensured military federalism at the grassroots and eroded State government power sharing with the local governments, transferring it to the center.

Furthermore, there was a heightened level of government instability during the military regimes that affected the political, social, economic and moral fabric of the nation. The period between December, 1983, and May, 1999, witnessed five different heads of States: the four already mentioned and Chief Ernest Shonekan whose leadership lasted five months (August, 1993–November, 1993) and involved the strangest military and civilian alliance ever witnessed in Nigeria's political setup.

The Buhari administration came to power like all military governments with the claim to salvage the nation from corrupt leaders and looters. However, the regime started to block noticeably various attempts being made to ground the Nigerian federation along confederal guidelines. In the midst of these challenges, the regime was short lived when Babangida came to power in August, 1985. The Babaginda administration was full of deceit, especially with regard to the transition program to democratic rule and the subsequent cancellation of the June 12 elections that would have ushered in M.K.O. Abiola as president. This singular act of Babangida will make it impossible for him to ever run for any political office in Nigeria. This is because Babangida is seen as undemocratic, autocratic, and self centered. Qualities which make it impossible for him to win any democratic elections. Also, the Structural Adjustment Program (SAP), initiated to boost the economy, was a major failure of this regime. Moreover, Babangida's administration opened the way for religious bigotry and antagonism in Nigeria with the decision of his government to secretly upgrade Nigeria's membership in the Organization of Islamic Countries (OIC) from that of an observer status to a substantive one. Christians saw this move as an attempt to turn Nigeria into an Islamic State thereby contravening the Nigerian constitution which upholds the secular nature of the country. The Shonekan administration was equally grandfathered by the military, and when it became clear that the consequences arising from the annulment of the June 12, 1993, election would not disappear, the military, this time under Abacha, took over as head of State. Abacha was confronted with the task of cleaning up the mess both he and Babaginda had created. The task proved very challenging because of several calls for a Sovereign National Conference to review the basis of Nigeria's federation before independence. The Abacha regime enforced military federalism to the letter and centralized the administration at his finger tips. He is also known to have been the most corrupt leader ever in Nigeria. His

49 Sam Oyovbaire, "New Guidelines for Local Government," *The Guardian* (Lagos), November 28, 1991, p. 17.

sudden death in June, 1998, was unofficially declared a day of rejoicing in many parts of the nation. Abacha had been planning to become a civilian president through another dubious democratic program. Abubakar, his successor, revised Abacha's transition program within a year and ushered in the Fourth Republic in May, 1999, with former General Obasanjo as civilian president.

The Fourth Republic: Obasanjo as Civilian President, 1999 to 2007

President Olusegun Obasanjo took his oath of office on May 29, 1999, having won the presidential elections under the ticket of the Peoples Democratic Party (PDP). There was much enthusiasm among Nigerians because Obasanjo was the first military leader to hand over power to civilians in 1979. He was also the first Nigerian leader to be "recycled" in what has now become a crisis of leadership. The nation expected Obasanjo, as a former leader, to run the nation in the right direction and to bring democratic principles of equal protection under the law, accountability, transparency, and good governance to bear on his administration.

Since Obasanjo had been imprisoned under the Abacha regime for his political views, the nation saw him as a Statesman who was familiar with the plight of the common person. Furthermore, Obasanjo and his party had received a national mandate of about 62% of the nation which showed that the PDP had majority acceptance. The only area where the PDP did not gain much support was in Obasanjo's home area, in the Southwest where the Alliance for Democracy (AD) had a strong ethnic base. The Obasanjo administration was confronted with complaints about marginalization and ethnic tension in different parts of the country. In the North, the challenge was to respond to the allegation that he has betrayed the political support he received when the North conceded political power to the South. This is because several military officers from the North were dismissed or retired, creating an imbalance in key ministerial appointments between the North and the Southwest, Obasanjo's home region where he had very little support. In the oil-rich Odi community in Bayelsa State, federal troops were ordered in to bring control to the communal uprising. Instead, they actually invaded and destroyed the property of people and killed some of them. There was no credible government explanation. There were ethnic clashes between the Jukun and Kuteb with over 200 people dead. In Kaduna, Christians and Muslims went to war killing several hundred over issues of Nigeria's hosting of the "Miss World Beauty Contest," that had a lot of political overtones.

Similarly, the Tiv people in the Middle Belt of Nigeria had more than their own share of invasion and destruction by federal troops who killed hundreds of people at random and destroyed much property on the excuse that nineteen soldiers were killed by people in the locality.[50] There were clashes involving the Ijaw, Itsekiri, and Urhobo communities of Delta State and ethnic militias of the Oodua Peoples' Congress, the Bakassi Boys, the Ijaw Youth Council and the Movement for the Actualization of the Sovereign State of Biafra.

The editor of a prominent news magazine[51] presented a review of the events of 2003 in Nigeria by looking at its politics, crime rate, judiciary, media, religion, corruption, and telecommunication system. In 2003, Nigeria was voted by Transparency International the second most corrupt country in the world, a position it has maintained in the last several years. In view of the above development, the following observation was put forward in connection with Obasanjo's administration:

> It is a kind of paradox, President Olusegun Obasanjo has expended so much energy and resources fighting corruption, but despite his efforts, Transparency International, rated Nigeria second most corrupt country in the whole world in year 2003. Nigeria has for many years maintained that position.
>
> Peter Eigen, chairman of Transparency International, said corruption was so deep-rooted in Nigeria that it would require many generations before it would be routed from Nigeria...Corruption bedeviled the May election that produced the present government. In so many states, it was widely reported that there were no elections at all and where elections were conducted, the ruling People's Democratic Party, (PDP) employed the services of soldiers and other law enforcement agencies to rig the elections.[52]

Some key members of the Obasanjo administration were implicated in another panel on corruption. The chairman of Independent Corrupt Practices and Other Related Offences Commission (ICPC) Nuhu Ribadu sought the arrest of seven Nigerians including Hussaini Akwanga, the former minister of labor and productivity. Others included Sunday Michael Afolabi and Mahmud Shata, former minister of internal affairs and minister of state in the same ministry, and R. O. Akerele, permanent secretary of the same ministry. There was also Okwesilieze Nwodo, former governor of Enugu State and former scribe of the ruling People's Democratic Party, PDP, Niyi Adelagun.[53]

Furthermore, Wilson Egbo-Egbo, a judge with an Abuja high court, was suspended indefinitely over his dubious role in controversial rulings and exparte motions. More specifically, the ruling ordering Governor Chris Ngige of Anambra State to vacate office was another major judicial rape of the precarious democratic process. Similarly, Chris Uba, financier of the PDP organized the abduction of

50 Iyorwuese Hagher, *Beyond Hate and Violence: Understanding the Tiv Struggle for Citizenship Rights and Social Justice in Nigeria* (Ibadan: Caltop Publications, 2002), pp. 93–169 for detailed analysis of the Tiv massacre.

51 Bala Dan Musa, *Newswatch*, January 12, 2004, p. 5. This book evaluates the Obasanjo administration in the year 2003, and it offers suggestions for the future.

52 Salif Atojoko, *Newswatch*, January 12, 2004, pp. 22–23.

53 Ibid. pp. 23–24.

Ngige. The ruling party, the federal government and the police have refused to take action on this matter. The other political landmark in Nigeria, apart from the precarious democratic elections and transition from one civilian administration to another, was the hosting of the Commonwealth Heads of Government Meeting, (CHOGM), in Abuja. The meeting lasted from December 3 to December 5, 2003, and was chaired by Queen Elizabeth II of England. The relevance of Nigeria's membership in the Commonwealth of Nations is best known to the leaders who benefit directly rather than the ordinary Nigerian citizen whose citizenship passport is subjected to much scrutiny in most European nations of the Commonwealth.

The prominent judicial victory was that of Amina Lawal, 31, a single mother condemned to death by stoning in March, 2002, by the *Shar'ia* Court in Katsina State. On September 25, a *Shar'ia* Appeal Court turned down this sentence. This ruling ended a 19-month battle for Amina's life which attracted local, national and international attention.

Another significant contribution being made in the Obasanjo administration is from Nasiru El-Rufai, the Minister of the Federal Capital Territory (FCT) in Abuja who is credited with a no nonsense approach to work. He challenged some key politicians over their request for bribe before his confirmation for ministerial appointment. He has also brought some sanity to the FCT by demolishing illegal structures put up by some former top military officers and some key people in government today. His goal is to make Abuja a less costly place to work and live in and to boost its tourism.[54] Time will tell whether these efforts would have the desired effects on ordinary citizens as they attempt to make a living in a capital city that was designed for the rich and famous.

Robert Rotberg, gave a very positive assessment of Obansanjo's administration that highlights the major events of the regime leading up to the 2007 elections:

> The professionalism of the higher judiciary, especially the Supreme Court, has by and large been a force for good, and for moderation at the national level. Important constitutional challenges have been debated and judged there rather than been settled in the streets or by coups. Obasanjo's administration has managed to institute budgeting practices, begin reforming the banking system and massively reduce foreign debt. Furthermore, probity in the petroleum sector has been enhanced thanks to the Nigerian Extractive Industries Transparency Initiative (NEITI). Outside of the government, Nigeria has a thriving civil society. Active nongovernmental organizations, and especially a vibrant media, mean that public accountability mechanisms function.[55]

Having accomplished all these endeavors, one wonders why Obasanjo did not leave office gracefully as a Statesman but was prepared to derail the democratic process

54 Ibid. pp. 10–19 for details of El-Rufai's interview.

55 Robert I. Rotberg, *Nigeria:Elections and Continuing Challenges* (New York: Council on Foreign Relations, April 2007), p. 5.

by pushing for constitutional changes that were to ensure a third term for him in office. Even after the defeat of his third term bid, Obasanjo schemed his way into becoming the chairman of the Presidential Campaign council for the People's Democratic Party so as to influence the choice of his successor. In the midst of all the candidates who were vying to be president, Umaru Yar'Adua emerged on the platform of the ruling party with Obasanjo's blessings. Why Umaru Yar'Adua? El-Rufai, Obasanjo's former minister and insider answers this question forcefully:

> Some years later in 2006, Umaru Yar'Adua was one of the few Northern Govenors who supported Obasanjo's bid for a Third Term in office. Indeed, he offered to host the zonal debates for the particularly sensitive North-West zone in Katsina. This led to protests in the city and at least two persons were shot and killed by law enforcement agents that confronted them. Umaru also directed all Katsina State representatives in the National Assembly to support the proposed constitutional amendment and expelled Aminu Bello Masari from K-34 for non-compliance with his wishes. One of the arrowheads of the Third Term in the National Assembly was Dr. Aminu Safana—Umaru's former Secretary to the state Government. All Katsina PDP legislators except Dr. Usman Bugaje lined up to support the Third Term project till its defeat in the Senate in May 2006.[56]

El-Rufai then goes on to show how Yar'Adua began to prepare to be president of Nigeria with the support of Obasanjo. One will expect that Obasanjo was supporting Yar'Adua in order for him to continue with the reforms he had started and not merely for supporting his third term bid for the office of president. However, why should one support a candidate who is not medically fit to run this office and who may not conclude his term in office due to his personal health? Was this a scheme by Obasanjo to install a sick Yar'Adua who would not be able to govern and make people wish Obasanjo were still in power?

> Umaru Yar'Adua's anointment by president was a double-edged sword. On the one hand, it almost ensured that he will be PDP's candidate in April 2007 Presidential elections, but throws up questions about Obasanjo's motives and Yar'Adua's suitability for the highest office in Africa's largest nation. Because Yar'Adua's medical history is fairly well-known, many Northern power brokers concluded that Yar'Adua's selection by Obasanjo had some ulterior motives.
>
> This concern came to the fore when Yar'Adua had to be flown to Germany for medical attention because of "a bad flu; arising from exhaustion" just before the primaries in December 2006. This is to happen again in March 2007, just weeks to the Elections. The failure of both Obasanjo and Yar'Adua to offer full disclosure about

56 Nasiru El-Rufai, "Umaru Yar'Adua: Great expectations, disappointing outcomes," *Newswatch*, June 24, 2009, p. 10. El-Ruai has offered the political and social context that brought Obasanjo and Yar'Adua as political bed fellows thereby ensuring Yar'Adu's succession as Nigeria's President after Obasanjo at the expense of moving Nigeria forward through credible elections, a dream that will take a long time to come.

> Umaru's health has led to all kinds of conspiracy theories that continue to haunt the Yar'Adua presidency till today.[57]

This is the scenario under which the 2007 selection/election process of Umaru Yar'Adua took place. The election proper was largely a disgrace of the very fragile democratic institution in Nigeria. The difference is that it was better than a third term for Obasanjo, and it was not a military coup. Given the Nigerian political set up, the People's Democratic Party is not willing to relinquish power to any other political party at least at the presidential level. Thus, the one party system operates at that level in practice though not in principle.

The Fourth Republic: The Presidency of Umaru Yar' Adua, 2007 to 2010

On May 29, 2007, Umaru Yar'Adua was sworn in as president of Nigeria's fourth republic. He gave an inspiring speech acknowledging the failures in the elections that brought him to power and promised electoral reform. The speech was largely an expansion of his seven-point agenda:

- Infrastructure particularly electricity and transportation
- Niger Delta regional development
- Food Security
- Human Capital–investments in health, education and training
- Land Reforms and home ownership
- National Security, and
- Wealth Creation

The declaration of assets by Yar'Adua was a novelty in the Nigerian political system by a president. We were hoping that this time around, Nigerians had found a leader who would take them to the Promised Land. The vice president, Jonathan Goodluck followed suit after much pressure from the media.

In my view, no one has so far given a better assessment of the Yar'Adua administration than Nasiru El Rufai, former minister of the Federal Capital Territory under Obasanjo and one who assisted in the transition from Obasanjo to Yar'Adua.

> It was in the reversal of the war against corruption that the Yar'Adua administration did the most damage to its credibility with Nigerians and the international community. The systematic destruction of the EFCC by the Yar'Adua administration began as soon as James Ibori—former governor of Delta State (and a recruiter, all and financier of Yar'Adua), was charged for money laundering and corruption at the Federal High Court in December 2007.[58]

---

57 Ibid. p. 11.

58 Ibid. p. 17.

George Mbah, writing about Yar'Adua's moral authority to govern challenged the president to earn the trust and confidence of Nigerians especially in fighting corruption. Indeed, he warned Yar'Adua that a year into his administration, it was clear that his anticorruption agenda was bleak.

> Nigerians thirst for that confidence and trust in his anticorruption battle. It is losing steam on the altar of party loyalty and threatening the president's moral grounds to assert his authority. The president once espoused that the only way any government can govern well is to command moral authority. Moral authority, he said, must be earned by a leader because it calls for a willingness by the people to submit themselves to leadership without coercion.[59]

Yar'Adua having lost the steam of his anticorruption fight, the rest of his seven-point agenda is equally lost. Even in the case where some minimal effort has been made like the Niger Delta regional development issue, the amnesty and peace pact with the militant groups in the Niger delta is very superficial and unlikely to pass the test of time. In other words, the removal of arms from the militants in exchange for money begs the question. The government must seek out the source for financing the purchase of arms by the militants and why this practice has continued to be a challenge for Nigerian governments. Similarly, the government's agenda for development in this region must be decisive, relevant, and beneficial to the majority of the people at the grassroots and not just the few who are well connected to people in government.

The other challenge with Yar'Adua's administration is that we are not sure whether his sickness will allow him to serve his term in office as president. Having not disclosed his sickness prior to his election, one questions the moral grounds upon which Yar'Adua and his associates stand to speak to Nigerians about moral authority.

Anayochukwu Agbo, writing on the lingering illness of Yar'Adua and its political implications for Nigeria opines:

> After nearly three years in office, marked by poor health and five controversial medical trips abroad, some people appear to be running out of patience with the hide-and-seek game over the health of the president and what they say is the consequent lull in the pace of governance. Reactions over his present hospitalization, "medical check-up" in official parlance, in Saudi Arabia climaxed with the audacious call for his resignation by a group of 53 eminent Nigerians from six geo-political zones of the country on Tuesday, December 1.[60]

When one reads the mystery and secrecy surrounding the illness of Yar'Adua, the feeling that Yar'Adua must have had a political score to settle in accepting to run

---

59 George Mbah, "Yar'Adua's Moral Authority," *Insider*, no. 29, August 4, 2008, p.15. This entire edition is dedicated to the crafty ways that Yar'Adua's administration has found ways of letting off the hook the conviction of ex-governors standing trial for corruption.

60 Anayochukwu Agbo, "Banking on a Morbid Assumption," *Tell*, December 14, 2009, p. 21.

for president is palpable. However with whom, or which group? We will know the answer to this question only in hindsight when the politics of Yar'Adua's sickness is all done hopefully sooner than later. Even so, there are still some pertinent questions: Is this the case of accepting a political office that his uncle Musa Shehu Yar'Adua came so close to but did not achieve because of Obasanjo? Is this the time for Obasanjo to compensate the Yar'Adua family for whatever contract he had made with the elder Yar'Adua during their military days? Why would a very sick man like Yar'Adua not take care of himself with all his millions but choose to be president with all the rigors of such an office? Is it that he wanted to be called president even if it meant doing nothing for Nigeria except for his family and friends and disgracefully leaving office prematurely? It does seem that at the moment we are in a political impasse where so many political options pile up by the day with no real solution in sight. Even the constitutional solution is lost in the details and jargon of legal interpretation. The military solution will take the Nation forty years back. The family solution may be the way out since Yar'Adua really listens to only his immediate family, friends, and political supporters. The epilogue by Dele Omotunde[61] narrating the supposed conversation between Turai Yar'Adua and Michelle Obama may be the key to unlocking the health/political logjam surrounding Yar'Adua's illness. The time has come for Turai if she really loves her husband to advice him to resign from office so that Nigeria can move forward, otherwise, Nigerian history will not be kind to the Yar'Aduas like the Abachas or will the personal ambitions for power by the Yar'Adua family cloud their vision for the common good of Nigeria?

The 'Doctrine of Necessity' in Nigerian Politics

On February 9, 2010, the National Assembly of Nigeria adopted a resolution by both Chambers of the National Assembly following a request by the Govenor's forum to empower the vice-president, Jonathan Goodluck, to act as the President and Commander-in-Chief of the Nigerian Armed Forces following the protracted illness (78 days out of office) of the substantive president who was not able to discharge the functions of his office as required by the constitution. The doctrine of necessity was adopted as a political solution to the constitutional logjam created by the failure of the president to follow the constitutional process and to avoid the lacuna created by his long absence from office. The doctrine was also used as a necessary measure to save Nigeria from imminent collapse in the face of the constitutional blockage and human contributions to the constitutional flaws.[62] The

61 Dele Omotunde, "Hello Turai, This Is Michelle Calling!" *Tell*, December 14, 2009, p. 54.

62 For details see "The doctrine of necessity in perspective," Sahara reporters, Tuesday, May 4, 2010; Chris Ajaero, "The Deal That Saved the Nation," News Watch, February 22, 2010, pp. 16–23.

doctrine of necessity is used to define and validate extra-constitutional issues that fall outside the purview of the constitution but are necessary to preserve political stability. The fundamental objective of the doctrine is to satisfy the exigencies that have been created by certain situations outside the contemplation of the constitution or rule of law, and its significant feature is the deliberate circumvention of the constitution or some aspects of the rule of law in order to get out of the political quagmire. It is also a situation where the rule of law and constitution has to be adulterated by extra-legal civil means in the short term in order to preserve the constitution, the rule of law, the government, and democracy in the long term. Simply put: to save the country, the constitution has to be dumped and the rule of law has to be slanted. In addition, the doctrine is not a legal theory but a concession to human weakness. It is also a political arrangement that has garnered some form of legal validation and global support.[63]

The doctrine of necessity is sometimes referred to as the "necessity defense" or "choice of evils defense." It was invoked to legalize government action in Pakistan in 1954 just seven years after the creation of Pakistan when the Pakistan Supreme Court gave legal support to the extra judicial action of the country's Governor-General who used extra-constitutional means of emergency power to dissolve the country's constituent assembly and appointed a new council of ministers on the ground that the constituent assembly no longer represented the people. In the action that followed, the then Pakistani Supreme Court Chief Justice not only validated the extra-constitutional action of the Governor-General but used Bracton's maxim: "that which is otherwise not lawful is made lawful by necessity." Similarly, the doctrine was used to justify an extra constitutional act in 1985 by the High Court of Granada to give legal backing to the existence of a special court trying the people who had conducted a coup against the ex-leader, Maurice Bishop.[64] The doctrine- of necessity as was applied in the Nigerian context was not timely, but morally and politically justified to move Nigeria forward beyond the politics of Yar'Adua's sickness; and to serve as an important lesson for Nigerian politicians to realize that any attempt to fulfill personal political wishes above and beyond the Nigerian project will be counteracted by all legal means necessary by the Nigerian people for the common good of the country. The Acting president in his acceptance speech said among other things: "We have all shown that our unity as a people, our love for this country and our hope for its great future cannot be shaken."[65] The death of President Yar'Adua on May 5, 2010, put an end to his presidency and ushered in Jonathan Goodluck as President.

63 Ibid.

64 See "The Lesser Evil," News Watch; Editorial, February 22, 2010, pp. 14–15.

65 See NewsWatch, February 22, 2010, p. 18.

The Fourth Republic: Jonathan Goodluck as President: 2010 to the Present

Jonathan Goodluck was sworn in as President and Commander-in-chief of the armed forces of the Federal Republic of Nigeria on May 6, 2010. In his inaugural address to the nation, he said that his administration shall focus resolutely on good governance, electoral reforms, and the fight against corruption. His administration will intensify efforts at sustaining peace and development in the Niger Delta; and he pledged to protect human lives and property in the country. He assured that the Federal Government will continue to support efforts being made to promote the socio-economic well-being of Nigerians through investing in electricity, water, education, health, and other social amenities. This administration is in its infancy which makes it very difficult to evaluate. However, there are some distinctive features that are noteworthy about the Jonathan administration. First, the presence of a lame-duck president is over. To have Jonathan Goodluck as president has been very refreshing considering the impasse one experienced with the sickness of Yar'Adua and the lack of responsible leadership that was associated with some members of his cabinet; second, there has been relative and steady supply of petrol and gas in Nigerian filling stations throughout the nation at the acceptable prize of N65 a liter that can be compared to the good old days of the late 1970's and early 1980's. Our hope is that this level of demand and supply in the oil sector will be sustained for a long period of time; third, the appointment of Prof. Attahiru Jega as chairman of the Independent National Electoral Commission (INEC) has been welcomed as a step in the right direction in preparing for the forthcoming 2011 elections. Given this initial beginning, one hopes that the same level of commitment will be extended to other aspects of the economy and development especially in the areas of electricity generation, education, and health care.

Similarly, a constitutional amendment that will significantly affect the timetable for elections has been passed by the national assembly. Based on the amendments, general elections will be held in January 2011 instead of April 2011. This is the first time in the history of Nigeria that a civilian administration has successfully made constitutional changes to the Nigerian Constitution. The major highlights of the Constitutional Amendments of the 1999 Nigerian Constitution are:

Section 66: Panel indictment can no longer be used to disqualify candidates.

Section 69: Recall of any member of house of representatives/senate will no longer go through a referendum.

Section 75: 1991 census not to be used as basis for delineating constituencies. Latest census figures should be used.

Section 81: Financial autonomy for judiciary, INEC and National Assembly

Section 84: Financial autonomy for the remuneration and recurrent expenditure of INEC board members.

Section 110: Recall of any member of state house of assembly will no longer go through a referendum.

Section 132: Presidential election to hold 120-150 days to the expiration of the tenure of the incumbent.

Section 135: No tenure extension for a president who wins a rerun election. Can serve only a maximum of four years (for a term).

Section 145: If the president does not transmit a vacation letter within 21 days, the National Assembly will pass a resolution making the VP acting president.

Section 156: Members of federal executive bodies, including INEC, must not belong to any political party.

Section 160: INEC to make rules for itself without presidential interference.

Section 178: Governorship election to hold 120-150 days to the expiration of the tenure of the incumbent.

Section 180: No tenure extension for sitting governors who win rerun elections. Can serve only a maximum of four years (for a term) in total.

Section 190: If the governor does not transmit vacation letter within 21 days, state assembly will pass a resolution making the deputy governor the acting governor.

Section 200: Members of state executive bodies, including the electoral commission, must not belong to any political party.

Section 239: Appeal Court to be the first court of jurisdiction for petitions on: president, vice-president, governor and deputy governor.

INEC has requested for an extension of time which by all indications will be granted by the National Assembly to ensure free and fair elections. This means that elections may now take place sometimes in March/ April 2011. As the electoral constitutional amendments are being debated, Nigerians have been assured by the Senate president that the May 29, 2011 handover date for a new president of Nigeria will not be changed.

Critical Implications and Perspectives

1. The major challenge before the nation is to determine its corporate existence in a way that would be acceptable to the different ethnic groups that make up Nigeria. It is clear that the amalgamation of Northern and Southern Nigeria by the British in 1914 was a tool of colonization meant

to benefit only the colonizers and not the citizens. In the end, this cosmetic arrangement has made strange bed fellows who are constantly at war with each other. There is an urgent need for renewed discussion and planning toward a sovereign national council of all ethnic tribes in Nigeria with the formula of proportional representation to discuss the future of this nation before the elections of 2011.

2. The system of centralization of power among the three major ethnic groups (Hausa-Fulani, Igbo and Yoruba), almost to the exclusion of all other ethnic minorities, has led to and encouraged political stratification on ethnic grounds. The power game among these three major ethnic groups as to who will control the political and economic life of Nigeria at a given time, has given way to exploitation and marginalized existence of minority ethnic groups. The rise in ethnic tensions is the direct consequence of this power play that has encouraged every ethnic group to protect its own base, since representatives fail to represent all Nigerians, except those of their ethnic affiliation. No wonder citizens have come to think first of ethnicity before realizing they are Nigerians. The emergence of Jonathan Goodluck as president from the Ijaw a minority tribal group from Bayelsa State, one of the oil producing States is a major breakthrough in Nigerian politics that one hope will begin the process of appeasing minorities in Nigeria and bring about peace and stability in the Niger delta region and Nigeria as a whole.

3. The basis for Nigeria's federation needs re-examination and re-evaluation. Since independence in 1960, the regional formulations have given way to the creation of States. However, the request for the creation of more States has become a political tool which the military has exploited so very well in the past and, perhaps, politicians will continue to exploit now and in the future. The time has come for proper boundary adjustments and assessment on the issue of creation of States. Closely related is the politicization of Local government reform in the nation. The arbitrary natures in which Local governments are governed deserve some review.

4. The role of the armed forces in the government of Nigeria is very ambiguous. The military succeeded in replacing Nigeria's federalism with military federalism that continues to derail the efforts to democratic rule. This situation, if left un-checked, will continue for many decades. At the present time, former military officers wish to rule and re-rule in Nigeria by using their ill-gotten wealth to their political advantage for election purposes. In the 2011 elections and beyond one hopes that former military leaders will step aside and give democracy a chance to operate in this nation. The citizens are tired of the travesty of democratic rule in this

nation which has merely been a change of dress code from the military "Khaki" to the civilian "Agbada."

5. The issue of corruption in Nigeria is largely due to the greed of political office holders who exploit the poverty of the majority of the people. Kwame Gyekye has written on the issue of "Political Corruption" by showing its devastating effects on African countries.

> Postcolonial Africa is undeniably among the worse victims of political corruption. For it cannot be denied that the most outstanding and resilient problem that has beset and blighted the politics of the new nations (or, nation-states) of postcolonial Africa is political corruption. It most probably constitutes the most serious source of the financial hemorrhage suffered by a developing nation in Africa, constantly gnawing at its developing efforts; it is undoubtedly the most common cause of the military overthrow of civilian governments in Africa, with the consequent disruption of the democratic political process: thus, it is the greatest and most serious disease of governments in Africa.[66]

In Nigeria, government property is nobody's property, so it is up for grabs, beginning with the office holders. Most go into politics with the intent of looting public funds and enriching themselves. Government contracts are inflated so that they can get their percentages up front, and the contractors are left to figure out what to do with the project. In many cases, they are not completed, but no one is held accountable in the process because the government officials have already been paid and paid well for that matter. Government officials do not obey traffic regulations; government drivers are at their worst when they carry their officers who encourage them not to follow the approved speed limits in the name of doing an important job for the government. Governors, Ministers, and other top government officials use the army and police to intimidate the masses as they drive on the road. The very people, who voted them to power, will usually have to move off the roads for them to pass with their entourage and body guards, always at alarming speeds. The corruption among the police and army on road blocks is unprecedented in the history of law enforcement. Those who are meant to protect the masses continually extort money and other goods from the common people, openly, and in most cases, with the approval of their supervisors. This study shows that the military have become even more corrupt in Nigeria and can no longer be trusted to take over a democratic government for the purpose of purifying it.

66 Kwame Gyekye, *Political Corruption*, p. 1.

6. The religious issues in Nigeria have been largely politicized through the involvement of politicians in government. While the Christian religion views the separation between Church and State as necessary to the peaceful co-existence of both, the Islamic religion considers the unity of Church and State essential for their existence. Given this problem, the Nigerian nation has been faced with many religious riots, especially between Christians and Moslems in the face of growing mistrust, marginalization, inhuman laws, and the call, in some cases, for a State religion. The tensions over the implementation of Islamic Law, known as *Shar'ia* in some parts of Northern Nigeria have raised both national and international outcry. It is a clear indication that the threat of unchecked religious zeal can destabilize the nation. The Boko Haram incident in Maiduguri led by one Mohammed Yusuf reveal the extent to which Islamic religious extremists are prepared to carry out their pathological ideology.

   Much more disturbing has been the religious and political tensions in the city of Jos, Plateau state. According to Tajudeen Suleiman, violence, carnage, arson and killing are not strange spectacles on the streets of Jos, the Capital of Plateau State, at least since September 7, 2001, when the first major crisis broke out. The crisis in Plateau State has re-occurred several times since these incidents (February 24, 2004-fighting between Christians and Muslims in Yelwa town, Plateau State; April 24, 2004-Clashes between Tarok and Fulani rivals at Bakin Chiyawa, Shendam Local government, Plateau State; May 1–2, 2004- renewed violence in Yelwa, Plateau State); However, the scale of violence that descended on the city on Friday, November 28, 2008, for three days, had never been witnessed before. There was another major disturbance on January 17, 2010 and since then skirmishes have taken place here and there in different parts of the state.[67] The consequences arising for the crisis in Plateau State has grave challenges that uproot social security of citizens in the State and throughout the nation.

7. Moreover, politicians take advantage of such opportunities to score cheap political points, and in the process fuel the religious sentiments therein. Nigeria is a secular nation that promises to respect the right of all Nigerians to practice their religion without coercion and does not support any State religion. The leadership of both the Christian and Islamic religions often advocates peace and admonish their followers to do the same. However, beyond the cameras and peace talks, there is constant killing and destruc-

67 The details of the crisis in Plateau State are contained in the write-ups by Tajudeen Suleiman, "The Fire This Time,":23–27; Adejuwon Soyinka, "Another Seed War?,": 28–32, TELL Magazine, December 15, 2008; Femi Adi, "Ethnic Cleasing," The News, February 01, 2010, 23–28.

tion of property from both sides, which may seem to suggest a major disconnect between what the leaders are proposing and what actually prevails in the minds and hearts of the followers that is so violently acted out in practice.

In essence, the role of government in dealing with religious and political issues at the federal, State and local levels needs some examination both in terms of the role played by security agents and those charged with the reconciliation efforts. Moreover, boundary issues and those of indigenes and settlers are all part of the complex mixture that continues to affect the many law abiding citizens in Plateau State. One would have expected that the National Assembly would be engaged in making constitutional changes that will deal with the threat to security and human life that religious and political tensions have caused and will continue to cause in different parts of the nation. The role the government continues to play by appointing pilgrimage board members in every State, and, subsequently, using a government fund to support both Christian and Muslim pilgrims is a major failure of government policy. Religious groups should be allowed to conduct and run pilgrimages for their worshippers without government intervention. This intrusion of government is precisely because pilgrimages have become money-making ventures for the privileged and a way of rewarding political party loyalists.

8. On Christmas day 2009, a 23-year-old Nigerian man by the name Umar Farouk Abdulmutallab shocked Nigerians and American society as he attempted to carry out a suicide bombing of an airplane Northwest Flight 253 that had taken off from Lagos to Amsterdam to Detroit. This is the first recorded terrorist act by a Nigerian. This issue has raised a lot of questions about the security system provided in Nigerian airports and how it was possible for Abdlmutallab to conceal dangerous explosives in his underpants without being detected in either Nigeria or Amsterdam. Umar Abdulmutallab is the son of a wealthy Nigerian, a Dr. Abdulmuttallab who was formerly manager of First Bank Nigeria, and who is currently chairman of Nigerian first Islamic Bank, Jaiz International Plc. Dr. Abdulmutallab had warned the United States Embassy officials in Nigeria about the radical views of his son and his suicidal intentions. This warning led to the sons's inclusion on a list of dangerous people with potential terrorist intent. Umar was an engineering student at University College London and he is said to be linked to an Al Qaeda cell in Yemen where he had spent several months supposedly studying at an Arabic institute. What propels a young man from such a solid family background with wonderful educational opportunities, an up-scale living standard, and a promising future turn terrorist and become willing to sacrifice his life as a suicide bomber to destroy Americans? Why was Umar not recognized

from this list by security agents at various airports? President Barack Obama described this incident as a systematic security failure in the handling of the information received prior to the bombing attempt by Umar.

The larger question this incident raises for Nigeria as a nation is how to deal with the volatile religious challenge in the country especially fundamentalism among some Muslim youth in Northern Nigeria. The time has come for exemplary Nigerians like Dr. Abdulmutallab who had the courage to report his son to the American embassy officials to be on the watch for the potential threat his son Umar might cause humanity, to lead the way in asking questions about the type of Koranic education his son might have received. Who are the Islamic leaders in Nigeria influencing this type of behavior from young people and what can be done to stop this trend? Aniagolu-Okoye has examined some of the lessons we can learn about the Umar Abdulmutallab case among other things as a failure of the Nigerian government security system: "The truth is that we do not have the government or security system to protect us from terrorism or any major guerrilla-like threats and should we become seriously challenged by such threats, with a government and security system so compromised, we are doomed".[68]

On the part of the United States, her embassy officials in Nigeria may consider stepping up the promotion of the International Religious Freedom (IRF) Act beyond the meeting of Religious leaders from both Christian and Muslim groups for photographs in front of the Television and Newspapers to concrete programs for youth development so that young people in Nigeria will understand that the United States is an agent for positive social change in the world. The challenges for the United States are: first, the promotion of religious freedom must go hand in hand with promoting democracy and good governance as central to her foreign policy with Nigeria; second, how will they promote religious freedom that will ensure stability in the religiously stable but politically volatile oil producing southern States as well as the politically savvy but religiously volatile northern States?

9. Decentralization and the balance of power between the Federal, State, and Local governments are necessary. The three-tier system of government is meant to provide opportunities for development at different levels where the citizens reside. The goal is that each tier will address the issues that are closer to its jurisdiction of governance. The challenge in Nigeria has been how to determine the balance of power between these levels of government, a balance that will promote an equitable level of productiv-

68 Chichi Aniagolu-Okoye, "What Umar Farouk Abdulmutallab Taught Me," TheNews, 01 February, 2010., p. 5.

ity. While government projects at the federal and State levels seem to draw some degree of supervision and support; projects at the local government level appear to be less and less supervised. This tendency has led to lopsided development and migration from local government areas to the State and federal capitals for white collar jobs. Thus, the local areas are mainly rural by nature while the State develops into township settlements. Nigerians need to channel their energies toward encouraging an even development in the nation. By so doing, citizens will benefit from government policies wherever they reside. This will discourage the clamor for being near the center of power in order to benefit from government programs.

10. The condition of the education system in Nigeria is as deplorable as are the other agencies. The largely government sponsored system of education is highly centralized and that is its bane. The State run schools, at the primary, secondary, and higher levels, depend largely on government funding for existence. This situation has led to manipulation of the education sector to the taste of different governments over the years. With centralized examination boards, admission policy into Universities, teachers' salaries, selection of University Chancellors and pro-chancellors, and mobile academic calendars, the nation's educational system is very unstable. In spite of great strides made in academia by Nigerians, the conditions under which students and teachers study are sub-standard. Thus, the illiteracy rate is growing more and more with the majority of the people now largely illiterate. This position may explain why the gullible public is easily manipulated by political office holders who belong to the elite class. Greater and purpose driven autonomy for Nigerian universities and other institutions of learning is necessary for expanding the educational system. Promoting civic education at the grassroots level is an essential policy issue for developing Nigerian civil society. This policy issue would address two needs: the alarming illiteracy rate and the need to build citizens that will cherish the land of their birth and promote the growth of a viable civil society.

11. The failure of Leadership is the most disturbing political challenge threatening the Nigerian State. Since Nigeria's independence in 1960, the country has enjoyed very limited stable leadership, due largely to military involvement in politics. This situation has enshrined a hybrid of military and democratic rule that continues to derail the nation for personal and selfish gains. Essentially, the Nigerian citizen has been socialized to accept as normal this military/democratic hybrid and to almost perpetually "vote" it into political power through the mockery of what appears to be an election and to continue the vicious cycle of misrule in the Country. A pos-

sible way of departing from this entrenched system of misrule is to embark on a constitutional reform that will make the elections administrative body truly independent from government control. This is the challenge before the Prof. Jega led Independent Electoral Commission as it attempts to conduct the 2011 elections.

Toward A Just Society: Subsidiarity and Federalism[69] in Nigeria

This study has uncovered that a federal political system may possess the theoretical framework for power sharing and governance at the local, State and federal levels of government without having, at the same time, the necessary capacity to accommodate for the cultural, ethnic, religious, and social differences, as is the case in the Nigerian political setup. Thus, in practice, one would embrace a federal type system of government with several adaptations which will make it possible to accommodate the multiplicity of differences within a particular historical and political setting. We embrace the federal political system because it offers some opportunities for the exercise of authority at different levels of government: local, state, and national levels. Apart from these entities, some power resides with social, economic, political and civil groups that are constituent parts of the entire nation.

---

69 The sources of the epigraphs to this section are the theoretical frameworks discussed in chapters one to three of the study and the following works: Paolo G. Carozza, "Subsidiarity As A Structural Principle of International Human Rights Law," *The American Journal of International Law* 97/38 (2003): 38–79; Thomas C. Behr, "Luigi Taparelli D'Azeglio, S.J. (1793–1862) and the Development of Scholastic Natural-Law Thought As a Science of Society and Politics," *Markets & Morality* 6/1 (2003): 1–12; Michael Novak, "Human Dignity, Human Rights," *First Things* 97 (November 1999): 39–42; Mark Friesen, "Subsidiarity and Federalism: An Old Concept with Contemporary Relevance for Political Society," http://cnfs.queensu.ca/federalgovernance/content/volume2/articles/Friesen_Mark.html (12/13/2003) from whom one borrowed some of the views on Federalism; Peter Schineller, (ed.), *The Church Teaches: Stand of the Catholic Bishops of Nigeria on Issues of Faith and Life* (Abuja: Gaudium Et Spes Institute, 2003), pp. 9ff.; Peter Schineller, (ed.), *The Voice of the Voiceless: Pastoral Letters and Communiqués of the Catholic Bishops' Conference of Nigeria* 1960–2002 (Ibadan: Daily Graphics, 2002), pp. 4ff.; James W. Skillen & Rockne M. McCarthy, "Three Views of Social Pluralism: A Critical Evaluation," *Political Order and The Plural Structure of Society*, (eds.), James W. Skillen & Rockne M. McCarthy (Atlanta, Georgia: Emory University/Scholars Press, 1991), pp. 377–417; James W. Skillen, *Recharging The American Experiment: Principled Pluralism for Genuine Civic Community* (Grand Rapids, Michigan: Baker Books, 1994), pp. 61–124; Paul Marshall, *God and The Constitution: Christianity and American Politics* (Lanham, MaryLand: Rowman & Littlefield, 2002), pp. 50–89, 157–168; Kwame Gyekye, *Political Corruption: A Philosophical Inquiry into a Moral Problem* (Accra: Sankofa, 1997), pp. 1–43.

The Correlation between Subsidiarity and Federalism in a Pluralistic Society

Roland L. Watts describes a federation as a political system that has both some degree of shared rule and common institutions while at the same time making room for some degree of autonomous rule of the constituency. In essence, the state or nation makes provision for diversity within the political structure. Thus, federal systems may take different forms such as "quasi-federations," "federations," and "confederacies."[70] The state in a federal system provides for some regional autonomy for the units that are so designated without sacrificing its central hold. The different regions or federations might have ethnic, cultural, religious, and social peculiarities, but the need to maintain some degree of autonomy in the regions or units remains paramount.

In addition, Carl Schmitt makes a pertinent distinction between a unitary state and a federal one that is worthy of note. The territorial state might be governed in two ways. On the one hand, the territorial power remains at the center and monopolizes control while allowing some of the units to be dependent on the center. On the other hand, both the center and the units depend on shared power which is distributed between the whole and the parts. The first is a unitary state, while the second is a federal one.[71]

The central question is whether the power that exists at the regional or local level is dependent on devolution from the federal central government or that such power is entrenched in the regions themselves. In some federal systems, some degree of sovereignty exists in the regions. However, it may also be the case that this sovereignty exists only through devolution from the central government. In such a case, the political legitimacy and mandate to exercise authority lies with the central government. However, if regional autonomy and sovereignty exist independently of recognition and affirmation from the central government, then the regions would have a legitimate mandate to govern and exercise political authority.

There are two fundamental perspectives that one has established. First, the nation-state is an aggregate whole, made up of different units within the society. Second, the question of whether the nation-state is always a legitimate aggregate whole is an open-ended one. Is the nation-state an authentic entity representing its sub-national parts? In theory, the aggregate whole exists as a manifestation of its constituent parts. Its existence should depend on continual affirmation and recognition from the parts. If it is not-then why is it? Federations are typically established because of a perceived need to share governance and institutions at

70 Roland L Watts, *Comparing Federal Systems* (Montreal and Kingston: McGill-Queen's University Press, 1999), pp. 6–7.

71 Luis Maria Bandieri, "Carl Schmitt and Federalism," *Telos* 22 (2002): 48.

some level and would likely not exist if there were no perceived need for some degree of unity. This study argues that in order for the Nigerian federation to continue to exist, there needs to be the continual perception of some necessary degree of unity. Such unity will give legitimacy to the existence of a federal national government that respects the sub-national parts as authentic, autonomous aggregates of the political society. The principle of subsidiarity provides the building blocks to best realize this type of political community.

Pope Pius XI captured well the vision of society being discussed here and defined the precise meaning of subsidiarity.

> ...One should not withdraw from the individual and commit to the community what they can accomplish by their own enterprise and industry. So, too, it is an injustice and at the same time a grave evil and a disturbance of right order to transfer to the larger and higher collectivity functions which can be performed and provided for by lesser and subordinate bodies. Inasmuch as every social activity should, by its very nature, prove a help to members of the body social, it should never destroy or absorb them.[72]

In general, human societies are composed of constituent parts. Nation-states also have sub-units that are parts of the whole. According to Requejo, the fundamental purpose of plural federalism is that it should reflect different types of arrangements, which correspond to the functions to be regulated by the character of the federated units.[73] Subsidiarity supports the view that federal national governments exercise political authority in a manner that respects the characteristics of both the federal and constituent units. Thus, Thomas Hueglin posits that, for Althusius, politics involved a "consociation" whereby a polity is a federally constructed edifice of consociations.[74] The consociations are the relationships and associations that are gradually fashioned at the family, kinship, civil association, and private association levels. Those who take part in these associations within a federation function in both the social and territorial levels in the political sphere.[75] Alain de Benoist opined that Althusius viewed society as organic and holistic, made up of different groups, not individuals, who could not fully develop without being autonomous, and viewed society from below, gradually reaching the top.[76]

Hence, society is organized by the people who belong to these associations and relationships. The different levels of society are aggregate wholes of these rela-

72 QA Par. 79, p. 60. In chapter two, the formal definition of subsidiarity by Pius XI was extensively discussed. Some parts of this principle are mentioned here to show the correlation of subsidiarity to federalism; cf., pp. 53-76 for details.

73 Ferran Requejo, "Federalism and National Groups," *International Social Science Journal* 53/167 (2001): 46.

74 Thomas O. Hueglin, "Federalism, Subsidiarity and the European Tradition: Some Clarifications," *Telos* 100 (1994): 43.

75 Ibid.

76 Alain de Benoist, "The First Federalist: Johannes Althusius," *Telos* 118 (2000): 33.

tionships. Indeed, the consociations between next of kin are the most recognizable. Thus, some consociations are natural in character like the family, community, ethnic group, or to some degree even a nation of peoples. Some consociations are not natural like civil associations. However, both natural and civil groups can enter into partnerships of cooperation for the common good of the society. In the case of Nigeria, subsidiarity will ensure that all the different ethnic communities are proportionately represented and that the majority ethnic groups do not absorb the minority ones as is the case in some parts of the country. Moreover, for the sake of the common good, civil associations based on mutual trust and respect would be formed across ethnic and social lines. While there have been some efforts in this direction in the formation of political parties in Nigeria, the parochial nature of some of the political party associations needs to be expanded. In this way, the autonomy of the natural groups or associations is not taken away but enlarged to embrace a plural social context. Thus, citizens are empowered through the practice of federalism and subsidiarity to accommodate their differences and enter into agreements at both the local and national levels that best serve their interests and promote the common good of all people. The issue of human rights in Nigeria is another major challenge to building a viable civil society. How might subsidiarity promote civil discourse and social justice in the nation?

The Building Blocks of Subsidiarity and the Promotion of Human Rights in Nigerian Society

While it is helpful to trace the history of human rights practice as a global ethic, such a study has been carried out by other scholars.[77] This study established the metaphysical basis for subsidiarity on four grounds in chapter one[78] that are intrinsic for discussing the issue of human rights, and analyzed the essential properties of subsidiarity in chapter two.[79]

The first foundation is that all human beings at the core of their existence, enjoy the capacity and freedom to choose how to go about attaining their ultimate end; hence, humans are able to claim inalienable rights in society. No society can interfere on this deeper level of their existence. This means that, though humans are in the State, it is impossible for the State to totally assimilate them. The worth

77 Michael J. Perry, *The Idea of Human Rights: Four Inquiries* (Oxford: Oxford University Press, 1998), pp. 11–41, 57–86; Jake O. Otonko, "Human Rights, Democracy and Religion: A Clash of Paradigms in the Quest for a Global Ethic and Religious Co-existence in Nigeria," (Ph.D. Dissertation, Katholieke Universiteit Leuven, 2002); Matthew Hassan Kukah, *Democracy and Civil Society in Nigeria* (Ibadan: Spectrum Books, 1999), pp. 37–66, 128–176.

78 See chapter one, pp. 8–9.

79 See chapter two, pp. 46–58.

of the individual person is both ontologically and morally prior to the State or any other social grouping. Since subsidiarity upholds that the human person toward whose growth the principle is aimed is naturally social, it means that human dignity requires relationship with others in various ways from the family, social, and political groups. This dynamic does not suggest in any way that the individual can be reduced to a single unit of the social whole, but it does mean that human self-fulfillment is better realized in community with other people. Thus, the challenge that such an understanding presents in the Nigerian social context is the recognition that individual rights and social rights are not opposed to each other. In fact,

> ...Association with others makes it possible for the person to become more authentically human, and her relationship with others cannot be separated from full expression and realization of her inherent and primary value. One could say that the existence and end of the community (and this can mean a "community" as intimate as a single friendship) is to help the individual flourish, to help create the conditions for her to reach her ultimate fulfillment.[80]

By so doing, subsidiarity expands the model of fulfillment through human relationships to different levels of assistance among social groups. Just as the individual realizes his or her fulfillment in community with others, so also do the smaller associations at the family, market, ethnic, and religious group levels, all part of the community effort for self-actualization. The majority tribal groups are called to help the minority groups with the necessary conditions for them to realize their own dignity and not to overrun them as is the case from the critical analysis of Nigeria's social context.

The second foundation for supporting the promotion of human rights in Nigeria is the recognition that the different human associations, in so far as they maintain and uphold the rule of law, fairness, and mutual respect, should be able to fit organically for the common good of all in the society. The different associations are meant to both serve their individual groups and at the same time support the smaller ones. In this way, the inter-connectivity between the social groups builds up the organic whole of the Nigerian society. The challenge has been that each social group in Nigeria (but most especially the larger ones) have operated on a winner takes all approach, that has made social groups isolated entities without major social links beyond the boundaries of their social group. Subsidiarity makes it necessary that some degree of social interaction exists between the groups just as it is necessary for the individual to be authentic in community. Thus, the individual social group becomes fully relevant in relation to the organic whole of the community without sacrificing its autonomy. That is why programs which encourage social interaction of the different ethnic groups such as the National Youth Service Corps, introduced by the Gowon administration after the civil war, needs more funding and

80 See Carozza, p. 43.

effective leadership to help build better partnerships of cooperation across ethnic, religious, and social barriers.

The third foundation is that human self-fulfillment requires some level of freedom to operate. Humans as thinking beings should be able to direct themselves to their end, struggling in their diversity toward a common ground. In other words, human beings are capable of deciding, through their own initiatives and the circumstances of their historical experience, the direction that their lives ought to take. The capacity to choose between right and wrong is at the heart of how human freedom is to be exercised in the direction of the principle of subsidiary function.

Thus, respecting the dignity of the human person and the integrity of the groups that constitute his or her personhood (and that themselves have a certain integrity) requires that all forms of society be oriented toward the freedom of "lower" forms of association, and ultimately toward the freedom of the individual. In short, subsidiarity takes the freedom necessary to human dignity and extends it to a regard for freedom at all levels of social organization.

This freedom, however, is not simply a negative notion of restraint from interference; it also encompasses an affirmative dimension. It means freedom to act in such a way as to participate fully in the goods of an authentically human life. Thus, since freedom is understood as the ability to reach one's complete flourishing, to realize the capacities of a being of inherent dignity, it can also be served by an intervention that creates the necessary conditions for the individual to lead a life of purpose and fulfillment.[81]

Some concrete examples in the Nigerian context might prove helpful. Each year many college graduates qualify in different educational and technical fields but only very few find jobs that relate to their areas of specialization. In order that their creativity and capacity to realize their human dignity be maintained, some form of assistance is necessary to support people seeking job placement so that they may not engage in destructive social acts against the common good of the society. In fact, one can argue that the increase in armed robbery, political mischief, and insecurity is a direct consequence of the inability of a large number of young people to receive gainful employment from both the public and private sectors. The area of job creation is one where subsidiarity would permit measured intervention by government or other higher associations in order that they might create the right set of conditions for stimulating the economy and providing jobs for the unemployed. In particular, both the "performance society" and "area society" would learn to work hand in hand. In Nigeria, the important role played by ethnic and social development associations could be enhanced to provide job opportunities. Perhaps, it is worth observing that the Obasanjo administration has put in place a reform strategy to address issues of poverty, unemployment, and development of the non-oil sector, and building partnerships for development. This initiative is called the National Economic Empowerment and Development

81 Ibid. pp. 43–44.

Strategy (NEEDS). The challenge lies in the practical commitment to this program by the facilitators. Will they put forward programs that will truly alleviate poverty or will this be another front for the well connected in society to amass wealth and engage in fraudulent contracts?

The Role of Self-Help Grassroots Associations as Agents of Social, Ethical, and Developmental Change in Nigeria[82]

John H. Hamer, writing on voluntary associations in sub-Saharan Africa, made a critical observation shared below:

> Increasingly it has become evident that programs planned and executed from the top down seldom result in significant change at the local level. When, however, people participate in the planning and creation of local level norms in voluntary associations, they take responsibility for inaugurating change.[83]

This is precisely why this study supports the position that, in order to bring about social and ethical transformation in Nigeria, there is great need to help the many existing ethnic, social, gender, development, religious, economic, cultural, human rights, grassroots, voluntary associations in the villages, towns, and urban centers to be able to help themselves and to participate in fashioning the type of society which would support the nation's citizens. In order to achieve such a goal, I have argued that the subsidiarity principle is indispensable in providing both the theoretical and practical platforms for organizing the relationships existing between the parts and the whole in the community.

In general, associations have been described as "shared interest groups established independently of ascribed membership in kinship or territorially based

82 The task here is carried out based on one's study of subsidiarity, the necessity for self-help associations at the grassroots and the insights drawn from these works. John H. Hamer, "Preconditions and Limits in the Formation of Associations: The Self-Help and Cooperative Movement in Subsaharan Africa," *African Studies Review*, XXIV/1 (March, 1981): 113–132; Graham B. Kerr, "Voluntary Associations in West Africa: 'Hidden' Agents of Social Change," *African Studies Review*, XXI/3 (1979): 87–100; Jeffrey Herbst & Charles C. Soludo, "Nigeria," *Aid and Reform in Africa: Lessons from Ten Case Studies*, (eds.),Shantayanan Devarajan; David R. Dollar; Torgny Holmgren (Washington, D.C.: The World Bank, 2001), pp. 645-678; Stephen N. Ndegwa, "Decentralization in Africa: A Stocktaking Survey," *Africa Region Working Paper Series*, No. 40, http://www.worldbank.org/afr/wps/index.htm, November, 2002, pp. 1–31; Adebayo Adedeji and Bamindele Ayo (eds.), *People-Centered Democracy in Nigeria?: The Search for Alternative Systems of Governance at the Grassroots* (Ibadan: Heinemann Educational Books, 2000), pp. 1–18, 87–97, 101ff.

83 See Hamer, p. 113.

groups."[84] Hoebel observes that "such groups form an exclusive membership in the larger society, are formally structured, and produce a sense of cohesiveness among the members."[85] Webster considered such groups as "arising out of a natural grouping together of men (women) of the same age who have similar duties and interests in life."[86] Schurtz, found the "origin of such groups in the antagonism between generations, leading to classification on the basis of age."[87] The different perspectives about what constitutes voluntary associations reveal the complex nature of the issue being considered.

Hamer has argued that the key to understanding the conditions necessary for the formation of voluntary associations involves three issues, namely, culture, social control, and authority.[88] First, Hamer and other scholars argue that the presence of multiple cultures within a society presents the situation where efforts are made by the people to interact at different levels within the community.

> Cultural homogeneity and a limited number of social rules are insufficient for the formation of associations. Rather, it is cultural heterogeneity and increasing complexity of existence that necessitate cross-cutting memberships for linking diverse groupings in opposition to members of the opposite sex, differing age groups, or outsiders in general.[89]

The Nigerian situation is akin to the type described above in some respects where some cultural practices have prevented in some cases both the growth of the individual and that of the community. The question of women's rights in the family vis-à-vis right to family inheritance; ethnic conflicts based on long standing myths and fears; the problem of illiteracy are but some of the issues that have formed and should continue to be addressed by self-help associations.

Second, the issue of social control as described by Hamer in terms of "a code of conduct sanctioned by gossip, ridicule, fear of avoidance, and other forms of diffuse sanctions,"[90] does not make much sense in the kind of society one is advocating with subsidiarity as the glue holding the community together. Instead, I would argue that any form of code of conduct proposed in these associations should respect the mutual rights of the members and needs to uphold the rule of law as agreed upon by the constitution rightly and fairly interpreted. Hence, any form of social control that seeks to bypass such due process is counter-productive and a negation of subsidiarity, which supports the inalienable rights of the human person.

---

84 Ibid. these works are cited in Hamer.

85 Ibid.

86 Ibid.

87 Ibid.

88 See Hamer, pp. 113–114 for details.

89 See Hamer, p. 113.

90 See Hamer, p. 114.

Third, on the issue of authority within self-help associations in the community, one agrees in part with Hamer that: achieved rather than ascribed positions are critical for the establishment of authority. Society leaders acquire their positions not on the basis of kinship rank or seniority, but on the ability to communicate with the spirit world, demonstrated acquisition of wealth, exercise of influence, and/or exceptional circumspection and neutrality in decision making. The influence of such leaders must extend beyond their particular descent group to the whole community.[91]

The issues one disagrees with concerning authority as described above include "the ability to communicate with the spirit world, demonstrated acquisition of wealth" and to some degree the "exercise of influence." This is because one major issue that has become a plague to the Nigerian society is the un-checked nature of wealth acquisition in the nation. People who have acquired wealth in dubious ways have several praise singers and appear in the public arena as people of great influence until the source of their wealth becomes public knowledge. The Obasanjo administration should be given some credit for establishing the Economic and Financial Crimes Commission, under the leadership of a fearless Nigerian policeman Nuhu Ribadu, which has been very proactive in detecting dubious wealth acquisitions by some un-patriotic Nigerians.

Apart from the three positions one has discussed above as necessary pre-conditions for effective self-help associations, there are other concrete issues worth examining in view of the historical circumstance of the Nigerian State one has extensively discussed. Adebayo Adedeji, in his critique of the Nigerian political structure, proposed a "People-centered development vision," that will support the governance structures in existence at the grassroots in the nation.

Popular participation is the *fons et origo* of a people-centered development vision that embraces the transformation agenda and is likely to achieve Africa's second liberation – its freedom from poverty, hunger, disease, ignorance and environmental degradation; and its emergence as a self-reliant and dynamic political economy, fully integrated and no longer marginalized, but rather participating actively in the community of nations. Popular participation, being at the heart of a people-centered development paradigm, looks up to justice, sustainability and inclusiveness as the defining principles of authentic development. Development—be it political, economic or social—becomes a people's movement rather than a foreign-funded initiative. Government's primary role is as an enabling one: to provide people with the opportunity and environment for self-development.[92]

Significantly, Adedeji acknowledged that two principles of Catholic social teachings are essential to realizing the vision of a people-centered development,

91 Ibid.

92 Adebayo Adedeji, "Renewal of the Search for Systems of Local Governance that can Serve the Common Good," *People-Centered Democracy in Nigeria*, p. 3.

namely subsidiarity and solidarity.[93] Adedeji proceeded to show how the existing community-based associations in Nigeria have been the major glue holding the people together in the face of government failure and reckless mismanagement of the resources at their disposal. Two independent researches were conducted by the "African Center for Development and Strategic Studies" and the "Research Group on Local Institutions" [LISDP], all based at the Obafemi Awolowo University in 1993. The following Local government areas and States were covered by both researches: Afijio, Oyo State; Dekina, Kogi State; Ethiope East, Delta State; Ijebu-Ode, Ogun State; Mbaitoli, Imo State; Ohaozara, Abia State; and Wurno, Sokoto State. Others included, Borno, Imo, Ogun, Kaduna, Benue, Ekiti and Osun States. In total, 12 States representing one-third of the States in different parts of Nigeria were covered.[94]

The research by LISDP discussed above made the following observations.

> The principal finding of all the researchers in all the local government areas in all the states covered is that the country's saving grace are the long-neglected traditional modes of social organization and civil society organizations. It is they that have successfully saved villages and towns from total collapse and have enabled the people to cope and survive. These modes of social organization consist of institutions centered around [on] traditional rulers, trade and professional guilds, age grade associations, town/village unions, community development associations, women's groups and associations, as well as religious and social organizations. There is no doubt that Nigerian communities are currently governed by these indigenous institutions.[95]

According to the observations made by the researchers above, findings which I share deeply, the hope of a bright future in Nigeria lies in community-based self-help associations. That is why I have made the case for government to support these associations as major partners in the building of Nigerian society. In so doing, one does not suggest in any way that government take over the running of these associations, for that will be a violation of subsidiarity. However, government can help organize these institutions and support the community projects which otherwise will be impossible for the associations to do for themselves. The National Orientation Agency which is responsible for promoting this type of grassroots networking is presently grossly under-funded, which is an indication of the lack of commitment by government to enter into these types of partnerships with community self-help associations.

Since there exist different types of community-based associations in Nigeria with divergent experiences and need, one cannot offer a general formula for the governance of these institutions. In fact, such a measure will be a violation of subsidiarity in terms of centralization. The proposals I am advancing will better be

93 Ibid. p. 3.

94 Ibid. p. 10 for details.

95 Ibid.

carried out through a process of dialogue, mutual trust, shared interests, and shared burdens, all with the goal of promoting the common good of the community. Thus, I have drawn from a variety of proposals made by scholars from the Nigerian experience[96] to put forward the following guidelines as the necessary pre-conditions, conditions, and limits in the strengthening and formation of self-help community-based associations that respect the principle of subsidiarity, promote social justice, bring about solidarity and promote the common good.

Proposed Guidelines for the Strengthening and Formation of Community-Based Self-Help Associations in Nigeria.

1. To uphold the priority of the human person over that of the State, realizing that the person is born to live in community with others. Thus, strengthening the family and extended family system is key to building healthy communities.
2. To promote the role of district heads and traditional council of chiefs.
3. To build on existing ethnic or tribal unions.
4. To maintain village and town unions as centers of community development.
5. To expand the existing local credit unions.
6. To elect transparent leaders and to maintain a transparent electoral process.
7. To practice accountability and self-reliance.
8. To promote formal and informal means of communication.
9. To promote the participation of women for concrete activities toward achieving specific objectives including seeking leadership roles in the community.
10. To promote both legal and social justice.
11. To exercise an open administration.

---

96 Mike Adeyeye, "Decentralization versus Local Level Governance: The Congruence Problem," *People-Centered Democracy in Nigeria*, pp. 115–128; Dele Gege, Shittu R. Akinola, "Balancing the Equation of Governance at the Grassroots," *People-Centered Democracy in Nigeria*, pp. 171–197; Aloy C. Nwosu, "Town Union Assembly as an Alternative to Local Government Council," *People-Centered Democracy in Nigeria*, pp. 199–204; Olu Okotoni, "Village Administration and Community Affairs," *People-Centered Democracy in Nigeria*, pp. 205–228; Bamindele Ayo, "Putting in Place People-Controlled Structural Frameworks—Which Way Forward?," *People-Centered Democracy in Nigeria*, pp. 231–234; Adebayo Adedeji, 'The Way Forward: Operationalizing the Six Fundamental Principles of People-Centered Systems of Local Government," *People-Centered Democracy in Nigeria*, pp. 235–251; Joy Ogwu, "Perspectives on the Critical Impediments to Women in the Decision-making Process," (eds.), Clara Osinulu & Nina Mba, *Nigerian Women in Politics* (1986–1993) (Ikeja, Lagos: Malthouse Press, 1996), pp. 35–42; Abiodum Idowu, "The Impact of Government-Sponsored Women's Organizations," *Nigerian Women in Politics*, pp. 43–63.

12. To practice consensus agreement as a means for collective-choice arrangements.
13. To encourage conflict resolution.
14. To respond to the benefits and burdens of the extended family system.
15. To be open to a balanced monitoring system.
16. To put forward realistic and attainable goals.
17. To practice and promote decision-making from the bottom rather than the top.
18. To form inter-ethnic, inter-communal, and inter-religious partnerships of cooperation.
19. To be open to limited and targeted intervention by a higher body as a last resort to promote the common good of the whole community.
20. To challenge over-centralization, anarchy, and corruption.

The Principle of Subsidiarity and the Catholic Church in Nigeria

The Catholic Church in Nigeria has made use of the subsidiarity principle as the hinge of the society at different times.[97] In particular, the laity in Nigeria has contributed immensely to building the Church, a fact, well documented.[98] The Catholic Bishops Conference of Nigeria (CBCN) has over the years commented on issues of Faith and Social Life, 1960–2003[99] that relate to subsidiarity.

The first indication of some use of subsidiarity does appear in the statements made by the bishops at the time of Nigeria's independence from British colonial rule on October 1, 1960 entitled: "The Catholic Church in an Independent Nigeria."[100] Since this was the first major pronouncement by the bishops in an independent Nigeria, their optimism for the future of the nation was very high as

97 See chapter two, pp. 99–21. Our task here is not to re-visit this question but to examine the extent to which the Catholic Bishops Conference of Nigeria has made use of subsidiarity in its Pastoral Letters and Communiqués.

98 Gabriel A. Ojo, *The Laity and the New Era of Evangelization* (Kaduna, Nigeria: Layon, 1987), pp. 12–25.

99 Peter Schineller, (ed.), *The Voice of the Voiceless: Pastoral Letters and Communiques of the Catholic Bishops' Conference of Nigeria* (1960–2002) (Ibadan: Daily Graphics, 2002), pp. 24ff.; Peter Schineller, (ed.), *The Church Teaches: Stand of the Catholic Bishops of Nigeria on Issues of Faith and Life* (Ibadan: Daily Graphics, 2003), p.86ff.; These two volumes contain 42 years of documented history of the developments that have taken place in the Catholic Church in Nigeria in the larger context of Catholic Social Teaching.

100 See *The Voice of the Voiceless*, pp. 1-46 for details of this document.

one takes a closer look at the document they put forward. At this time, it is significant to note, the majority of the bishops were missionaries working in Nigeria prior to independence (sixteen out of the nineteen existing bishops were missionaries and three Nigerians). It would be fair to say that the document under review was produced by those who were not completely immersed in the struggle for independence and those who may be wrongly perceived as an extension of the colonial administration. But in general, they produced a beautiful document, guided by some of the major papal social encyclicals.

The bishops, while discussing the important role of the State, maintained that the government exists for the people: hence institutions such as the family and private property derive from the natural law to help foster human ends and fulfillment. Thus, "the State may regulate such institutions in view of the common good. But it cannot eliminate or supersede them."[101] Clearly, the bishops use here the subsidiarity principle that one has discussed at great length in this book. The point is that the bishops understood the relevance of this principle for governance in Nigerian society. While discussing the social problems of the nation, the bishops specifically called for unity in diversity:

> Right from the start it is well to recognize that Nigerian unity includes a great deal of diversity. The country is one state. But it includes many nations. Each one of the several large groupings in our multi-national state possesses a language and traditions that are its own; each people owns a certain group loyalty; and the members of each ethnic group have a natural tendency to associate with one another, even when they are away from their state of origin...It is perfectly legitimate to suggest that the future development of Nigeria should respect the different national traditions of our people. However, above the fellowship of these particular traditions stands the greater fellowship of the state. Nigerians, especially the country's leaders, must primarily look to the common well-being of all the members of the political community.[102]

The above mentioned position of the bishops encouraged community-based associations that may be ethnic in character but they also encouraged the autonomous pursuits of these groups be channeled towards the common good of the larger political community. In fact, they challenged Catholics to be respectful of their fellow citizens and not to engage in divisive practices: "We insist that no Catholic can with a good conscience indulge in a policy that sets one section of the state against another – 'tribalism' as this attitude is usually called."[103] Unfortunately, both the issue of Nigeria's unity and tribalism coupled with bad leadership has been the bane of the nation as I have indicated in this work.

---

101 Ibid. p. 6.

102 Ibid. p. 7.

103 Ibid. p. 8.

The emphatic mention and attempt to apply the principle of subsidiarity by the bishops took place in their February, 1972 Pastoral Letter.[104] The bishops made a statement on the present social situation in the nation and stated two positive developments mixed with some degree of difficulty.

1. [A] Nation which is passing through an important spiritual experience; there is growing awareness of the intrinsic value of the human person and of the inviolable rights of the individual human person.
2. [On] this positive side, too, we see the ever expanding process of a just "socialization" assisted by government finances, through individual human strivings in a widening range of commodity projects, and institutionalized community services. We see the writing on the wall, too, in an increasing number of African countries, of expanding state-control and government take-over in matters where the Christian social principle of subsidiarity (of social help and not state domination) should apply. The gradual state take-over of denominational schools is but one instance of this emerging pattern of thought. We must be prepared always to raise our cry against any form of dictatorship before it becomes a too strong and stifling reality.[105]

The discovery that the bishops in Nigeria in the early 70s attempted to apply the subsidiarity principle was a hopeful development in supporting the type of vision for a just society I am proposing. The bishops proceeded from the initial premise under review to state the social problems in the country and to make recommendations for resolving the social crisis. Among other things, the bishops supported rural development, social movements, workers' unions, social justice, and partnership between religious groups and government to bring about social change in the nation. Specifically, they addressed issues such as unemployment, adult education, and agriculture.[106] In retrospect, I can now see the context in which the Church in Nigeria has made much contribution in the areas of education, health care and social mobilization of the people. The Church can still do better, especially in participating as a Non-governmental organization (NGO) that has the trust of the people and the human resources to open up the villages to positive social transformation as echoed by the bishops in their February 10, 1979, Pastoral Letter, section 43 entitled "Self–Help and the State."

> A principle of good government in a free society is dependence on the people to achieve their own solutions—if necessary, with government subvention and encouragement, though without government takeover or law-making. Again, a political astuteness which assists non-governmental sectors of the society to be responsible for social goals can

104 *"The Church and Nigerian Social Problems," The Voice of the Voiceless*, pp. 58–74 for details.

105 Ibid. p. 58.

106 Ibid. pp. 69–72.

> leave government free to apportion its resources to more intractable problems. Achieving a more balanced sharing in national wealth and resources, better urban industries on the one hand and rural farm communities on the other [hand] will require a great infusion of government help. The nation's food supply and the stability of its dominant rural population are at stake.[107]

Furthermore, it is important to state that the bishops had indicated their willingness to cooperate with government as active partners in grassroots initiatives with past regimes but did not receive a very favorable response. Most of the theoretical projects such as MAMSER for social mobilization, reconstruction and education of the citizens, DFRRI which stands for the Directorate for Food, Roads and Rural Infrastructure, NDE for the National Directorate for Employment, Better Life for Rural Women, and the People's Bank have all collapsed due to lack of responsible accountability and partnership with grassroots oriented non-governmental agencies such as churches, community associations, and other people-oriented agencies. Thus, I will re-echo the position of the bishops in their Pastoral Letter of March, 1990.

> As Church, with our wide and effective rural network of facilities and structures, we are ready to cooperate with government in promoting the objectives of these people-oriented schemes. We hope that our hands of collaboration will not be rejected[108].

The "Prayer against Bribery and Corruption in Nigeria," issued by the bishops in their Pastoral Letter at Ibadan in 1998, is a classic case of the bishops attempts to respond to the socio-political and ethical challenges facing the nation by appealing to a higher source. This prayer is constantly been recited in all parishes and out-station Churches at every Eucharistic celebration nationwide. It is one instance when the people are properly mobilized to address an intractable issue that continues to derail the nation and give her people bad publicity both nationally and internationally. I am of the opinion that this method of creating public awareness be utilized in discussing not only government matters but also Church policy.

Specifically, there are two documents issued by the bishops that capture the practical implications for the Church's engagement in social issues based on Gospel values. In their meeting at Abuja in February 2002, the bishops put forward one of the more balanced positions on both the roles of government and the Church in meeting the common good. In the sub-section 4 entitled "Action to Be Taken," the bishops called on the government to make these commitments.

- We renew our call for a national conference that will examine the sources of conflict and propose measures to heal the divisions. To say "no" to dialogue is to say "yes" to violence.
- We call on government to put in place qualitative and functional education at all levels, which should include sound moral and religious instruc-

107 "Civic and Political Responsibility of the Christian," *The Voice of the Voiceless*, p. 98.

108 "The Winds of Change in Nigeria," *The Voice of the Voiceless*, p. 237.

tion. In this connection, we renew our demand for the return of schools to their legitimate owners.

- We reaffirm the secular nature of the Nigerian State as enshrined in the Constitution of the Federal Republic of Nigeria.
- Government should intensify efforts at creating job opportunities for the unemployed.
- Government should not only allow but foster the creation of more political parties so that more options are available to the public.
- Insecurity in the land is not solved by the proliferation of dubious vigilante groups. There is no civilized alternative to a well-trained, well-equipped, and well-paid Police Force.
- We call on government to conduct its business in the open, and not as if it were a secret cult. People have the right to full knowledge of what programs and plans are discussed in the halls of government.
- The war against corruption has so far proved ineffectual, partly because many of the principal actors in government are themselves not free from corruption. Good intentions are not enough. An independent body should be given full power and authority to wage an effective war against corruption at all levels of government and business.[109]

On its part, the bishops pledged to make these commitments.

- We reaffirm the indispensable role of the Justice, Development, and Peace Commissions/Committees (JDPC) at the parish, diocesan, provincial and national levels. These Commissions/Committees are not simply another group or society in the Church but are to oversee and take leadership responsibility in the struggle to heal the wounds of the nation. In accord with the Social Teaching of the Church, we encourage Catholics to enter the difficult world of politics. Through the Justice, Development and Peace Commissions/Committees and the Catholic Social Forum (CSF) the Church will provide political education formation both for candidates vying for office and the electorate. Catechesis in parishes should include the Church's teaching on the social dimension of sin and grace, and on how Catholics should be agents of healing and reconciliation, standing for non-violent action for justice and peace.
- The Church will continue and intensify its efforts to complement the programs of government in providing health care, education and other social services.
- The Church commits itself to establishing centers of vocational, functional education that will lead to gainful employment.

---

109 "Healing the Wounds of the Nation," *The Voice of the Voiceless*, pp. 434–435.

- Working with government we will put in place programs to combat the HIV/AIDS pandemic. These programs will aim at creating AIDS awareness, arresting the spread of the virus, and extending pastoral care to infected individuals and their families.
- We remind all God's people and the laity in particular, that they are to be salt of the earth and light of the world. All Catholics must be seen to be part and parcel of the healing process of the nation.
- The Church will continue to set an example for the nation by renewed efforts to follow the example of Jesus by preaching the good news to the poor (cf. Lk. 4:18), and looking after those who are most neglected. If a nation cannot truly be great when it neglects the needs of its poorest members, how much more true is that of the Church, the family of God?[110]

The partnership discussed above between government and the Church is one major step forward to bringing about the type of social justice oriented civil society I have put forward here. The practical realization of these goals will take place when both the government and the Church allow the subsidiarity principle to operate by providing support to communities at the grassroots to help themselves without interference except for the sake of promoting the common good of all the society.

The partnership approach between government and Church was again adopted by the bishops in dealing with the issue of young girls and women taken to serve as prostitutes in the Western world, particularly in Italy. The Church leaders affirmed:

> We will collaborate with governments here and abroad, and with security officials in freeing women who are enslaved in sex exploitation overseas and returning them to their homes. In pursuit of this, we encourage our faithful towards effective collaboration with existing national networks of Church societies, NGOs, and other established organizations. We support the efforts of the Nigeria Conference of Women Religious in spearheading this campaign.[111]

This type of approach to confront a major issue such as prostitution is remarkable. But beyond this effort, one will hope that at the grassroots level, citizens will begin to address some of the cultural practices which continually place women as second class citizens in their families, villages, communities and the society. Here, I will recount issues such as the right to inheritance in the family, the right to participate in family meetings and have an active voice, the right to education, the right to be respected in marital commitments especially in case of polygamous marriages, the right to be respected in the public space of politics and social engagement, and, of course, the right to play a more active role in the Church beyond roles traditionally associated with women. The extent to which the partnership between the government and the Church will be measured will depend on the

110 Ibid. pp. 435–436.

111 "Restoring the Dignity of the Nigerian Woman," *The Voice of the Voiceless*, pp. 454–455.

extent to which these issues are carried out in the families, villages, local associations, Churches, local governments, states and the larger society.

Questions for Further Reflection

1. Does the critical reflection on the Nigerian state provide some balanced nuance of the complex issues involved in building homogenous and just society? Describe and discuss these issues?
2. Do you support or disagree with the thesis that subsidiarity and federalism can promote grass-roots self-help development and social change in Nigeria?
3. How is your local Church/Mosque community involved in issues that connect faith to social, ethical, economic, political, judicial, and public policy activities?
4. How do you understand the role and responsibility of elected government officials to their constituency?
5. How do you understand your responsibility as a citizen in shaping the type of elected government of your choosing?

5

TOWARD THE FUTURE OF SUBSIDIARITY IN CHURCH/ STATE RELATIONS IN NIGERIAN SOCIETY

The extent, to which the principle of subsidiarity can be sustained as a tool for promoting a just Nigerian society, will depend on how it is practiced at the local levels by social groups such as the family, churches, mosques, communities, associations, and non-governmental organizations. It will also involve some degree of practical commitment by people who are willing to allow this principle of natural social philosophy to operate, without losing sight of its main goal: to help persons in community to help themselves and to promote the common good of all.

Subsidiarity and Structural Organization in the Church

Kaufmann has raised a fundamental question about the extent to which the historical and social reality of the Church is at the heart of ecclesiology. According to him, there is some confusion between the essence of the 'social' and the 'sociological' reality of the Church that needs some clarification in order to understand discourse about the Church's social reality. The former, that is the social aspect, can be understood in this way: "The social reality of the Church is the Church in action, what is visibly happening in Rome and elsewhere in the context of what is called 'the Catholic Church.' It is also the context of the experience of the Church's members and the context of religious socialization, that is, the transmission of the faith to successive generations."[1] The Latter, that is the sociological aspect, is viewed this way: "The sociological reality of the Church is a quite narrow reality, the sum of statements which have been formulated about the social reality of the Church from a sociological perspective. These sociological propositions, of course, are also a social fact and by chance they may influence the social reality of the Church."[2] Hence, the social reality of the Church is a complex phenomenon that takes different forms in different situations of the lived experience of Church. Similarly, sociological propositions of the Church's social reality are varied precisely because of the complex nature of the Church's social reality. Kaufmann posits that one should not take for granted the social reality of the Church as if it were secondary to the spiritual reality of the Church.

> This devaluation of social reality, that is, of the field of lived experience, is dangerous for the transmission of the faith in modernizing societies. For the transmission of the faith has to be [effected] by social mechanisms which themselves are becoming more complex, and more dependent upon the lived experience of the Church. This experience is interpreted not only by the ecclesiastical authorities but also by public opinion and above all by the persons in charge of the education of successive generations.[3]

The necessity to interpret the social reality of the Church through a sociological lens does not make the sociologist an expert on Church matters; rather, it underscores the fact that lived human experience is at the heart of any social reality including that of the Church. Thus, the social context in which the Christian reality is experienced as Church requires constant study, reflection, meditation, and practice. I do realize that in the Church, one is dealing with both a temporal and transcendent reality, hence the need for a balance between these perspectives of Church.

> Although the spiritual, sacramental, mystical reality of the Church is not accessible to sociological analysis, the sociologist must take note of the social fact that the Church is constituted by faith in its transcendent reality; otherwise he lacks an adequate understanding of what he is studying.[4]

---

1 Franz-Xaver Kaufmann, "The Principle of Subsidiarity Viewed by the Sociology of Organizations," *The Nature and Future of Episcopal Conferences,* (eds.), Herve Legrand, Julio Manzanares, and Antonio Garcia y Garcia (Washington, D.C.: The Catholic University Press of America, 1988), p. 276.

2 Ibid.

3 Ibid. p. 277.

4 Ibid. p. 278. The perspectives of sociologists vary depending on the extent to which they understand the social reality they are analyzing. Perhaps, it is necessary to say that sociological analysis that is done from a distance of the social reality is more likely to be controversial. "Thus, sociologists must consider themselves and explain to others their positions

The transcendent nature of the Church is the life wire for its existence and relevance in society. If the faith of the Church were to lose its core dynamic spirit, some loss of religious identity might be manifested that would provide a major challenge to the Church. In society, this type of challenge be it in economics, politics, or family relationships, has been met with some degree of resolution by appealing to structural differentiation and relative autonomy in the public square. The major challenge for the Church seems to be to what extent will the continuous articulations of subsidiarity within purely hierarchical terms, without any type of functional and structural complementarities, respond to the decentralizing tendencies of civil and political structures today. Thus, without going into details about the modern theory of organizations which makes one to realize the complex nature of organized social reality today, it is necessary to propose that some attempt be made in the Church's structural organization to respond to the complex nature of its social reality and that of the larger society. In view of this complexity, the reasonable approach appears to be maintaining the balance between a more elastic organization and a rigid organization.

> The principle of hierarchical organization has not been abandoned in the process, but it has itself become more complex. The elementary principle of all formal organization, that is, the specialization and combination of differentiated functions, today is typically repeated at several levels of the organization, so that there are different levels of control in the cybernetic sense. These systems try to combine the advantages of both centralization and decentralization.[5]

Does the Church have something to learn from society in terms of how the nature of the Church's hierarchical structural organization has affected and may continue to affect the understanding of subsidiarity proposed for the social order?[6] Is the hierarchy of the Church open to making the necessary changes in its structural organization that respects the dignity of the people of God? These questions raise some concrete issues from a sociological or even theological perspective about the applicability of subsidiarity in the Church.[7]

---

with regard to any social reality. We know that certain sympathy (even at some distance) with a social phenomenon usually contributes to a better understanding of it. Moreover, any communication with the actors at work in a certain social sphere makes a certain sharing in fundamental perspectives necessary, if the communication is going to succeed." p. 278, note. 5.

5 Ibid. p. 286.

6 In chapter one this study explained the nature of subsidiarity as an organological principle with both a vision of society and association with an innate relationship between the parts and the whole, as a unity, and as a system where the parts and the whole have different functions but are mutually dependent on each other in a non-hierarchical fashion. See chapter one, pp. 10-16.

7 Joseph A. Komonchak, "Subsidiarity in the Church: The State of the Question," *The Nature and Future of Episcopal Conferences*, pp. 298-349 for a detailed analysis of the central issues

Is the Church's hierarchical structure too simple from an organizational point to face the complex tasks confronting the Church in pluralistic modern societies? Have the Church's administrative structures become much more complex than the original sense of *hierarchia ordinis* from a sacramental perspective? Perhaps, this is a matter reserved for theological, pastoral, and canonical discussions. Kaufmann puts it poignantly:

> It is probable that the centralizing tendencies proper to any hierarchical organization also operate within the Catholic Church. The violations of the principle of subsidiarity which result from them are hidden in the case of the Catholic Church by the idea of a sacramental hierarchy...one of the most important tasks of ecclesiology is to distinguish more clearly between the essentially hierarchical functions of the Church, which arise from its sacramental order, and those which are only accidentally hierarchical and arise from its administrative order.[8]

There are two implications arising from the above question. First, there is no doubt that the distribution of competencies requires a central administration. The challenge is the degree of power which a central administration should have on concrete local issues like those between the Roman curia and regional or national bishops' conferences for "it is quite clear that a central administration will always be more insensitive to regional particularities."[9] But these reflections are not limited only to the relations between Rome and Episcopal conferences, but can be applied to relations between the parish and the central administration in a diocese and even among individual dioceses. The struggle for autonomy and communion in African Churches, especially from the central administration of Rome, is a case in point.

> The whole debate on inculturation, which has been the dominant theme of theology in Africa and which the 1994 Synod of Bishops for Africa supports as the organizational metaphor for evangelization, is finally an issue of power. Who decides how the Church should live in the context of Africa? Who makes decisions about marriage, liturgy, canon law, spirituality, and theology? The Roman technocracy which interferes in the free experience of the life of the Church in particular contexts of Africa is not qualified to do so. The pro-nuncio whose opinion carries more weight in the Roman scheme of things than the pastor of a diocese is not really qualified to speak for the Church [in Africa]. The assembly effectively convoked to listen to the Word of God and to keep the memory of Jesus, the community which welcomes the Word and proclaims and bears testimony to him as the Savior of the world must not be confused with

of this debate from the time of Gundlach, Heinrich Pesch, Bishop Ketteler, Nell-Breuning, Pius XII to John Paul II. In the course of the study, one will highlight some of the conclusions which one is more interested in at this time.

8 See Kaufmann, pp. 288-289.

9 Ibid. p. 289.

> the offices of congregations or secretariats in Rome nor with a pro-nuncio who does not preside over an assembly.[10]

Second, the apparent tension between sacramental hierarchy and administrative hierarchy may be resolved in one way by decentralization which makes room for the expansion of relevant administrative roles within the Church that are not tied to the sacraments. The attempts being made today toward lay administrative roles in the Church is a step in the right direction, especially in the developed countries of the West. In African Churches, clericalism is still the order of the day. The challenge in African countries will be how to open up parish and diocesan centers for lay persons with the qualified training to bring their competency to the table and help build the local Church.

At this juncture, it will be helpful to emphasize two practical conclusions made by Komonchak in an essay mentioned earlier. First, he challenged all interested in the issue of the applicability of subsidiarity in the Church to examine the origin of the principle.

> The principle was elaborated and formulated in response to the growing centralization of state authority, which was absorbing the legitimate roles of other communities and reducing the freedom and self-responsibility of individuals...Within the Church, this problem needs to be addressed in the broad context not only of the powerful centralizing tendencies of the last two centuries but also of the social theory, imported from without, which legitimated them.[11]

The second point of Komonchak emphasizes the relevance of subsidiarity in helping to check some of the centralizing tendencies in the Church: "the persistence of the same complaints over these fifty years suggests that some fundamental structural problems remain in the Church...I do not believe that it was subsidiarity which first put people in mind of the problems, but the problems which suggested the usefulness of the principle."[12]

Lastly, it is reasonable to say that an overly centralized view of subsidiarity is inadequate to show how competencies should be distributed. That is why it is necessary to analyze the problems, structures, social context, and means of control, communication and development in each particular case in order to ascertain how these contribute toward or away from the common good. Indeed, "the expansion of the means of control was the historical reason why it was just and necessary to formulate the principle of subsidiarity with regard to the state. The Church has to

10 Elochukwu E. Uzukwu, *A Listening Church: Autonomy and Communion in African Churches* (Maryknoll, New York: Orbis Books, 1996), p. 61.

11 See Komonchak, pp. 342-343. The social theory referred to is that of the view of the Church as *societas perfecta* and the model of sovereignty, cf. Komonchak, p. 343, note 116.

12 Ibid. p. 343.

keep in mind that the very secular means of control today are growing so fast that it cannot consider them indifferent to its spiritual and social task."[13]

The Second Vatican Council's[14] document on the Church, *Lumen Gentium*, in chapter three entitled "The Church is Hierarchical," (LG 8) discussed the leadership structure of the Church and affirmed Jesus Christ as the eternal pastor who sends out his apostles on a mission to preach the kingdom of God (Mt. 10: 1-42). The document makes it clear that the Church's hierarchy is called to a pastoral function in varying degrees depending on their particular calling and function in the hierarchical order. The image of the Good Shepherd, who came not to be served but to serve and lay down his life for his sheep (Mt. 20:28; Mk. 10:45), is set before the hierarchy in their pastoral duties to the people of God (LG 27-29). Thus, the issue of charism and institution in the Church has become the object for controversy which is beyond this study except to say that Dulles has proposed the context for addressing this issue in the Christian community that is related to subsidiarity. According to Dulles, Vatican II left two unanswered questions: "Is the charismatic superior or inferior to the hierarchical? Is the charismatic a free and unpredictable outpouring of the Spirit or a permanent gift associated to certain offices?"[15] Dulles proposed a synthesis that will address these issues by upholding "unity in distinctness, sacramentality, necessity of institution, and of the charismatic."[16] He upheld the mutual dependence of charism on institution and institution on charism.

> The charismatic, by offsetting the vocational hazards of the official, helps to prevent the institution from becoming rigid, mechanical, routinized, and domineering. Office-holders who try to quench the Spirit (cf. 1 Thess. 5:19) are subject to correction. Criticism, however, can have no place in the Church unless it proceeds from faith, from love, and from recognition of the rights of office, and unless it aims to build up the body of Christ in unity.[17]

This is precisely the role of subsidiarity in acting as a stabilizing principle in the Church and society. In this connection, the pastoral office of Church leaders demands that the leaders be Good Shepherds who are not "rigid, mechanical, routinized, and domineering," but people open to the Spirit rather than seeking to quench it. Pastoral leadership demands that office holders in the Church be accountable to the People of God by the manner in which they carry out their

---

13 See Kaufmann, p. 290.

14 "Dogmatic Constitution on the Church Lumen Gentium (LG)," *Vatican Council II: Constitutions, Decrees, Declarations*, (ed.), Austin Flannery (Newport, New York: Costello Publishing Company, 1996), pp. 1-95.

15 Avery Dulles, *A Church to Believe In: Discipleship and Dynamics of Freedom* (New York: Crossroad, 1983), p. 26.

16 Ibid. pp. 29-35.

17 Ibid. p. 37.

spiritual and social mission. This is the proper context in which the Church's articulation of subsidiarity for the social order in society would make any sense. What is the point of calling on the political and public office holders to practice accountability, if the same practice is not promoted in our parishes, diocesan offices, and among the leaders of the Church? The recent sexual abuse of minors by some members of the clergy in the Catholic Church in the United States is a case in point where the People of God in the Archdiocese of Boston brought to bear their collective voices to force Cardinal Bernard Law to resign. The lesson from this action is clear that the Laity should no longer be viewed as a passive group in the Church. To this extent there is great need today and always to maintain some balance between the genuine response from the Laity and the openness from Church leaders.

> There is no question but that the church is not built up "from below" by the religious needs and wishes of the people according to their taste and feelings. At the same time, the church "from above" should not be misunderstood in the sense that all power and all truth flow from the top. It has never been maintained that the Spirit of truth and holiness is active only in church officials...The ethical consciousness of today's young people is concerned not only with the correct actions of individuals within a given institution, but with justice in the social institutions themselves. The church's future depends on whether its institutional structure gives witness to the teaching it proclaims. More subsidiarity within the church might make it even more credible in the eyes of modern man (woman).[18]

In the Nigerian context, where corruption has eaten deep into the fabric of the nation, the Church leaders need to be accountable at the parish, diocesan, and national levels to the people they have taken an oath to serve. In this way, the Church will lead by example and stand a better chance of being an efficacious sign of Christ as the "Light of the Nations," in this part of the world. When the Church fails to lead in areas of accountability, fight against corruption, and social justice issues, people will find it difficult to distinguish between actions of Church leaders and those of leaders of the State. This will be an unfortunate and sad development in our attempt to making Nigeria a less corrupt nation.

Subsidiarity and Nationalism

The other issue implicated in the operation of the principle of subsidiary function is the question of nationalist sentiments and Church practices. Since subsidiarity promotes the fact that decisions be made by those who are closer to the social context where such decisions are being made, how will this impact some issues involving cultural, ethnic, national, and regional developments? In the Nigerian context,

18 Walter Kerber, "The Principle of Subsidiarity within the Church," *Theology Today* 32/3 (Fall, 1985): 228-229.

the period of mission territories is almost over in many dioceses. The local leadership is in charge of the Church. Yet, there have been situations where the Vatican, in consultation with some bishops who claim to be speaking for the people, made appointments of bishops across ethnic and cultural lines that have created some degree of instability for the local Church. One is aware that promoting cultural and ethnic reconciliation and understanding is a necessary task of the Gospel. However, this type of evangelization needs to be gradual, open, realistic, fair, and just. The Vatican should not be viewed as forcing ethnic groups who have not resolved long-standing tensions, both in their civic relationships and in the Church, to start working together overnight with the hope that somehow the deep seated ethnic tensions of so many generations will be pacified. This was one of the mistakes made by the colonial powers in Africa, and, in situations like the one described above, it is reasonable to understand when people make an obvious connection with the Vatican as a colonial power. In such a case, the people's allegiance is obviously to the land of their birth and not to the Church. The point one has made here can be applied to related issues such as loyalty to one's nation or Church; loyalty to the extended family system or Church; loyalty to the Church's call for abstinence in the face of genocide resulting from the spread of AIDS, which may be helpful in the long term, but in the short term, does not help address the calamity of many African countries. The words of Kerber speak volumes:

> Thus, the church's organizational structure must be such that it allows human beings to participate in church life. Human beings have a right to expect every kind of help for their Christian lives from the community of believers. This help should not be tied to conditions which are impossible to fulfill by individuals or the entire culture. Inculturation, then, is an absolute necessity.[19]

The challenge and fear associated wirh applying subsidiarity at the Local level, that these churches could somehow become nationalist churches is unnecessary. Rather, by applying subsidiarity, local churches are empowered and supported to act more effectively and to carry out the mission of the church in view of local conditions.

Subsidiarity and Sphere Sovereignty: The Ecumenical Task

The question of the relationship between subsidiarity and sphere sovereignty has been a major concern of some scholars[20] who have attempted to show the rele-

19 See Kerber, p. 228.

20 Jonathan Chaplin, "Subsidiarity and Sphere Sovereignty: Catholic and Reformed Conceptions of the Role of the State," Francis P. and Samuel M. Natale, (eds.), *Things Old and New: Catholic Social Teaching Revisited* (Lanham, Maryland: University Press of America, 1993),

vance and challenges of providing an ecumenical perspective for ethical principles in the plural public square. Chaplin has shown the interaction that exists between the Catholic vision of subsidiarity and associational autonomy and the Reformed Dutch neo-Calvinism vision of 'sphere sovereignty,' articulated by Abraham Kuyper and Herman Dooyeweerd. According to Chaplin: "This pluralistic Reformed conception, although not widely known outside the Netherlands, is arguably the most substantial example of a Protestant social and political theory in the twentieth century...Although rooted in quite different theological and philosophical foundations, it shares a great deal with the Catholic conception."[21]

The Reformed concept of 'sphere sovereignty' is a Dutch phrase *souvereiniteit in eigen kring* which is literally translated 'sovereignty in one's own sphere.'[22] According to Chaplin the term received its classic formulation in the writings and speeches of Abraham Kuyper (1837-1920). Kuyper stated in a classic statement at the Free University of Amsterdam in 1891 while proposing a Christian approach to the problem of poverty that: "Against both of these (referring to the state and society), we as Christians must hold that the state and society each has its own sphere, its own sovereignty, and that the social question cannot be resolved rightly unless we respect this duality and thus honor state authority as clearing the way for a free society."[23] Chaplin then identified four major parallels between the Reformed Calvinist concept of sphere sovereignty and the Catholic social thought principle of subsidiarity.[24] First, each of these concepts denounced both individualistic and totalitarian theories. Second, they both upheld the individual as a social being created by God to live in different communities, and not to be taken over by others. Third, they both developed pluralist views of society, consisting of different groups or parts, but with a coextensive harmony. Fourth, they both viewed the state as having the primary responsibility of protecting these communities, and challenged the state not to override these communities and that the individuals may not be dominated by stronger communities. These points provide some opportunity for ecumenical dialogue between both traditions in the continual quest to discover better ways of organizing complex societies in view of the common good.

---

pp. 175-202; James W. Skillen and Rockne M. McCarthy, "Three Views of Social Pluralism: A Critical Evaluation," *Political Order and the Plural Structure of Society*, (eds.), James W. Skillen and Rockne M. McCarthy (Atlanta, Georgia: Emory University/Scholars Press, 1991), pp. 377-417. What follows is an attempt to evaluate some of the views expressed in these works.

21 See Chaplin, p. 177.

22 Ibid. p. 187.

23 Abraham Kuyper, *The Problem of Poverty*, (ed.), James W. Skillen (Washington, DC / Grand Rapids: The Center for Public Justice & Baker Book House, 1991), p. 65.

24 See Chaplin, p. 188.

There are some areas of differences between the two traditions being discussed. The Reformed tradition has challenged the Catholic notion of hierarchy in relation to subsidiarity. This is a legitimate issue which has been raised within the Catholic Church as well. In this study, I have discussed the fact that subsidiarity is in favor of the bottom up approach rather than the top down approach. There will always be the need, both in the Church and society, of some type of structural arrangement. The real challenge is to fashion a structure that promotes human self-actualization in view of the common good. This may yet be another point for an ecumenical dialogue where the experiences from both traditions may lead to mutual enrichment and development. In fact, Chaplin made the connection between subsidiarity and sphere sovereignty in the context of public law that is open to different types of structural arrangements, including some type of limited hierarchy.

> Each social relationship possesses original rights deriving from its 'juridical sphere sovereignty' which may not be overridden by the state. Nonetheless, with respect to public law, the state does indeed stand above all other communities in a hierarchical relationship. Its sphere sovereignty is a public legal sovereignty. This is not a general hierarchical priority, only a functional legal, and hence a limited, one.[25]

Both Skillen and McCarthy have criticized subsidiarity and autonomy as inadequate tools to the task of guaranteeing a real pluralism in the temporal social order.

> In our judgment, influenced as it by Herman Dooyeweerd's contrast between "sphere sovereignty" and the "whole-part" relation, the principle of autonomy in a subsidiarity framework does not adequately define or safeguard the identities, tasks, and rights of multiple societal institutions. Autonomy can provide for the relative independence of parts within a whole, such as different government units within a state, or different academic units within a university, or different ecclesiastical offices within the church. It does not, however, provide an adequate basis for distinguishing the identities and responsibilities of different spheres of human life. A family, a school, a church, a business enterprise, a state, each has a different identity, requiring uniquely different human roles and responsibilities within it. These different social entities should not be viewed as parts of one another as autonomous subunits in a larger whole.[26]

The criticism leveled against subsidiarity and autonomy from the perspective of this study is based on a partial reading of the internal logic undergirding the principle. I have pointed out in chapter two that there are three major principles on which subsidiarity rests. These are: autonomy, hierarchy, and intervention.[27] All these three principles act as a dynamic whole to present the authentic meaning of subsidiarity. Thus, any reading of this principle which does not articulate

25 See Chaplin, p. 194.

26 Ibid. pp. 384-385.

27 See chapter Two, pp. 44-45.

all three principles is merely an abstraction. In this sense, one can understand the confusion about the true nature of subsidiarity in serving as a basis for differentiating temporal social institutions. Similarly, it is a matter of debate whether institutions like the family, school, church, business, and state, while maintaining their distinct identities, require unique roles and responsibilities such that they could not be considered as parts of the larger social order. The claim that subsidiarity appears not to recognize the ontological role of institutions stems from the same partial understanding. Indeed, if subsidiarity accepts the relative independence of the different parts, how could it hold back their ontological status as suggested by Skillen and McCarthy?

> A truly pluralist social order seems to require recognition of the fundamental and not merely the relative independence of the different spheres and institutions in a differentiated society. To achieve this recognition, the ontological status of institutions must be grasped and upheld. In our opinion, the subsidiarity-autonomy framework does not do this.[28]

There are two traditions at work here with their specific assumptions about how best one could approach the issues involved in a complex plural social order. The progressive Calvinist tradition out of which has emerged the concept of "sphere sovereignty," while upholding the Trinitarian basis for the correlation between culture and society, differs in the understanding associated with the state by Catholics.

> For Kuyper, the state takes its place not above all other spheres, but rather next to them. Its high and overarching position is due not to a natural hierarchy but to the state's peculiar character as public authority. At this point Kuyper, like Calvin, stands at a considerable distance from Aristotle and Thomas. The state is in no way self-sufficient; it is not the natural telos of other associations or spheres of social life; it is not the whole of which the latter are parts.[29]

This study has presented the ontological basis for subsidiarity in Aquinas and the subsequent papal social encyclicals beginning with that of Leo XIII that does not in any way grant absolute power to the state. Rather, the basis for subsidiarity and the social teachings comes from the Christian vision of the dignity of the human person which has revelation as its foundation as one has discussed extensively in previous chapters. The ecumenical task for both traditions is to engage in what Chaplin called "communitarian pluralism" which has two major ideas:

> First, there exists a diversity of essential, divinely created, human purposes each of which needs to be concretely pursued within a corresponding community with a distinctive character appropriate to that purpose; second, each of these communities must be enabled by the state (and indeed by everyone) to pursue its particular purposes in responsible freedom and security.[30]

---

28 Ibid. p. 385.

29 Ibid. p. 398.

30 See Chaplin, pp. 196-197.

The principles of subsidiarity and sphere sovereignty rightly understood and practiced might form the basis for genuine presentation of Christian social and ethical views that address the issues and needs in complex pluralist societies.

Subsidiarity and Some Canonical Implications

The preface to the Latin edition of the 1983 Code of Canon Law has stated that some guidelines were approved unanimously in the revision of the whole Code at the request of the Supreme Pontiff, by a general session of the Synod of bishops in October, 1967[31]. Thus, guideline no. 5 which was used for the revision of the Code is central in this study and is quoted in full:

> Careful attention is to be given to the greater application of the so-called principle of subsidiarity within the Church. It is a principle which is rooted in a higher one because the office of bishops with its attached powers is a reality of divine law. In virtue of this principle one may defend the appropriateness and even the necessity of providing for the welfare especially of individual institutes through particular laws and the recognition of a healthy autonomy for particular executive power while legislative unity and universal and general law are observed. On the basis of the same principle, the new Code entrusts either to particular laws or to executive power whatever is not necessary for the unity of the discipline of the universal Church so that appropriate provision is made for a healthy "decentralization" while avoiding the danger of division into or the establishment of national Churches.[32]

The above guiding principle recognized the need to apply subsidiarity in the Church and upheld that the foundational basis for applicability be tied to the office and powers of bishops which is a reality of divine law. Here, the Synod of bishops acknowledged the fact that subsidiarity is to be applied in the Church without prejudice to the hierarchical structure of the Church[33]. I have discussed the implications arising from the continual articulation of subsidiarity with the present hierarchical structure of the Church and the inherent challenges. Guideline no. 5 sought to discuss the necessity for particular laws but cautioned that there was the need for "healthy autonomy." The issue of autonomy as an integral component of subsidiarity has been discussed. But unlimited autonomy is not in the spirit of subsidiarity and that is why "intervention" is a necessary component. Thus, both autonomy and intervention as necessary parts of subsidiarity are always geared

31 John Paul II, "Preface to the Latin Edition," *Code of Canon Law: Latin-English Edition* (Washington, D.C.: Canon Law Society of America, 1983), p. xx.

32 Ibid. p. xxi.

33 Pius XII is quoted to have made the first magisterial statement that subsidiarity applies to the Church in his address to newly created cardinals on February 20, 1946. See Pius XII, Consistorial Allocution, February 20, 1946: *Acta Apostolicae Sedis* (AAS) 38 (1946): 144, and the English translation in *The Catholic Mind* 44 (April, 1946) cited in Joseph A. Komonchak, "Subsidiarity in the Church: The State of the Question," pp. 302-305.

toward the common good. The directive in the guideline that the new Code ensure that either "particular laws" or "executive power" be the custodian of "whatever is not necessary for the unity of the discipline of the universal Church," appear vague. Is the guideline no. 5 seeking the unity of the Church's discipline on universal uniformity? This may seem to be the case, since the guideline goes on to mention the need for "healthy decentralization," and then concludes with what seems to be its greatest fear, namely "the danger of division into or the establishment of national Churches." I have previously discussed both the issue of decentralization with regard to subsidiarity and the relationship of subsidiarity to nationalism. The challenge posed by these issues with regard to the applicability of subsidiarity in the Church by guideline no. 5 must have led to the complete disappearance of subsidiarity in the 1983 Code of Canon Law.

John A. Alesandro has acknowledged that, while most of the guidelines were helpful during the revision process of the 1967 Code, subsidiarity was completely left out of the new Code's judicial process.

> These principles were a helpful tool for those drafting the revised law. The final version of the canons illustrates the effectiveness of the principles in inculcating the spirit and directives of the Council into the Code's juridic framework. Many of the principles had a direct influence on the revision and most, although not all were substantially implemented. (The most notable exceptions are the directives concerning subsidiarity in the judicial process and the establishment of administrative tribunals).[34]

Thus, in 1985 when the Synod of bishops[35] requested that further research be carried out on the applicability of subsidiarity in the Church, they were attempting to revisit the missed opportunity that the 1983 Code had provided on discussing the nature of subsidiarity in the Church. Essentially, it would seem that the central canonical challenge for subsidiarity in the Church is the failure of official Church pronouncement on its applicability within the Church's administrative and pastoral structure beyond the stand taken by some of the social encyclicals I have discussed in great detail.

Ad Leys has studied the new Code and made some connection with subsidiarity in terms of the role of the institutional Church as communion of the faith-

---

34 John A. Alesandro, "General Introduction," *The Code of Canon Law: A Text and Commentary*, (eds.), James A. Coriden, Thomas J. Green, & Donald E. Heintschel (New York/Mahwah: Paulist Press, 1985), p. 7.

35 1985 Synod of Bishops, "The Final Report," 8, c: *Origins* 15/27 (December 19, 1985): 449: "It is recommended that a study be made to examine whether the principle of subsidiarity in use in human society can be applied to the Church and to what degree and in what sense such an application can and should be made." Since then several suggestions showing how the principle could be applied in the Church have been made but there has been no official pronouncement from the Church's leadership on this subject.

ful.[36] Generally, Leys attempted to respond to the question raised by Sobanski in the context of the ecclesiological and canon law issues of today: "Considering the Christian claim to truth and the authoritative mediation of it, can there be in the Church an autonomous freedom and is it possible to offer that in ecclesiastical institutions?"[37] Leys then raised some further questions: "The constitutional value of the basic rights of the faithful in the Church, the relationship between spiritual authority and Christian freedom, the tension between the right to truth and the rights of the subject, the tension between the community and the faithful who belong to it."[38] Leys then discussed the implications arising from the rights of all the Christian Faithful as formulated in the Code, Canons 208-223. According to Leys "these are sacramentally established basic rights (c. 204 par. 1), which are a foundation of the legal system. They must guarantee personal freedom in the Church."[39]

In view of the Nigerian social context and the social reality of the Church, the following two recommendations are made that should become part of the much needed canonical reform that will respect local needs of the Church in Nigeria and other African countries with subsidiarity as the guiding principle.

1. The universal canonical age for the retirement of the clergy, fixed at seventy-five by canons 538/3 and 401/1, needs to be reformulated to respect the particular retirement age in different countries. The case of African countries particularly is very unique and demands special attention. In these developing countries where medical facilities are lacking, the conditions of service are very poor, there are little or no retirement benefits for the secular clergy, and above all the average life expectancy age is 53 years, it is unreasonable, unrealistic, and even unnatural to expect the clergy working in these conditions to fit the universal age of seventy-five, knowing full well that the majority of them will die working in the most inhuman situations. The matter of retirement age should be left in the hands of local and regional conferences of bishops.

2. The local bishops' conferences in Africa need to take into consideration the challenges which the extended family system presents to those who aspire to and become secular clerics in the African context. Most of these

36 Ad Leys, "Structuring Communion: The Importance of the Principle of Subsidiarity," *The Jurist* 58 (1998): 84-123, especially 116-122.

37 Ibid. p. 116.

38 Ibid.

39 Ibid. p. 118. The canonical details provided by Leys are beyond the scope of this study but the conclusion provided is significant: "The principle of subsidiarity gives the particular churches, individually but also in larger associations such as bishops' conferences and continental synods, the task to profile themselves more clearly as churches which are rooted in their own culture, or should be." p. 123.

persons are often the major source of well-being and support to their families in their social, health, and educational needs. There needs to be in place an organized support system following canon 281/1 and 281/2, rather than the practice which exists in most dioceses in Nigeria, whereby, the parish priest is left to determine what amounts to reasonable stipends for associates in parish situations. These are not matters for which, in the spirit of subsidiarity, local bishops require Rome's blessing nor is it necessary.

Subsidiarity and Islam: The Inter-religious Task

Robert D. Crane[40] makes a significant connection between the principle of subsidiarity and Islam within the context of the theoretical framework for political rights in Islam. According to him, three human rights are emphasized today namely, political rights, religious rights, and gender equity.

> The universal principle of political freedom, known as haqq al hurriya in Islamic jurisprudence, has always been understood as a call for self-determination by individual persons and by the communities in which they find their social identities. The secondary level of *hajjyat* calls first of all for *khilafa*. This provides that the highest responsibility both of those who govern and those who are governed is to God. The idea is that people should be governed by people who are governed by God. This is basic to Thomas Jefferson's teaching that a people can remain free only if they are educated, that education consists primarily in learning virtue, and that a people can remain virtuous only if both their private and their public lives are infused with awareness of God. The next of the second-level principles of *haqq al hurriya* or political freedom is *shura*, which calls for responsive governance and for political institutions to assure that the government is a servant of the people rather than the reverse. The third requirement is known as *ijima*, which is the duty of every citizen and especially of the opinion leaders to seek consensus on a preferred political agenda and to reach compromises on the means to pursue this agenda in specific policies and courses of action.

Having made the case for understanding political freedom as a call for self-determination, responsive governance and consensus, and the implications associated with this call, Crane then argues forcefully in favor of subsidiarity in this way:

> Institutionalizing these three second-level requirements of political freedom is important because self-determination as the framework of *haqq al hurriya* is based on the

40 Robert D. Crane, "Human Rights and Tolerance within Islam: Legal, Political, and Spiritual Perspective, *The American Muslim*: February 7, 2010 for details see www.theamericanmuslim.org/tam. I have attempted to articulate the Islamic notion of subsidiarity presented in this essay as a first step to inter-religious dialogue on this subject matter. All quotations are cited from the same essay and no page numbers were included in the original and so are not available here in the text or in the notes.

> principle known in Western moral theology as "subsidiarity". This provides that all problems should be resolved at the lowest political levels, with resort to higher levels only when resolution is otherwise impossible. The concept of subsidiarity comes from two of the other primary principles in the Islamic code of human rights. The first of these two is *haqq al haya*, which provides that the highest level of human sovereignty, subject only to the Sovereignty of God, is the human person. This, in turn, gives rise to the correlative principle of *haqq al nasl*, which provides for the derivative sovereignty of the human community in ascending levels all the way to entire civilizations and even to the human species.

Crane, further explains the practical implications for subsidiarity within Islam: "Respect for both personal and community-based sovereignty is the root of the Islamic concept of *ittihad*, which refers to the unity that can result from the decentralization of political power through federalism or the looser concept of confederalism". On the contrary, Crane identifies the role of the state as a major challenge in contemporary Muslim thought:

> Like human rights, the concept of the state is a relatively recent Western construct. It arose as a means to end the Thirty Years War at the Treaty of Westphalia in 1648 by accepting human power rather than God as the highest authority in human affairs. The state is a secular construct that recognizes the corporate or collectivist identity of its citizens as the basis of legitimate power...the state by definition has a monopoly of coercion, and its geographical jurisdiction extends as far as it can control more than fifty percent of the population in a given territory.

Hence, for Crane, "The very concept of an Islamic State and even of political Islam is a prime example of 'Westoxification,' especially in its jihadic incarnation as the pursuit of justice through power and the pursuit of power eventually as an end in itself. By drawing religion into the pursuit of power such political Muslims preempt those who would bring wisdom of higher religion into the public square. The very concept of political Islam reveals a Western mindset with a totalitarian leaning based on a level of tolerance that denies the very concept of human rights". Crane offers an Islamic spiritual perspective on human rights as the way forward for counteracting the Western ideology of Statecraft. This view posists that Islam recognizes "a direct relationship of the person with God and therefore conceive of human rights as sacred, including the right of persons and communities to a government that is limited by the sovereignty of God". It also affirms that the practice of morality, traditionally referred to as the virtues, is at the core of spiritual wisdom. In this connection, Crane opines that the issue of Justice as the will of God is important for Islam.

> Justice is important for Muslims because they consider that it is the translation of truth into practice and that therefore justice is nothing more than the Will of God, as indicated in the *Qur'anic ayah* from *Surah al An'am*, :115, *tama'at kalimatu Rabbika sidqan wa 'adlan*, "The word of Your Lord is perfected and completed in truth and justice". Its nature and substance, however, must be sought out through deduction from the three sources of knowledge, namely, 1) *haqq al yaqin*, known as revelation; 2) *'ain al yaqin*,

known as natural law or the *sunnatu Allahi*; and some jurists would say also from 3) *'ilm al yaqin*, which is the human intellectual processing of the first two sources.

There are four questions I will raise in view of Crane's positions: first, since Islam considers the state as a secular construct arrogating onto itself the sovereignty due only to God, and since Islam does not make the distinction as in Christianity between the sacred and the secular, how can both Moslems and Christians function in a state such as Nigeria by affirming the principle of subsidiarity and promoting human rights and social justice without resulting to a theocracy but actually practice democracy? Second, how does the call to respect personal and community sovereignty in Islam translate in practice to non Moslems who live within a given state where shari'ah laws are applied without regard to their personal sovereignty? Third, what is the extent to which Islam is prepared to go in order to do away with Western-Christian trappings such as the concept of a secular state and yet remain faithful to the league of nations in this modern and postmodern world that is fast becoming a global village each day? Fourth, how does the promotion of gender rights in Islam account for the treatment of women and men in predominantly Muslim states in Nigeria as a practical way of enforcing sahr'ia law?

Questions for Further Reflection

1. How might Church/Moseque/State relations be promoted in Nigeria?
2. What type of structural adjustments if any does either the Church/Mosque or Society need to make in order to bring about a just Nigerian society?
3. To what extent can a local Church/Mosque identify with the national identity of her social, cultural, political and economic contexts?
4. How does one promote a pluralist vision of society in a given social context that is saturated with ethnic and religious bias?
5. How might the bottom up organizational approach instead of the top down one positively change Nigerian society?

CONCLUSION

Synthesis and Major Findings

Subsidiarity is a natural principle of organizing and ordering individuals and groups to pursue common purpose and objectives in community. The term connotes notions of support from below, aid, and help to self-help. It points to a particular way of organizing a community so that the members can assist each other from the grassroots in the task of standing up and pursuing their common goals. The principle affirms that there is something inherently good about groups organizing around interests and helping each other seek common ends. While recognizing that communities are made up of people with different interest groups, the principle promotes the healthy interaction of these varying interest groups with a view toward the common good of all. The principle of subsidiarity articulated by Pius XI involves three core ideas which form a dynamic whole in explaining how the principle works. These are autonomy, intervention, and hierarchy. Autonomy stresses the limited degree of independence necessary for groups and individuals to be able to operate in a given context. It helps persons to make free choices without any form of external coercion. Intervention specifies the non-absolute nature of autonomy, both for the individual and the group. Independence must be accountable to the common good of the entire society. Mutual interaction and cooperation is intrinsically required. Thus, when there is a clear case of violation against the common good, some limited form of intervention is permitted by the social body. Hierarchy helps to explain the levels of responsibility in society. Authority is defined in terms of the level of participation among the social groups that promote the individual's values in their associations, while at the same time upholding the social objectives of the larger society. This understanding of authority calls for limited power sharing in view of the common good of all, while leaving some room for putting in check any arbitrary use of such powers. It is in the nature of subsidiarity to intervene in the case of hierarchical abuse to act as a stabilizing principle in the social order.

The articulation of subsidiarity provided by Pius XI in QA has universal appeal and significance in every social arrangement of persons in community. This is because subsidiarity emphasizes the priority of the person in communion with others to bring about the *bonum commune*. The vision of the common good sees in the human person the personal dignity proper to one's nature but directed essentially to others in the society. Hence, the common good and the good of the individual do not oppose one another, but the good of the individual whose nature is personal has a dignity proper to itself, but nonetheless is social in character, that is, it is directed to the well-being of others. Hence, the common good is realized through the participation and contribution of the individual to others in society. In this way, the relationship of the individual to the social group remains an issue for everybody in a given social context.

Social justice is a multi-dimensional concept. From a theological perspective, the biblical meaning of social justice as fidelity to the demands of a covenant relationship challenges one to engage in some form of concrete manifestation of this relationship. In examining some of the history and practice of social justice in the Bible, one is able to conclude that the central thrust for social justice is respect for the dignity of the human person who is created in the image and likeness of God. Thus, wherever and whenever that dignity is marginalized, the demands of social justice come into operation to restore and fashion the human person toward his or her God-given dignity. Furthermore, the study discovered that the mission and message of Jesus affirm the revelation of God and make ethical demands centered on the commandment to love God and neighbor as primary to participation in God's Kingdom. Moreover, the Kingdom of God has social, economic, political, cultural, and religious consequences that the followers of Christ would have to deal with on a day-to-day basis as they encounter the present, imminent, and eschatological dimensions of the Kingdom.

Another dimension of social justice is how to respond, on the one hand, to the reality of innocent suffering of individuals and groups, and, on the other hand, to explain the reality of the goodness of God in creating the world good. This issue is the age-old problem of theodicy. From this study, it was clear that there are several complex questions that are implicated in the issues of theodicy in the face of injustice in the world. How does one simply explain, for instance, that some persons who find themselves in situations of desperate poverty are paying the price for their bad actions? Human experiences inform us that while this might be true in some cases, there are instances when this argument is very untrue. How does one explain natural phenomena like drought, earthquakes, tornadoes, and hurricanes that bring unbearable hardship on people? Thus, one is able to conclude that while it is true that there are some phenomena in the world that transcend human understanding, which are attributed to some divine power, one may and must not absolve human beings from their responsibility to be co-creators with God. In this way, the challenge to take up the task of providing social justice in one's community remains very much a partnership of cooperation between persons among themselves and between them and God. Hence, in concrete terms, the practice of social justice must be geared toward the common good of all. The demand to achieve the common good makes it imperative to pay just wages to workers, to promote servant leadership, to promote purposeful dialogue between the employer and the employee, to set forth the right conditions that respect, enable, and ensure the proper working situation for workers. In this way, institutional reform is not only required but necessary where needed to fulfill the demands of social justice as the universal standard to all social relationships which lead them to the common good.

The practice of social justice in a pluralistic society such as Nigeria needs some foundational structure which will provide some stability and order to the social body. The common sense of the laws and values of the people, which are grounded in the day-to-day interrelationships in terms of their beliefs, family, clan and ethnic structures, cultural practices, political and economic arrangements, and generally accepted social practices are central to the type of society one is fashioning. To the extent that most people live by the acceptable norms of society and see them as useful and true, social order is maintained. However, to the extent that social norms are grossly violated, there exists generally social disorder. Therefore, there needs to be in Nigeria healthy interaction between social order and cultural values because culture is developed over long periods of struggle, exchange and interchange. Consequently, when the culture of a people is disconnected as is the case in Nigeria by corruption, misrule, and ethnic and inter-ethnic and religious conflicts, the building process might be overwhelming as is the present situation with a precarious democratic process that is bedeviled with uncertainty and lack of direction. It is obvious that naïve and unconstructive arrangements which have failed to recognize the cultural make-up of the nation are having a field day.

Another key issue central to building of community is moral and ethical responsibility of the citizens. While to some degree morality springs out of the cultural experiences of the community, it is not limited to human individual choices, lifestyles, values, and interpretations, though all these are implicated in the type of moral practice that exists in a nation. Morality, as I have investigated, is also revealed and is grounded in nature and the Creator of the Universe, whom we call God. In essence, the divine law envisions a moral order that promotes the common good and respects all human life and is able to serve as corrective to the moral order of society. The attempt to build a prosperous socio-economic and political community without moral standards in Nigeria may be likened to building a house without a solid foundation. Hence, I abhor the lack of moral transparency by some of the citizens, including those in leadership positions, as a major threat to building a social justice oriented society.

In the attempt to re-build Nigerian society to the point where it is able to accept and celebrate its multicultural, multi-religious, and multiethnic makeup, some of the traditional community will continually undergo a process of rebuilding and reformulation of its shared values, beliefs, and cultural practices. Some of the most cherished values will be passed on to the next generation with renewed vigor and meaning. Other beliefs and cultural practices will become obsolete and irrelevant, losing their meaning in view of new realities. In the midst of these challenges, the role of the extended family system with its benefits and burdens and the levels of support it provided or did not provide for the social structuring of the society would play a vital role in reshaping new models of social groups in the Nigerian society. Essentially, a philosophy of pluralism is the key to maintaining the balance between diversity and wholeness. Such a philosophy will make allowance for open dissent and critical comments without sacrificing one's identity in the process. More specifically then, minority ethnic groups would be allowed to present their vision within the setting of larger groups. Here, concrete grassroots arrangements for groups to dialogue with one another are fundamental to community rebuilding. The process might lead to the emergence of a new crop of leaders, both in government and within civil society, that will engage in broad-based initiatives rather than engage in divisiveness by exploiting the diversity in the nation.

Having examined the history of Nigeria with a critical lens and having recognized the enormous task before the citizens in re-building up a social justice oriented society, it is necessary to engage four approaches that will help support the complex nature of the Nigerian situation. First, the correlation between subsidiarity and federalism was established as integral to the building of a viable civil society. The situation where majority ethnic groups absorb minority ones in some parts of the nation is a violation of subsidiarity and injustice that breeds social disharmony and jeopardizes the common good. Rather, minority groups in Nigeria must be supported and enabled with the right set of conditions—mutual trust, mutual respect, and participation to make their choices in view of the common good. Second, the promotion of human rights which are inalienable in society with the recognition that individual rights and social rights are not opposed to each other but need to work together to build the common good. Thus, building trust across ethnic, religious, cultural, and social barriers is central to promoting individual and group rights. That is why programs which encourage this type of interaction of the different groups should be promoted. The National Youth Service Corps, introduced by the Gowon administration, was a novelty in this sense. I support the promotion of programs for young people across ethnic and socio-cultural backgrounds on a nation-wide scale as a vehicle for building and fostering communion. Third, self-help grassroots associations are supported to serve as agents of social and ethical development. These associations exist at the village, clan, and town levels where the majority of Nigerians reside. It is these basic structures existing in the communities that need support to stand up. These structures affect the lives of the people on a daily basis in the market squares, town meetings, religious gatherings, and local development initiatives. These are the same structures where citizenship education should be promoted. Here, the problem of good leadership that has plagued the nation could be discussed. Furthermore, the unchecked nature of the power of wealth acquisition demands some attention. Moreover, since main line religious organizations, both Christian and Moslem, have some level of trust with the people and have been able to engage most of the rural areas through the provision of schools, clinics, and churches/mosques, it may form some partnership of cooperation with government acting as mediating structures in communities where this type of arrangement is considered beneficial to the social body.

Future research needs to address the applicability of the principle of subsidiarity in the Church and society. These involve some structural organization in the Church, particularly to answer the question whether the Church's administrative structures have become much more complex than the original sense of *hierarchia ordinis* from a sacramental perspective. In addition, there is the issue of the extent to which the central administration of the Church should have control on concrete local issues of national and regional bishops' conferences. The role of the Laity in the Church demands some attention in view of the subsidiarity principle in terms of the common good of the Church. Is this to be determined by the administrative body alone or ought it to be a joint venture between responsible leaders and the Laity together acting as the people of God? Does the applicability of subsidiarity promote nationalism or encourage local initiative and decision making by those present in the social reality where the Church is rooted? There is a need for ecumenical dialogue to understand the relationship existing between subsidiarity and sphere sovereignty. Moreover, there needs to be some canonical review in the light of some local issues existing in the Nigerian and African context. Finally, the connection between subsidiarity and Islam has been established, but this connectedness also raises challenges for inter-religious dialogue in terms of a secular understanding of state, justice, self-determination, promotion of human rights, and good governance.

BIBLIOGRAPHY

Achebe, Chinua. *Things Fall Apart. London: Heinemann, 1958.*

———. *The Trouble with Nigeria.* Enugu: Forth Dimension Publishers, 1983.

Adedeji, Adebayo., and Bamidele Ayo. (Eds.). *People-Centered Democracy in Nigeria? The Search for Alternative Systems of Governance at the Grassroots.* Ibadan: Heinemann Educational Books, 2000.

Adeoye, Oladimeji. *The Morning of A Coup: The Dictatorship of Nigeria's Ibrahim B. Babangida.* Evanston. Illinois: Chigaco Spectrum Press, 1995.

Aguh, Philip. O and A. Ngindu Mushete. (Eds.). *The Voice of the Symposium of Episcopal Conferences of Africa and Madagascar for the Evangelization of Africa.* Accra, Ghana: SECAM Secretariat, 1987.

Akaabiam, Terwase H. *The Proclamation of the Good News: A Study of LK 24 in Tiv Context.* Frankfurt Am Main: Peter Lang/European University Studies, 1999.

Alesandro, John A. "General Introduction." *The Code of Canon Law: A Text and Commentary.* (Eds.). James A. Corien, Thomas J. Green, and Donal E. Heintschel. New York/Mahwah: Paulist Press, 1985.

Amadi, Elechi. *Ethics in Nigerian Culture.* Ibadan: Heinemann Educational Books, 1982.

Aquinas, Thomas. *De Regime Principum.* Rev. Ed. Trans. Gerald B. Phelan. London/New York: Sheed & Ward, 1938.

———. *On Politics and Ethics.* Trans. Paul E. Sigmund. New York: W. W. Norton & Company, 1988.

———. *Summa Contra Gentiles.* Trans. Vernon J. Bourke. New York: Image Books, 1956.

———. *The Summa Theologica.* Trans. Fathers of the English Dominican Province. New York: Benziger Brothers, 1947.

Augustine, Saint. *City of God.* Trans. Henry Bettenson. New York: Penguin Books, 1984.

Badru, Pade. *Imperialism and Ethnic Politics in Nigeria.* Trenton: Africa World Press, 1998.

Baum, Gregory. "The World Bank's New Interest in Religion." *The Ecumenist* 36/2 (1979): 6–18.

———. (Ed.). *The Twentieth Century: A Theological Overview.* Maryknoll, New York: Orbis Books, 1999.

Beabout, Gregory R. "The Principle of Subsidiarity and Freedom in the Family, Church, Market, and Government." *The Journal of Markets & Morality* 1/2 (1998): 1–10.

Benedict XVI, *Caritas In Veritate.* Vaticana: Libreria Editrice, 2009.

Benestad, Brian J. "The Catholic Concept of Social Justice: A Historical Perspective." *Communio* 11/4 (1984): 364–381.

Beyer, J. "Le Principe de Subsidiarite: Son application en Eglise." *Gregorianum* 69/3 (1988): 435–459.

Bodunrin, P. O. (Ed.). *Philosophy in Africa: Trends and Perspectives.* Ile-Ife: University of Ile-Ife Press, 1985.

Boff, Leonardo. *Church: Charism and Power.* Trans. John W. Diercksmeier. New York: Crossroad, 1985.

Bohannan, Laura and Paul. *The Tiv of Central Nigeria.* London: International African Institute, 1969.

Bokenkotter, T. *Church and Revolution: Catholics in the Struggle for Democracy and Social Justice.* New York: Image Books, 1998.

Bole, William. "Tales of Globalization." *America* 181 (1999): 14-16.

Bovens, Mark. *The Quest for Responsibility: Accountability and Citizenship in Complex Organizations.* Cambridge: Cambridge University Press, 1998.

Boxx, William T. "Building the Well-Ordered Society: Subsidiarity and Mediating Structures." *Building A Community of Citizens: Civil Society in the 21st Century.* (Ed.). Don E. Eberly. Lanhan, Maryland: University Press of America, 1994.

Briefs, Goetz A. "Social Encyclicals and Liberal Ethics." *Social Order* 6/1 (1956): 13–20.

Brown, Raymond E. *The Churches the Apostles Left Behind.* New York/Mawah: Paulist Press, 1984.

———. *The Community of the Beloved Disciple.* New York/Mahwah, New Jersey: Paulist Press, 1979.

———. *An Introduction to the New Testament.* New York: Doubleday, 1997.

Browne, Maura. (Ed.). *The African Synod: Documents, Reflections, Perspectives.* Maryknoll, New York: Orbis Books, 1996.

Bujo, Benezet. *African Christian Morality: At the Age of Inculturation.* Nairobi: Paulines Publications Africa, 1998.

Cahill, Edward. "The Catholic Social Movement: Historical Aspects." *Readings in Moral Theology No. 5: Official Catholic Social Teaching.* (Eds.). Charles E. Curran and Richard A. McCormick, New York: Paulist Press, 1986, 3–31.

Calvez, Jean-Yves, and Jacques Perrn. *The Church and Social Justice: The Social Teaching of the Popes from Leo XIII to Pius XII.* Chicago: Henry Regnery Company, 1961.

Carrier, Herve. Gospel *Message and Human Cultures: From Leo XIII to John Paul II.* Trans. John Drury. Pittsburgh, Pennsylvania: Duquesne University Press, 1989.

Catechism of the Catholic Church. Image Books Edition. New York: Doubleday, 1995.

Catholic Bishops of Africa Speak. *The Voice of SECAM for the Evangelization of Africa.* (1969–1985) Accra, Ghana: SECAM Secretariat, 1987.

Chaplin, Jonathan. "Subsidiarity and Sphere Sovereignty: Catholic and Reformed Conceptions of the Role of the State." (Eds.). Francis P. and Samuel M. Natale. *Things Old and New: Catholic Social Teaching Revisited.* Lanham, Maryland: University Press of America, 1993.

Charles, Rodger. *Christian Social Witness and Teaching: From Biblical Times to the Late Nineteenth Century.* Vol. 1. Trowbridge, Wiltshire: Cromwell Press, 1998.

———. *Christian Social Witness and Teaching: The Modern Social Teaching: Contexts, Summaries, Analysis.* Vol. 2. Trowbridge, Wiltshire: Cromwell Press, 1998.

Carozza, Paolo G. "Subsidiarity as a Structural Principle of International Human Rights Law." *The American Journal of International Law* 97/38 (2003): 38–79.

Carter, Warren. *What Are They Saying About Matthew's Sermon on the Mount?* New York/Mahwah, New Jersey: Paulist Press, 1994.

Chossudovsky, Michael. *The Globalization of Poverty: Impacts of IMF and World Bank Reforms.* London and New Jersey: Zed Books Ltd., 1998.

Clarke, Thomas E. (Ed.). *Above Every Name: The Lordship of Christ and Social Systems.* New York/ Ramsey: Paulist Press, 1980.

Coleman, J. A. "Development of Church Social Teaching." *Readings in Moral Theology No. 5: Official Catholic Social Teaching.* 169–187.

———. (Ed.). *One Hundred Years of Catholic Social Thought: Celebration and Challenge.* Maryknoll, New York: Orbis Bzoks, 1991.

Comaroff, John. and Jean C. (Eds.). *Civil Society and the Political Imagination in Africa: Critical Perspectives.* Chicago: The University of Chicago Press, 1999.

Cook, Michael I. *The Jesus of Faith: A Study in Christology.* New York: Paulist Press, 1981.

Coulibaly, Cheibane. "On Subsidiarity in Western Africa: A Contribution to Institutional Problem-Solving in Africa." Paper for the Workshop on the Workshop 2. Bloomington, Indiana: Indiana University, June 1999.

Crenshaw, James L. (Ed.). *Theodicy in the Old Testament.* Philadelphia: Fortress, 1983.

Cronin, John F. "sForty Years Later: Reflections and Reminiscences." *Readings in Moral Theology No. 5: Official Catholic Social Teaching.* 69–76.

———. "The Message of Quadragesimo Anno Today." *Social Order* 6/1 (1956): 2-12.

DeBerri, Edward P. et al. *Catholic Social Teaching: Our Best Kept Secret.* 4th. Rev. & Exp. Ed. New York/Washington, D.C.: Orbis/Center of Concern, 2003.

De Benoist, Alain. "The First Federalist: Johannes Althsius," *Telos* 118 (2000): 33.

Diamond, Stanley. "Tribal Society." *A Dictionary of Marxist Thought.* 2nd Ed. (Ed.). Tom Bottomore. Oxford: Blackwell Publishers, 1991.

Dillon, M. A. "The Common Good: A Catholic Theological Contribution to the Search for A Moral Basis For the Allocation and Rationing of Health Care Resources." Ph. D. Dissertation, Duquesne University Pittsburgh, 1994.

Dollen, Charles J. et al. (Eds.). *The Catholic Tradition: Social Thought.* Vols. 1 & 2. USA: McGrath Publishing Company, 1979.

Donahue, John R. "Biblical Perspectives on Justice." *The Faith That Does Justice: Examining the Christian Sources for Social Change*. (Ed.). John C. Haughey. New York: Paulist Press, 1977.

———. "The Parable of the Sheep and the Goats: A Challenge to Christian Ethics." *Theological Studies* 47 (1986): 3–31.

———. *What Does the Lord Require? A Bibliographical Essay on the Bible and Social Justice*. St. Louis: The Institute of Jesuit Sources, 2000.

Dorr, Donal. *Option for the Poor: A Hundred Years of Catholic Social Teaching*. Maryknoll, New York: Orbis Books, 1992.

———. *The Social Justice Agenda: Justice, Ecology, Power and the Church*. Maryknoll, New York: Orbis Books, 1991.

Dorrien, Gary J. *Reconstructing the Common Good: Theology and the Social Order*. Maryknoll, New York: Orbis Books, 1990.

Dostoevsky, Fyodor. *The Grand Inquisitor*. New York: Continuum, 1998.

Drane, James. *Authority and Institution: A Study in Church Crisis*. Milwaukee: Bruce, 1966.

Droel, William M. "The Delivery of Human Services: Mediating Structures and Catholic Social Thought." *Communion* II (1984): 89–94.

Drummond, William F. *Social Justice*. Milwaukee: The Bruce Publishing Company, 1955.

Dulles, Avery. *A Church to Believe In: Discipleship and the Dynamics of Freedom*. New York: Crossroad, 1983.

———. *Models of the Church*. Garden City, New York: Doubleday & Company, 1974.

———. *The Resilient Church*. Garden City, New York: Doubleday and Company, 1977.

Dwyer, Judith. (Ed.). *The New Dictionary of Catholic Social Thought*. Collegeville, Minnesota: The Liturgical Press, 1994.

Eberly, Don E. (Ed.). *Building A Community of Citizens: Civil Society in the 21st. Century*. Lanham, Maryland: University Press of America, 1994.

Egendorf, Laura K. (Ed.). *The Third World: Opposing View Points*. San Diego, California: Green Heaven Press, 2000.

Ehrenberg, John. *Civil Society: The Critical History of An Idea*. New York: New York University Press, 1999.

Elaigwu, Isawa J. et al. (Eds.). *Federalism and Nation Building in Nigeria: The Challenges of the 21st Century*. Garki, Abuja: National Council on Intergovernmental Relations, 1994.

Etzioni, Amitai. (Ed.). *Rights and the Common Good: The Communitarian Perspective*. New York: St. Martin's Press, 1995.

Ferree, William. *The Act of Social Justice: A Study in Social Philosophy*. Washington, D. C.: Catholic University of America Press, 1942.

Filibeck, Giorgio. (Ed.). *Human Rights in the Teaching of the Church: from John XXIII to John Paul II*. Vatican City: Libreria Editrice Vaticana, 1994.

Finn, James. (Ed.). *Private Virtue & Public Policy: Catholic Thought and National Life*. New Brunswick, New Jersey: Transaction Publishers, 1990.

Fiorenza, Elisabeth S. *In Memory of Her: A Feminist Theological Reconstruction of Christian Origins*. 10th. Ed. New York: Crossroad, 1983.

Fiorenza, Joseph. "The Principle of Subsidiarity in the Church." *Origins* 31/19 (October, 2001): 317–320.

Fitzgerald, Garrett. "Toleration or Solidarity?" *The Politics of Toleration in Modern Life*. (Ed.). Susan Mendus. Durham, NC: Duke University Press, 2000.

Flannery, Austin. (Ed.). *Vatican Council II: Constitutions, Decrees and Declarations*. Northport, New York: Costello, 1996.

Freire, Paulo. *Pedagogy of the Oppressed*. New Revised 20th Ed. Trans. Myra Bergman Ramos. New York: Continuum, 1997.

Fretheim, Terrence E. *Exodus*. Louisville: John Knox Press, 1991.

Friesen, Mark. "Subsidiarity and Federalism: An Old Concept with Contemporary Relevance for PoliticalSociety,"http://enfs.queensu.ca/federalgovernance/content/volume2/articles/Friesen_Mark.html (12/13/2003).

Gaudium ET. Spes. *Vatican Council II*. Trans. & Ed. Austin Flannery. Northporth, New York: Costello Publishing Company, 1996.

Gellner, Ernest. "Civil Society in Historical Context." *International Science Journal* 43 (1991): 495–510.

George, Joseph S. "The Principle of Subsidiarity with Special Reference to Its Role in Papal and Episcopal Relations in the Light of Lumen Gentium." Ph. D. Dissertation. The Catholic University of America, Washington, D.C., 1968.

Glenn, Paul J. *A Tour of the Summa*. Rockford, Illinois: Tan Books and Publishers, 1978.

Gove, Philip B. (Ed.). *Webster's Third New International Dictionary of the English Language*. Springfield, Massachusetts: Merriam/Webster Publishers, 1993.

Gowon, Donald E. *Theology in Exodus*. Louisville, Kentucky: Westminster John Knox Press, 1994.

Grassi, Joseph A. *Informing the Future: Social Justice in the New Testament*. New York/Mahwah, New Jersey: Paulist Press, 2002.

Greeley, Andrew M. "What is Subsidiarity? A Voice from Sleepy Hollow." *America* 153/13 (1985): 292–295.

Gremillion, Joseph. *The Gospel of Peace and Justice: Catholic Social Teaching Since Pope John*. Maryknoll, New York: Orbis Books, 1976.

Grey, Michael T. "The Concept of Christian Citizenship in the Declaration on Religious Liberty." Ph. D. Dissertation, Duquesne University Pittsburgh, 1997.

Gula, Richard M. *Ethics in Pastoral Ministry*. New York/Mahwah, New Jersey: Paulist Press, 1996.

———. *What Are They Saying About Moral Norms?* New York/Mahwah, New Jersey: Paulist Press, 1982.

Gutierrez, Gustavo. *A Theology of Liberation*. Rev. Ed. Trans & Ed. Caridad Inda and John Eagleson. Maryknoll, New York: Orbis Books, 1988.

Handy, Charles. *The Age of Paradox*. Boston, Massachusetts: Havard Business School Press, 1994.

Hanigan, James P. *As I Have Loved You: The Challenge of Christian Ethics*. New York and Mahwah: Paulist Press, 1986.

———. "Militant Nonviolence: A Spirituality for the Pursuit of Social Justice." Horizons 9/1 (1982):7-32.

Harbeson, John W. and Donald R. (Eds.). *Africa in World Politics: Post-Cold War Challenges.* Boulder, Colorado: Westview Press, 1995.

Haring, Bernard. *The Law of Christ.* Vol. 1. Trans. Edwin G. Kaiser. Westminster, Maryland: The Newman Press, 1961.

Hayek, Friedrich A. *The Mirage of Social Justice.* Vol. 2. Chicago: The University of Chicago Press, 1976.

Haynes, Jeff. *Religion and Politics in Africa.* Nairobi: East African Educational Publishers, 1996.

Henriot, Peter J. "Cologne Debt: Initiative Falls Short." *America* 181 (1999): 18-19.

———. "Social Sin and Conversion: A Theology of the Church's Social Involvement." *Theological Studies* 11 (1972): 115–130.

———. "Who Cares about Africa? Development Guidelines from the Church's Social Teaching." *Catholic Social Thought and the New World Order: Building on One Hundred Years.* (Eds.). Oliver F. Williams and John W. Houck. Notre Dame: University of Notre Dame Press, 1993.

Henriot, Peter J. et al. (Eds.). *Catholic Social Teaching: Our Best Kept Secret.* Maryknoll, New York: Orbis Books, 1992.

Hillman, Eugene. *Toward an African Christianity: Inculturation Applied.* New York & Mahwah, New Jersey: Paulist Press, 1993.

Himes, Kenneth R. Responses to 101 Questions on Catholic Social Teaching. New York/Mahwah, New Jersey: Paulist Press, 2001.

Himes, Michael J., and Kenneth R. *Fullness of Faith: The Public Significance of Theology.* New York/Mahwah, New Jersey: Paulist Press, 1993.

Hobbes, Thomas. *Leviathan.* (Ed.). Crawford Macpherson. London: Penguin Books, 1968.

Holland, Joe. *Modern Catholic Social Teaching: The Popes Confront the Industrial Age 1740–1958.* New York/Mahwah, New Jersey: Paulist Press, 2003.

Holland, Joe, and Peter Henriot. (Eds.). *Social Analysis: Linking Faith and Justice.* Washington, D.C.: Center of Concern, 1983.

Hollenbach, David. *Claims in Conflict: Retrieving and Renewing the Catholic Human Rights Tradition.* New York: Paulist Press, 1979.

———. "The Common Good and Urban Poverty." *America* 180/20 (1999): 8-11.

———. *The Global Face of Public Faith: Politics, Human Rights, and Christian Ethics.* Washington, D.C.: Georgetown University Press, 2003.

———. "Global Human Rights: An Interpretation of Contemporary Catholic Understanding." *Readings in Moral Theology, No. 5: Official Catholic Social Teaching.* 366–383.

———. *Justice, Peace, & Human Rights: American Catholic Social Ethics in a Pluralistic Context.* New York: Crossroads, 1988.

Hueglin, Thomas O. "Federalism, Subsidiarity and the European Tradition: Some Clarifications," *Telos* 100 (1994): 43.

Hughson, Thomas. *The Believer As Citizen: John Courtney Murray in a New Context.* New York/Mahwah, New Jersey: Paulist Press, 1993.

Ike, Obiora F. (Ed.). *Catholic Social Teachings En-Route in Africa.* Enugu: Snaap Press, 1991.

Jibo, Mvendaga. *Tiv Politics Since 1959.* Katsina Ala: Mandate International, 1993.

John XXIII. Mater ET Magistra. *Catholic Social Thought: The Documentary Heritage*. (Eds.). David J. O'Brien and Thomas A. Shannon. Maryknoll, New York: Orbis Books, 1992.

John P. II. Centesimus Annus. Catholic Social Thought: The Documentary Heritage.

———. Code of Canon Law: Latin-English Edition. Washington, D.C.: Canon Law Society of America, 1983.

———. Laborem Exercens. *Catholic Social Thought: The Documentary Heritage.*

———. Motu Proprio: On the Theological and Juridical Nature of Episcopal Conferences. Boston: Pauline Books & Media, 1998.

———. Sollicitudo Rei Socialis. *Catholic Social Thought: The Documentary Heritage.*

Kammer, Fred. *Doing Faithjustice: An Introduction to Catholic Social Thought*. New York/Mahwah, New Jersey: Paulist Press, 1991.

Kant, Immanuel. *Critique of Judgment*. Trans. Werner S. Pluhar. Indianapolis/Cambridge: Hacket Publishing Company, 1987.

———. *The Metaphysics of Morals*. Trans. & Ed. Mary Gregor. Cambridge: Cambridge University Press, 1996.

Kasper, Walter. "The Principle of Subsidiarity Within the Church." *Theology Today* 32/3 (Fall, 1985): 225–229.

Kavanaugh, John F. *Following Christ in A Consumer Society (Still): The Spirituality of Cultural Resistance*. Rev. Ed. Maryknoll, New York: Orbis Books, 1999.

Keane, John. *Civil Society: Old Images, New Visions*. Stanford, California: Stanford University Press, 1998.

Kelley, John J. *Freedom in the Church: A Documented History of the Principle of Subsidiary Function*. Dayton, Ohio: Peter Li, 2000.

Kerber, Walter. "The Principle of Subsidiarity Within the Church." *Theology Digest* 32/3 (Fall 1985): 225–229.

Kern, Walter, and Jorg Splett. "Theodicy." *Encyclopedia of Theology: The Concise Sacramentum Mundi*. (Ed.). Karl Rahner. New York: Seabury Press, 1975.

Kohler, Thomas C. "Quadragesimo Anno, (1931)." (Eds.). George Weigel and Robert Royal. *A Century of Catholic Social Thought*. Washington, D.C.: Ethics and Public Policy Center 1991, 27-44.

Komonchak, Joseph. "Subsidiarity in the Church: The State of the Question." *The Jurist* 48 (1988): 298–302.

Kossel, Clifford. "Global Community and Subsidiarity." *Communion* VIII (1981): 37–50.

Kukah, Matthew H. *Democracy and Civil Society in Nigeria*. Ibadan: Spectrum Books, 1999.

———. Religion, Politics and Power in Northern Nigeria. Ibadan: Spectrum Books, 1993.

Kung, Hans., and Leonard Swidler. (Eds.). *The Church in Anguish: Has the Vatican Betrayed Vatican II?* San Francisco: Harper and Row, 1987.

Kuyper, Abraham. *The Problem of Poverty*. (Ed.). James W. Skillen. Washington, D.C./Grand Rapids: The Center for Public Justice & Baker Book House, 1991.

Land, Philip S. *Catholic Social Teaching: As I Have Lived, Loathed, and Loved It*. Chicago: Loyola University Press, 1994.

Lane, Dermot A. *Foundations for a Social Theology: Praxis, Process, and Salvation*. New York/ Ramsey: Paulist Press, 1984.

Legrand, Herve, Julio Manzanares, and Antonio Garcia y Garcia. (Eds.). *The Nature and Future of Episcopal Conferences*. Washington, D.C.: The Catholic University of America Press, 1988.

Leo XIII. Rerum Novarum. *Catholic Social Thought: The Documentary Heritage.*

Lerner, Natan. *Religion, Beliefs, and International Human Rights*. Maryknoll, New York: Orbis Books, 2000.

Lewis, Peter M. et al. *Stabilizing Nigeria: Sanctions, Incentives, and Support for Civil Society*. New York: The Century Foundation Press, 1998.

Leys, A. *Ecclesiological Impacts of the Principle of Subsidiarity*. Trans. A. Van Santroord. Kampen, Netherlands: Kok Pharos, 1995.

———. "Structuring Communion: The Importance of the Principle of Susidiarity." *The Jurist* 58 (1998): 84–123.

Llamzon, Benjamin S. "Subsidiarity: The Term, Its Metaphysics and Use." *Aquinas* 21 (1978): 44–62.

Local and Regional Authorities in Europe, No. 55. *Definition and Limits of the Principle of Subsidiarity*. Strasbourg Cedex: Council of Europe Press, 1994.

Lohfink, Gerhard. *Jesus and Community: The Social Dimension of Christian Faith*. Philadelphia: Fortress Press, 1982.

MacIntyre, Alasdair. "Toleration and the Goods of Conflict." *The Politics of Toleration in Modern Life*.

———. *Whose Justice? Which Rationality?* Notre Dame, Indiana: University of Notre Dame Press, 1988.

Mahoney, Jack. "Subsidiarity in the Church." *The Month* 21/11 (1988): 968–974.

Maier, Karl. *This House Has Fallen: Midnight in Nigeria*. New York: Public Affairs, 2000.

Makar, Tesemchi. *The History of Political change Among the Tiv in the 19th and 20th Centuries*. Enugu, Nigeria: Fourth Dimension Publishers, 1994.

Maldonado, Carlos E. *Human Rights, Solidarity and Subsidiarity: Essays toward a Social Ontology*. Washington, D.C.: The Council for Research in Values and Philosophy, 1997.

Maly, Eugene H. *Prophets of Salvation*. New York: herder and Herder, 1967.

Manno, Bruno V. "Subsidiarity and Pluralism: A Social Philosophical Perspective." *Toward Vatican III: The Work That Needs To Be Done.*

Marty, Martin E., and Jonathan Moore. *Politics, Religion, and the Common Good*. San Francisco: Jossey Bass Publishers, 2000.

Mazrui, Ali A. and Alamin M. *The Power of Babel: Language and Governance in the African Experience*. Chicago: University of Chicago Press, 1998.

Mbaku, John M. (Ed.). *Preparing Africa for the Twenty-First Century: Strategies for Peaceful Coexistence and Sustainable Development*. Aldershot/Brookfield: Ashgate Publishing Company, 1999.

Mbiti, John S. *African Religions and Philosophy*. London: Heinemann, 1969.

McBrien, Richard P. "An Ecclesiological Analysis of Catholic Social Teaching. *Catholic Social Thought and The New World Order.* (Eds.). Oliver F. Williams and John W. Houck. Notre Dame, Indiana: University of Notre Dame Press, 1993.

McCormick, Richard A. "Changing My Mind about the Changeable Church." *ChurchWatch* 3 (October-November, 1990): 3–7.

———. *Corrective Vision: Explorations in Moral Theology*. Kansas City, MO: Sheed & Ward, 1994.

McGoldrick, Terrence. "Episcopal Conferences Worldwide on Catholic Social Teaching." *Theological Studies* 59 (1998): 22–50.

Mckenna, Joseph C. *Finding A Social Voice: The Church and Marxism in Africa.* New York: Fordham University Press, 1997.

McKenzie, John L. *Authority in the Church*. New York: Sheed and Ward, 1996.

———. *Dictionary of the Bible*. New York: MacMillan, 1973.

McLean, Iain. (Ed.). *The Concise Oxford Dictionary of Politics*. Oxford: Oxford University Press, 1996.

Meany, John O. *The State and the Principle of Subsidiarity in Quadragesimo Anno*. Notre Dame, Indiana: University of Notre Dame Press, 1949.

Mendus, Susan. (Ed.). *The Politics of Toleration in Modern Life*. Durham: Duke University Press, 2000.

Metz, Helen C. (Ed.). *Nigeria A Country Study*. Washington, D.C.: Library of Congress, 1992.

Mich, Marvin L. K. *Catholic Social Teaching and Movements*. Mystic, CT: Twenty-Third Publications, 2001.

Miller, David. *Principles of Social Justice*. Cambridge, Massachusetts: Harvard University Press, 1999.

Miller, Raymond J. *Forty Years After: Pius XI and the Social Order*. St. Paul Minnesota: Radio Replies Press, 1947.

Misner, Paul. *Social Catholicism in Europe: From the Onset of Industrialization to the First World War*. New York: Crossroads, 1990.

Monitoring European Integration, No. 4. *Making Sense of Subsidiarity: How Much Centralization for Europe?* London: Center for Economic Policy Research, 1993.

Morisi, P. "The Principle of Subsidiarity and European Union." *The Month* 28/1 (January, 1995): 32–33.

Morsink, Johannes. *The Universal Declaration of Human Rights: Origins, Drafting & Intent*. Philadelphia: University of Pennsylvania Press, 1999.

Moti, James S., and Shagbaor Francis. W. *An Encounter Between Tiv Religion and Christianity*. Enugu: Snaap Press, 2001.

Moyniham, Daniel P. "Social Justice in the Next Century." *America* 165/6 (1991): 132–137.

Mulcahy, R. E. "Subsidiarity." *New Catholic Encyclopedia*. Vol. 13. (Ed.). William J. MacDonald et al. New York: McGraw Hill Book, 1967.

Murphy, Charles M. "Action for Justice as Constitutive of the Preaching of the Gospel: What Did the 1971 Synod Mean?" *Theological Studies* 44 (1983): 298–311.

Murphy, Francis X. "Oswald von Nell-Breuning: Papal Surrogate." *America* 165 (1991): 293–295.

Murray, Charles. *In Pursuit Of Happiness and Good Government*. San Francisco, CA: Institute for Contemporary Studies Press, 1994.

Nash, Ronald H. *Social Justice and the Christian Church*. Michigan: Mott Media Publishers, 1983.

Nell-Breuning, Oswald V. "The Drafting of Quadragesimo Anno." *Moral Theology No. 5: Official Catholic Social Teaching*. 60-68.

———. *Reorganization of Social Economy: The Social Encyclical Developed and Explained*. Trans. Bernard W. Dempsey. Milwaukee: The Bruce Publishing Company, 1936.

———. "Social Movements." (Ed.). Karl Rahner. *Encyclopedia of Theology: The Concise Sacramentum Mundi*. New York: The Seabury Press, 1974.

Newsom, Carol A., and Sharon Ringe H. (Eds.). *The Women's Bible Commentary*. Louisville, Kentucky: Westminster/John Knox, 1992.

Nichols, T. L. "Aquinas's Concept of Substantial Form and Modern Science." *International Philosophical Quarterly* XXXVI/3 (September, 1996): 303–318.

Niebuhr, Richard H. *Christ and Culture*. New York: Harper & Row Publishers, 1956.

Nolan, Albert. *Jesus Before Christianity*. Maryknoll, New York: Orbis Books, 1978.

Noonan, John T. *Bribes: The Intellectual History of a Moral Idea*. Berkeley and Los Angeles: University of California Press, 1988.

Novak, Michael. *The Catholic Ethic and the Spirit of Capitalism*. New York: The Free Press, 1993.

———. *Catholic Social Thought & Liberal Institutions*. New Brunswick and Oxford: Transaction Publishers, 1989.

———. *Free Persons and the Common Good*. New York: Madison Books, 1989.

———. (Ed.). *Democracy and Mediating Structures: A Theological Inquiry*. Washington, D.C.: American Enterprise Institute for Public Policy Research, 1980.

Oakley, Francis and Bruce Russett. (Eds.). *Governance, Accountability, and the Future of the Catholic Church*. New York/London: Continuum, 2004.

O'Brien, David J. and Thomas A. Shannon. (Eds.). *Catholic Social Thought: The Documentary Heritage*. Maryknoll, New York: Orbis Books, 1992.

O'Donovan, L. J. "A Dialogue in Hope: Reflections on Ethical Issues in a Globalizing Economy." *America* 181 (1999): 18–21.

Okome, Mojubaolu. *A Sapped Democracy: The Political Economy of Structural Adjustment Program and the Political Transition in Nigeria 1983-1993*. Lanham: University Press of America, 1998.

Okure, Teresa. *The Johannine Approach to Mission: A Contextual Study of John 4:1-42*. Tubingen: J.C.B. Mohr/Paul Siebeck, 1988.

Olowu, B. "Toward Resolving the Nigerian Governance Crisis." Paper for Workshop on the Workshop. Bloomington, Indiana: Indiana University, June 1999.

Osaghae, Eghosa E. *Crippled Giant: Nigeria Since Independence*. Bloomington and Indianapolis: Indiana University Press, 1998.

Ottaway, Marina. *Africa's New Leaders: Democracy or State Reconstruction?* Washington, D.C.: Carnegie Endowment for International Peace, 1999.

Outhwaite, William and Tom Bottomore. (Eds.). *The Blackwell Dictionary of Twentieth-Century Social Thought.* Oxford: Blackwell Publishers, 1994.

Parsons, Wilfred. "The Pope and the Depression." *America* 47 (1932): 37–39.

Paul VI.Populorum Progressio. *Catholic Social Thought: The Documentary Heritage.*

———. Evangelii Nuntiandi. Catholic Social Thought: The Documentary Heritage.

———. Octogesima Adveniens. *Catholic Social Thought: The Documentary Heritage.*

Paulhus, Normand J. "Social Catholicism and the Fribourg Union." *The Society of Christian Ethics,* (1980): 63–88.

Pearce, J. "Civil Society: Trick or Treat?" *The Month* 30/2 (March 1997): 101–106.

Perkings, Pheme. *Reading the New Testament.* New York/Mahwah, New Jersey: Paulist Press, 1988.

Perry, Michael J. *Morality, Politics, and Law.* New York: Oxford University Press, 1988.

———. *The Idea of Human Rights: Four Inquiries.* Oxford/New York: Oxford University Press, 1998.

Phan, Peter C. *Social Thought: Message of the Fathers.* 20. Wilmington, DE: Michael Glazier, Inc., 1984.

Pius XI. Quadragesimo Anno. *Catholic Social Thought: The Documentary Heritage.*

———. Divini Redemptoris. *Reorganization of Social Economy: The Social Encyclical Developed and Explained,* 443–475.

———. *Social Wellsprings: Eighteen Encyclicals of Social Reconstruction.* Vol. II. (Ed.). Joseph Husslein. Milwaukee: The Bruce Publishing Company, 1940.

Pixley, George V. *On Exodus: A Liberation Perspective.* Trans. Robert R. Barr. Maryknoll, New York: Orbis Books, 1987.

Pontifical Council for Justice and Peace. *Compendium of The Social Doctrine of The Church.* Vaticana: Libereria Editrice, 2004.

Powell, Mark A. *What Are They Saying About Acts?* New York/Mahwah: Paulist Press, 1991.

———. *What Are They Saying About Luke?* New York/Mahwah: Paulist Press, 1990.

Rahner, Karl. *Theological Investigations XXII: Humane Society and the Church of Tomorrow.* New York: Crossroad/Continuum, 1989.

Rausch, Thomas P. *Authority and Leadership in the Church: Past Directions and Future Possibilities.* Wilmington, Delaware: Michael Glazier, 1989.

———. *Catholicism: At the Dawn of the Third Millennium.* Collegeville, Minnesota: The Liturgical Press, 1996.

Rawls, John. *A Theory of Justice.* Rev. Ed. Cambridge, Massachusetts: The Belknap Press of Harvard University Press, 1999.

Reese, Thomas J. (Ed.). *Episcopal Conferences: Historical, Canonical and Theological Studies.* Washington, D.C.: Georgetown University Press, 1989.

Riordan, Patrick. *A Politics of the Common Good.* Dublin, Ireland: Institute of Public Administration, 1996.

Ropke, Wilhelm. *The Moral Foundations of Civil Society.* New Brunswick: Transaction Publishers, 1996.

Rotberg, Robert I. *Nigeria: Elections and Continuing Challenges*. New York: Council on Foreign Relations, 2007.

Rotberg, Robert I. (Ed.). Crafting the New Nigeria: Confronting the Challenges. Boulder, Colorado: Lynne Rienner Publishers, 2004.

Rousseau, Jean-Jacques. *The Social Contract*. Trans. Christopher Betts. Oxford: Oxford University Press, 1994.

Rubingh, East. *Sons of Tiv: A Study of the Rise of the Church Among the Tiv of Central Nigeria*. Grand Rapids: Baker Press, 1969.

Sanks, T. Howland. "Globalization and the Church's Social Mission." *Theological Studies* 60 (1999): 624-651.

Schilling, Theodor. "Subsidiarity as a Rule and a Principle, or: Taking Subsidiarity Seriously." *Havard Law School*: The Jean Monnet Chair.http://www.jeanmonnetprogram.org/papers/95/9510ind.html, 1995.

Schineller, Peter. (Ed.). The Church Teaches: Stand of the Catholic Bishops of Nigeria on Issues of Faith and Life. Abuja: Gaudium Et Spes Institute, 2003.

———. (Ed.). *The Voice of the Voiceless: Pastoral Letters and Communiques of the Catholic Bishops' Conference of Nigeria 1960-2002*. Ibadan: Daily Graphics, 2002.

Schuck, Michael J. *That They Be One: The Social Teaching of the Papal Encyclicals 1740–1989*. Washington, D.C.: Georgetown University Press, 1991.

Seligman, Adams B. *The Idea of Civil Society*. Princeton, New Jersey: Princeton University Press, 1995.

Senior, Donald, et al. (Eds.). *The Catholic Study Bible*. New York/Oxford: Oxford University Press, 1990.

Shields, Leo W. *The History and Meaning of the Term Social Justice*. Indiana: University of Notre Dame Press, 1941.

Shorter, Aylward. "Ancestor Veneration Revisited." *African Ecclesial Review* 25/4 August, 1983:198.

Simpson, J. A. and E.S.C. Weiner. (Eds.). *The Oxford English Dictionary*. 2nd ed. Vol. XVIII. Oxford: Clarendon Press, 1989.

Sirico, R. A. and Maciej Z. (Eds.). *The Social Agenda: A Collection of Magisterial Texts*. Vaticano: Libreria Editrice Vaticana/Pontifical Council for Justice and Peace, 2000.

Skillen, James W. and Rockne M. McCarthy. (Eds.). *Political Order and the Plural Structure of Society*. Atlanta, Georgia: Emory University/Scholars Press, 1991.

Solomon, Robert C. and Mark C. Murphy. (Eds.). *What Is Justice? Classic and Contemporary Readings*. New York/Oxford: Oxford University Press, 2000.

Soyinka, Wole. *The Open Sore of a Continent: A Personal Narrative of the Nigerian Crisis*. New York: Oxford University Press, 1996.

Stagaman, David J. *Authority in the Church*. Collegeville, Minnesota: The Liturgical Press, 1999.

Staley, Ronald. *Catholic Principles of Social Justice*. Los Angeles: Lawrence Publishing Company, 1964.

Stelten, Leo F. *Dictionary of Ecclesiastical Latin*. Peabody, Massachusetts: Hendrickson Publishers, 1995.

Strain, Charles R. (Ed.). *Prophetic Visions and Economic Realities.* Grand Rapids, Michigan: William B. Eerdmans Publishing Company, 1989.

Suberu, Rotimi T. *Federalism and Ethnic Conflict in Nigeria.* Washington, D.C.: United States Institute of Peace Press, 2001.

Synod of Bishops, Justitia in Mundo. *Catholic Social Thought: The Documentary Heritage.*

Townsend, Henry. *Society and the Gospel.* Hales Corners, Wisconsin: Clergy Book Service, 1976.

Tracy, David. et al. *Toward Vatican III: The Work that Needs to Be Done.* New York: The Seabury Press, 1978.

Ukpong, Justin S. *Proclaiming the Kingdom: Essays in Contextual New Testament Studies.* Port Harcourt, Nigeria: Catholic Institute of West Africa Press, 1993.

Uzukwu, Elochukwu E. *A Listening Church: Autonomy and Communion in African Churches.* Maryknoll, New York: Orbis Books, 1996.

Vacek, E. "Popular Ethical Subjectivism: Four Preludes to Subjectivity." *Horizons* 11/1 (1984): 42–60.

Valls, Andrew. (Ed.). *Ethics in International Affairs: Theories and Cases.* Lanham, Maryland: Rowman & Littlefield Publishers, 2000.

Walgrave, John H. *Person and Society: A Christian View.* Pittsburgh, PA: Duquesne University Press, 1965.

Walsh, Michael and Brian Davies. (Eds.). *Proclaiming Justice and Peace: One Hundred Years of Catholic Social Teaching.* London: Cafod/Collins, 1991.

Westphal, Jonathan. (Ed.). *Justice.* Indianapolis/Cambridge: Hackett Publishing Company, 1996.

White, Dale C. *Making A Just Peace: Human Rights & Domination Systems.* Nashville: Abingdon Press, 1998.

Wincott, Daniel. "Subsidiarity." *Oxford Concise Dictionary of Politics.* (Ed.). Iain McLean. Oxford: Oxford University Press, 1996.

Wright, Nicholas T. *Jesus and the Victory of God.* Minneapolis: Fortress Press, 1996.

Yves, R. Simon. *A General Theory of Authority.* Notre Dame: University of Notre Dame Press, 1980.

INDEX

www.ingramcontent.com/pod-product-compliance
Ingram Content Group UK Ltd.
Pitfield, Milton Keynes, MK11 3LW, UK
UKHW021828100926
8556IPUK00003B/218

9 781433 110115